The Return of Light

The Imminent Restoration Of Earth
And Liberation Of Humanity

THE RETURN OF LIGHT

Revelations From The Creator God Horus
With Karen Kirschbaum
and Elora Gabriel

First Edition

To order additional copies, please visit www.returnoflight.com or
call Green Willow Publications at 1-877-968-4337.

Cover art: "Trinity Logos" by Maia Christianne Nartoomid
www.spiritmythos.org
krystos@spiritheart.org

This book is dedicated to all those beings
who held enough light to make the salvation
and restoration of this Creation possible.

TABLE OF CONTENTS

INTRODUCTIONS

Celestial Light Healers

presents

PRELUDE TO CHANGE
COUNTDOWN TO 2012

PAOLA SANI   ROSEMARY STEPHENSON   EDWIN COURTENAY

In this unique and powerful one day event Rosemary Stephenson – Sacred Sound Teacher and Sound Healer, Paola Sani - Mayan Expert and Aura Soma Teacher and Edwin Courtenay - Clairvoyant Channel and Spiritual Teacher will combine their considerable talents to offer an enlightening and experiential journey into the heart of the mysteries of the Mayan prophecies. Revealing the truth behind the speculation and misunderstandings, offering clarity and practical guidance for 2012 as well as direct experience of the energies that are to come.

QUEENS HOTEL LEEDS
SUNDAY 19TH JUNE 2011
10AM TO 5PM

£54 or 2 for £99 until May 31st

FOR TICKETS CONTACT
ROSEMARY 07775 854640
KATE 07732042589
CAROLINE 07960202391

REFRESHMENTS AVAILABLE
BOTTLED WATER PROVIDED
BRING YOUR OWN LUNCH

For further information go to www.celestiallighthealers.com

PRELUDE TO CHANGE

Much has been spoken of 2012 and what it might hold in store for humanity and the world, much has been said about the Mayan prophecies and the end of the Mayan calendar and what this truly might indicate. Much has been said about the Galactic alignment of our Earth with the centre of the Galaxy, the movement of the Sun into the "dark rift", much has been said about endings and new beginnings, "re creation day", ascension and the evolution of the planet.

But what do we really know for sure? What do we really understand about the Mayan people and their predictions? Where did their prophecies come from and what is the truth behind them? What advice did they leave behind as their legacy for the rest of the world?

In this unique and powerful one day event Rosemary Stephenson – Sacred Sound Teacher and Sound Healer, Paula Sani - Mayan Expert and Aura soma Teacher and Edwin Courtenay - Clairvoyant Channel and Spiritual Teacher will combine their considerable talents to offer an enlightening and experiential journey into the heart of these mysteries. Revealing the truth behind the speculation and misunderstandings, offering clarity and practical guidance for 2012 as well as direct experience of the energies that are to come. This wondrous day will include …

❑ Lectures on decoding the Mayan mystery and understanding fully for the first time the true significance of 2012 and what it means for all of the world.
❑ Meditations with the Crystal singing bowls to unlock hitherto hidden codes of ascension that require priming now in time for 2012.
❑ Live channellings directly from the spiritual hierarchy of the Ascended Masters and Archangels offering practical guidance as to what needs to be done to prepare for 2012 and what to expect as we approach this time.
❑ Group rituals and exercises to activate the power needed to endure the roller coaster ride that will lead up to 2012 and become beacons of light, healing and calm for the humanity as Lords and Ladies of Order.

This promises to be a truly transformational day, exciting, educational and inspirational in the extreme, the must do event of the year not to missed!

AUTHOR'S INTRODUCTION
by Elora Gabriel

Please read this introduction.

In many books, introductions are breezed through or skipped entirely. We hope, however, that you will take the time to read these few pages. Otherwise you will find yourself with many unanswered questions as you proceed to read the book itself. In addition, please note that there is a Glossary at the end of the book, which will be of help if you encounter unfamiliar terms.

Who are we, and who is Heru?

This book was compiled by four people: Karen Kirschbaum, Elora Gabriel, Shakura Rei, and Marjorie Bair. Karen is the crystal clear channel who brought through all the information recorded in these pages. It is her superlative ability as a channel which made this work possible. I am generally (though not always) the voice who asks the questions. I have also written a short narrative which introduces each chapter; and in places my comments are inserted within the body of a chapter. Shakura submitted many questions and wrote much of the Meditations section. She also made and contributed the illustrations and helped with publishing the book. Marjorie served as consulting editor for the book, asked her own insightful questions, and generously shared her expertise in the publishing field.

Heru is best known to our world as Horus, the Egyptian God of light, wisdom, spiritual vision, and protection. Heru (pronounced HAY-ru) is the Egyptian form of his name and is preferred by him to the Latinized Horus. Like Jesus of Nazareth, Heru was called the redeemer and embodied himself in a physical incarnation in the distant past. Like Jesus, he conquered death and ascended, thus holding the title and powers of an Ascended Master. In Egyptian mythology Heru was known as the son of Isis and Osiris; and defeated Set, the

God of darkness and chaos, in a great battle. Heru was a solar and sky God and was associated with the falcon. He was known for his great wisdom and for the quality of spiritual sight. The Eye of Horus is a powerful esoteric symbol which was used for protection in ancient Egypt and is still commonly seen today. Heru was said to have been the first pharaoh of Egypt and was considered the protector of all the pharaohs. The ancient Egyptians called Heru "Lord of Light", and this title strongly resonates with my experience of who he is.

Heru and his twin flame, the mighty Creator Goddess Sekhmet, have long been active in assisting humanity and the evolution of this planet. Sekhmet was known as the Lion Goddess in Egypt. She has also appeared as the Goddess Durga in India, as White Jaguar Lady in Central America, and as the lion-headed dakini Senge Dong-ma in Tibet. She has asked that we refer to her as Durga/Sekhmet, to honor both of the major traditions in which she has appeared. Heru was known in Greece as Apollo and in India as Satyanarayana, Lord of Truth. Each of these aspects reveals a different facet of the being in question.

First and foremost Heru is a Creator God, one of those beings who, in his words, "is capable of taking the stuff of Creation, the plasma from Prime Creator, and manifesting it into form. These forms may be as large as universes and may be as small as micro-cosms." Heru is one of the greatest of all Creator Gods in that he is capable, in working with other Creator Gods, of creating both human souls and vast universes. These mighty beings are even older than our current Creation, as they derive from an earlier Creation cycle, and were created by Prime Creator Himself/Herself.

Because of his stature as one of the greatest of the Creator Gods, Heru's perspective is truly vast. There is very little that he does not know, although he will readily admit ignorance if the occasion arises. In addition, he has the capacity to organize and synthesize his knowledge into a form that is clear and meaningful.

How did this book come about?

In the winter of 2003-2004, Karen and I discovered that she could channel with amazing clarity and precision. We spoke to a number of beings, but ended up working with Heru because of his all-encompassing knowledge and because he is part of my own cosmic lineage. As our conversations proceeded, we began to delve into the mysteries of life, of our universe, and beyond. Heru also answered a great many personal questions for us and never scorned to help us with the problems and perplexities of our lives. As time went on and as we were able to verify the accuracy and consistency of his information in many ways, our trust in him increased. We also came to love this magnificent being for his gentle courtesy, his love, his wisdom, and the greatness of his heart. Perhaps above all, we found Heru to be unremittingly truthful, knowledgeable, and consistent. In the cases where we could test the accuracy of his statements, we found them to be correct.

During the summer of 2004, Heru stated to us that he had "been too long away" from Earth and wished to offer his teachings and his knowledge to humanity once again. He laid out a series of subjects that he wished to speak on, and in addition gave us three powerful meditations which have been life-changing for those who have used them. Thus this book was born. Heru also told us that there is an urgency to offer this material to humanity at this time, given the intensity and power of changes which are already occurring in our universe and are soon to occur on our planet.

This book is not linear.

I nearly tore out my hair in my first attempts to edit and organize the mass of material which Heru had given us. A helpful friend pointed out the fact that the information had been received in a series of conversations rather than in a linear, point-by-point fashion, and that therefore the book itself should be presented in a non-linear fashion. I would like our readers, therefore, to envision this book not so much as a progression from A to Z, but as something more like a tapestry. Parts of the tapestry tell a story. Parts of it are complete unto themselves. However, once the whole is put together, all parts are related. We suggest that you read the book in the order which it is presented, but please bear in mind that the book is an organic whole rather than a sequential narrative.

We have chosen to retain the question and answer format in which the information originally came. We could have re-written everything into a standard text format, but we felt that by so doing many of the precise shades of meaning in Heru's words would have been lost. At times, grammatical correctness has been sacrificed for the purpose of retaining as much of the original flavor and flow of our conversations as possible.

You will encounter not only Heru, but from time to time will meet other beings in these pages.

Karen has the capacity to channel almost any being. We have spoken with Sananda (also known as the Master Jesus) a number of times, as well as Durga/Sekhmet and others. <u>Unless otherwise noted, it is Heru who is answering our questions.</u>

Heru's teachings conclude with glory, but they are not for the faint of heart.

I will take some of the blame for the relentless pursuit of information in this book, not all of which is pretty. I simply insist on getting to the bottom of things. Much of the substance of this book is wonderful and uplifting, and much of it may be shocking and deeply disturbing, at least while it is being absorbed and processed. Heru does not sugar-coat the truth. He presents it without garnishment, and without the saccharine, flowery language or vague platitudes which are so often found in channeled works. Some of Heru's messages took us days and cost us deep emotion to process. However, even the most difficult portions of information were oddly reassuring at the same time, for we sensed that here was someone who was willing to tell us the whole truth and nothing but the truth. There was something about this material which felt like reaching bedrock.

Once we had integrated the more difficult parts of Heru's teachings, we found that the view of God and the cosmos which he presented was, in fact, preferable to our former beliefs. Ultimately his cosmology is more positive and infinitely more uplifting than anything that the sugar-coated rationalizations could provide. And the ultimate conclusion to which Heru takes us, at this time in the history of Earth and of Creation, is one of hope, glory, healing, and restoration.

Indeed, the reality of the Creation we live in is revealed by Heru to be one which is so far beyond our wildest dreams that it is only matched and comprehended by the deepest longings which are buried in our hearts and souls. Our Creator has brought into manifestation, for all living beings, a paradise of intoxicating diversity and matchless harmony. However, the fact is that we're not living in such an environment now. For those who wish to understand why not, who want to know where we have been as well as where we are going, Heru rips away the veils, shredding them layer by layer. "It is time for the truth to be known," he says. It is time because the hour of our redemption has finally arrived. The teachings which are recorded in this book can be a beacon of clarity in the times of intense change which we are entering.

If you thirst for truth, read on!

For me Heru's teachings have been, not a mouthful of cloying cotton candy, but a clear, cold, draught of truth, like crystal pure water from a deep well. Truth, of course, can assume many aspects in this multi-faceted Creation. It can, for example, appear as a welter of correct but bewildering detail. What Heru has given us here is a map—a map of reality as seen through the eyes of a Creator God. Details have been drawn in here and there. But in general you will find in this book that you have been taken high above the Cosmos, flying on the wings of the divine falcon, so that looking down upon Creation the clarity and coherence of cosmic patterns, and the epic of Creation itself, can be seen.

I almost envy you the journey of reading this information for the first time—a journey which ends with the restoration of our planet, our universe, our Creation, and our own selves, to the magnificence and perfection for which they were created. The most exciting, most stirring and most joyous time in our entire history is at hand.

Further information will be forthcoming from Heru.

As we receive updates, they will be posted at www..returnoflight.com.

HERU'S INTRODUCTION

[Heru:] Greetings, dear reader. It is my wish that you would take deeply into your heart the messages put forth in this book.

We are now at the tipping point of the history of this planet, and also the tipping point of so many larger cycles and systems. I would have you know it is no accident that you are here on this planet at this time and it is no accident that you are reading these words.

This is the time of miracles. This is the time that has been fore-told by many prophets. And yet, we have a little ways still to go where it would appear that the forces of dark have the upper hand. I say "appear", for there is a revolution afoot the likes of which is beyond comprehension, because the foundation of this revolution starts out-side this Creation—it starts with Prime Creator Itself, and it is the reclamation and restoration of this entire Creation.

Can you say something about who you are as a being?
I, Heru, am one of the Creator Gods. We are a group of beings that Prime Creator created prior to this Creation, and so we are older than this universe. When Prime Creator said, "Let there be light," we were the instruments through which that was manifested. We are the weavers of this magical substance that Prime Creator pours forth endlessly. And we weave and we shape that sacred substance into forms, into elements, into worlds, into universes, into souls. We are the beings who create the soul inside the sun, and we create the sun. All substance that we create with is of Prime Creator. I personally, along with others, was involved in the creation of this universe, the creation of this planet, and the creation of many of the souls who inhabit this planet. So I am father, uncle, and great uncle to many of you. And I would like to reclaim my own—to lift up, embrace, and heal my children.

Why have you chosen to give these teachings at this time?
First, I would like to say that, as one of the Creator Gods who was involved in the creation of this world and this universe, I am a respon-sible party in its reclamation. Even though I have not been very active

on this planet for several thousand years, it is my intent to bring forward a perspective on this Creation that does not currently exist on this planet; and in so doing, become reactivated in all aspects of the reclamation. As I do so, even all of the sweet Eye of Horus charms that exist throughout this world are being activated by my presence. So I am truly returning to this planet, not just in dry text, but in actual presence.

What would you like this book to accomplish?

Hope, joy, self healing, and the beginning of the accolades that will be heaped upon all of those that held to the light. I want the unvarnished truth to be revealed so that full true healing can take place. This is not about putting band-aids on a tumor, but it is about restoration of true health.

It is my wish to draw people to this material, and have it be available as a teaching for many.

Is there an urgency to get this material out quickly?

Yes, there is. For with the advent of the Light Warriors and the turning of the tide, there will be people still laboring under beliefs that were fostered by the dark—religious beliefs, philosophical beliefs, and self image beliefs. As these are ripped away, they will need to have a foundation for understanding what is left. Therefore both the teachings contained within this book, as well as the meditation techniques I offer, will give people a way to not despair, to not shatter, to not cling to falsehoods that would drag them down.

You have spoken often of the corrupting nature of darkness. How do we and the readers of this book know that you are uncorrupted? How can we know that what you are speaking is the truth and that you are fully trustworthy?

That is a most important question. And perhaps there is truly no way to know, outside of what resonates within your heart. It is my hope, my intent, and my dedication, to make this as pure a teaching as possible. Perhaps it is not possible in this world to have any teaching that is a hundred percent pure. But I know that I have done the best that I could. And those working with me—Elora, Karen, Marjorie and Shakura, have all made great efforts to ensure that their integrity is intact at all times. Can I guarantee this? I cannot. Can I hope? Yes. Do I think that this will resonate in the depths of the purest part of the souls of the people who read it? I believe it will.

In this book, you speak of the invasion of the dark, and the rescue that is upon us. Why has none of this information been available in any form until now?

Until the recent advent of the Omniversal Energy, the dark was able to block access to the cellular memory within each individual. In doing so, access to the entire story was successfully suppressed.

Heru, what would you wish to convey to humanity at this time?

Beloved humans, I would have you know that many of you have come into this universe with missions of light and healing and hope. Because of the degraded nature of where this planet and this whole sector are, most of these plans have not been fulfilled. Therefore there is a deep frustration, anguish, pent up creativity, and so on, that is very heart wrenching to witness on my part. I know that for each of you to have had your highest dreams of service subverted and perverted and stopped has to be painful beyond words. And first, I want to say that the most important thing that all of you have done collectively and individually is to hold enough light, enough truth, and enough integrity so that this world and this universe are salvageable and will be restored. That is a service above and beyond any of your individual dreams of service, and this is the most important thing that you have done.

Though some of you may at this point be heartsick, weary, soul fatigued, and damaged, you have been successful. <u>You are the Great Heroes.</u> There is no medal or commendation that could honor you enough. *Please take this deep within your heart: that each and every* one of you who has held onto even a speck of light, even a particle of integrity, have been victorious. The promise of restoration and restitution is at hand, and the time that you will actually be able to see this is very near.

Some of what you will read in this book is a frank and unveiled look at the past of humankind on this planet. It may be somewhat disturbing to you to read this, but I want you to know that the only reason this stark truth is being allowed to come forward at this time is because of the certainty and the nearness of the dissolving of all that is dark. It is truly very close to us now, and even upon us. And as part of the healing, it is necessary for us to take a good strong look at where we have come from, and how close we have come to annihilation. Much of this was withheld until now, for the purpose of not driving people into despair by the extent to which the dark energy had corrupted this Creation. But now that we are at the turning of the tide, we can express to you simultaneously both the harsh danger we have all been in, and the rescue that is at hand.

For you, dear reader, as you take into your heart the entirety of this picture, it will trigger very deep emotions for many, as it has for the people involved in bringing this book forward. For there has been much damage and hardship and loss for so many of you. This will touch upon the very deepest buried memories that you carry within you—in your personal records, in your cellular DNA, in your bones. And it is stored in the very stones of this Earth. As you walk upon her battered soil, you cannot help but pick up the anguish that is every-where around you, including the many battlegrounds—some of them physical, some etheric—that were never healed.

As these emotions surface, what I would recommend to you first and foremost is not to despair. For the great light has returned. And it will help you to feel that light within you, to feel it supporting you. Secondly, to practice self forgiveness, for many have done acts that would never be in their true nature to do. Self forgiveness is one of the first steps in healing.

I would have you understand that in order for the healing to take place, it is necessary to some degree for each of you to look directly at how the dark has impacted your life, how it has distorted who you are. This is not to jump into a quagmire and spend twenty-five years in therapy working through these realizations. What is being asked is for you to take a brief, concise, self-evaluating look at who you are in the moment and who you would be in an unfallen Creation. You have that blueprint within you, within every cell and every atom of your body. And you have the capacity to call that up and see it.

It is important to look at the past because in order to release what is there, it is necessary for it to first come into conscious awareness. I would add that it is not necessary to relive every single cut and scrape and broken arm throughout the millennia. What is needed for each of you is to look at your current lives and the imbalances in them —the big stories, the big heartaches, the big frustrations—and to understand that they fit into the overall pattern that you have carried with you for many thousands or millions of years.

Again, hold up your current imbalanced state, and compare it with who you would be in an unfallen world—that original blueprint that is so perfect, that is so beautiful, that is such an elegant and elo-quent expression of Prime Creator. Your heritage, your lineage, and your destination all pertain to that perfection. That is who you are. Embrace it. And as you embrace it, what you need to process and look at the imbalances will naturally well up from within you as you are ready to heal them. Imagine if you would that there are two blueprints we are looking at, the perfected one and the distorted one. And as you pull your distorted blueprint into alignment with the perfected one, piece by piece, issue by issue, and atom by atom, you will naturally process, in an ordered pattern, what needs to be done. Let me add to this that much help is here for you, and that you may call upon it freely.

Why is it necessary for us to know that we had come close to annihilation?

First, because it is the truth, and secondly, because it will give you a true understanding of the whole picture. Embedded in many beliefs and philosophies on this world is the concept that darkness is an illusion—that this is all maya and a play of the Gods, that this is the Creator Gods having sport. And that illusion will persist unless a person truly understands the magnitude of this horrific invasion. As a result of living in a fallen world, each one of you will have, to some extent, compromised pieces of truth, pieces of the light, and pieces of yourself. Therefore, to hold onto that false belief is to still leave room for the dark to act within you. And this is part of the necessary identification of the dark, in order for it to be eradicated.

Can you speak about the relevance of your three meditations to the rest of this material, and why they might be especially useful through this time?

These meditations are tools. They are not a path or a dogma or a religion to follow. They are merely offered to you as an assist at this time, to draw to you sufficient energy to proceed through these changes, and to give you many creative opportunities to process and manifest what will bring you back into alignment. The third technique is the heart of these meditations, and it may be used in an infinite variety of ways as needed. It can be simply a place of refuge and peace, nurturing and healing, or it can be used to manifest deep and powerful healings and transformations. It can also serve as a room within which to dialogue with many of the helpers who are here at this time.

Heru, would you like to conclude this introduction with anything further for our readers?

Beloved reader, I call you forth to stand in front of myself and in front of Prime Creator; to hold forth your genuine heart and receive within it my blessing, my love, my acknowledgement of your tribulations and your ultimate triumph. I add that the same is extended from Prime Creator. I fill your heart with a golden transforming love that is the promise of full redemption, and I ask that you receive this and let it grow.

[Elora:] We will conclude this introduction with a few words from Durga/Sekhmet.

Sekhmet, is there anything that you wish to convey to humanity at this time?

Yes. I would like to convey the absolute and complete joy in my heart for the advent and the return of the light, and the reclamation of all beings large and small in this universe. And I would also extend my hand to any who read this, that I make myself available for help and protection. For this next little while may be somewhat trying, and sometimes a comforting hand in a dark corridor can make all the difference. I extend my hand to all.

I also bring to you the message of hope beyond hope. It is certainty; it is really beyond words to convey to you the incredible magnitude of the change that is at hand and very near. For those of you who are reading this: ask for help in any time of doubt and despair, to be given a vision of how close indeed we are to the point at which humans on this Earth will be able to perceive that in reality the great change is happening. ***And this great change is the blessed return of all light.***

SECTION ONE
THE EPIC OF CREATION

CHAPTER ONE
PARADISE REMEMBERED

This chapter, like most, begins with an introduction by Elora.

Throughout my lifetime, I have continually worked to push back the veils obscuring my memory of other worlds and other existences. Once I had conquered the barriers to past life memory on this Earth, I found that I could go further back in time and could remember lives in other star systems and galaxies. It was not until the spring of 2002, however, that I began to recall what life was like outside this universe.

At that time I was contacted in spirit by a beautiful young man who seemed deeply familiar to me. He told me he was my brother, from an existence in a universe called Virqie and a planet known as Atia; and that he and my other two brothers had arrived in this universe to take me home. Despite the fact that many scientists now recognize not only the possibility but the inevitability of multiple universes, I had a hard time believing all of this. Still, he was adamant that this was the truth of the matter. With the help of my brothers, I began to remember what it had been like in Virqie. I have also been able to compare my memories with those of other friends who know that they come from light universes. While the details of their remembrances differ, their overall stories are very similar to mine.

As I explored my memories of Virqie, I was stunned to realize that none of them contained pain or disharmony, even in the slightest way. Most of my past life memories are traumatic, partly because Earth life tends to be that way and partly because it is the unresolved traumas that we remember most. However, in accessing my memories of Virqie, I simply could not uncover any remembrances of sorrow, suffering, fear, illness, aging, or even of discontent. I realize how incredible this sounds, yet it is the truth of my recollection. I am not speaking of some remote heavenly realm here, or some between-life paradise, but day to day life on a planet, a world just as concrete as Earth. A common reaction may be that this sounds boring. It was not. I have experienced a great deal of tedium in my lives on Earth, but I remember none in Virqie. Another reaction may be that it requires some amount of pain to appreciate joy. I also found this to be entirely untrue.

In the Virqie universe, all is beauty, harmony, and love. Evolution occurs through joy, not through suffering and struggle. The presence of God flows through that universe like a great golden tide that is always at the full. While there is the free will to choose among many possibilities in life, the thought of doing anything negative, hurtful, or in any way outside of the flow of God's Will is simply not conceived of. Nor is there any fear of being harmed, either by other humans or by nature. Perfection reigns—and yet not a static, lifeless, and tedious perfection, but one which contains vibrancy, joy, and great creative challenges.

On the planet of Atia where I lived, human relationships are considered a high art. Intimacy and love exist in exquisite delicacy and profound depth. Male/female relationships are practiced within a free-flowing yet committed structure which ensures that love and partnership are always available to all, as are times of aloneness and communion with nature and God. Loneliness, abusive or unfulfilling relationships, and emotional pain of all types are unknown. The decision to bring forth a child is considered a sacred act, and each child is seen as a precious manifestation of the divine.

From my memories of Atia, I know that nature thrives there in resplendent beauty. Trees, flowers, grass, birds, sea creatures, and land animals live there just as they do here, yet in complete harmony and glorious vibrancy. All forms of life, from the tiniest to the greatest, are honored, and all are part of the great tapestry of life. The whole universe evolves together. None are left behind, not the tiniest insect or flower. All beings are conscious, and all matter is filled with awareness; even the grains of sand shimmer with life as they lie on the shores of the jade-green ocean. It is as if the whole universe is one great symphony. There is no illness, and death is simply a conscious releasing of one form to move on to a higher one.

Fear, pain, anger, and grief do not exist in the normal course of evolution—although my family did grieve, and did fear for my safety, when I left to travel to this universe and did not return as expected.

As I accessed these memories, I knew that I had come to this universe along with many others in an attempt to set things aright in this part of Creation. I also knew that life in Virqie was life as the Creator designed it to be. This book contains a great deal of information on what is commonly called the Fall, which will be discussed in detail in the next chapter. Therefore, we have chosen to begin by taking a good look at the original design of Creation and the nature and purpose of our Creator.

THE NATURE AND STRUCTURE OF OUR CREATION

Heru, let us begin this discussion by defining several terms. Please define the term "Creation".

Creation is the manifested will of Prime Creator. It is a vast system of universes and is structured, as you have seen, in the form of a flower. Prime Creator, or the Godverse, is the central source around which the petals of Creation bloom.

Please define "Godverse".

The Godverse is the dwelling place of Prime Creator, although Prime Creator is not limited or encapsulated by the Godverse. It is the place from which all energy originates, and all of the cosmic plasma that we Creator Gods use to create form originates in the Godverse. It is at the center of all Creation.

Please define "universe".

A universe is a structure contained within a membrane. It is created out of the Omniversal matter which is a free flowing, unformed, plasmic cosmic material that Prime Creator has made. The Creator Gods take that plasma, create a membrane around it, and structure it. *[Are all the universes set up as vast collections of galaxies?]* Most are, but some are quite tiny, as the one I told you about that Durga/Sekhmet and I created. There are microcosmic universes as well. All of them have a certain similarity in structure in terms of the way matter and the elements are structured. There are considerable variations in size and theme, but the larger universes you would recognize. *[Do they each have a great Central Sun?]* Yes. That is integral to holding them together, and actually is integral in holding the outer membrane together.

Please define "Prime Creator."

God is that which creates, sustains, and permeates all.

Please tell us about the nature of Prime Creator; about who and what Creator is, from your own knowledge and experience.

My eyes may see what yours do not, and that is the direct vision of the wondrous nature of our beloved Creator. This is a being without beginning or end, formless and yet formed at the same time, wondrous to look upon, brighter than all of the suns put together. And not only the brightness but the purity of that light is incredible to behold. Out of Creator streams limitless light, streams infinite energy, streams the very space upon which matter hangs. That space is the thought projection of Prime Creator; and so Creator, being infinite, has created infinite space.

Within that infinite space, Prime Creator has made many Creations, of which this system of universes is but one. And within the space of this Creation are hung, like the petals of a jeweled lotus, universe after universe after universe, suspended in this infinite space and hung with sustaining lines of energy. Then within each universe, as you know, many are the worlds and galaxies.

So varied is this Creation that I would compare it to one of your deliciously beautiful floribunda roses, where the bushes cascade blossom after blossom after blossom, each one so exquisite in its patterning and its fragrance and its individuality.

Creator has imbued, within every atom and every universe, its own consciousness, its own connectedness to itself. It is almost a holographic mirror that you could look into. You could look into any part of this Creation and know that Creator is there—present, seeing you look, looking through your eyes, looking at Creation, and mirroring back and forth—and offering you this kaleidoscopic experience that is never ending.

Please say more about the structure of this Creation.

The basic structure of Creation, from the tiniest particle to the alignment of the universes, is all built upon the sacred geometric principles that are taught in some of your esoteric circles. Much has been written on sacred geometry, and it would benefit the reader to at least take a look at some of what has been written—to understand the divine nature of the human body in its proportions, and how that is a reflection of Prime Creator's infinite loving wisdom.

The older universes, closer to the center of Creation, are more basic and simple in their expression of the sacred geometric principles. As one travels outward into the newer universes, each arm of the spiral, so to speak, would show universes more and more complex and diverse in nature. The universe you are living in is towards the edge and has a greater degree of complexity. This process is designed to be a never ending spiral, to continue forever with an increasing complexity and increasing beauty. And there is designed to be communication between the universes—ambassadors, educational exchanges, all of that—so that there might be pleasure taken in the experience of each new facet as it is created, each new color that is discovered, each new form that can be created, "fractalling out" from the original forms into infinite variation. And in this there is no end to what can be created and discovered.

I have noticed that forms repeat themselves within this Creation, in the microcosm and the macrocosm. For example, the Great Central Sun of this universe has the form of a lotus, and the whole Creation itself looks like a flower.

That is based on the sacred geometries which were set in motion with the first burst of Creation. The plasma that the Creator Gods use to create with has, imbedded within it, certain structures and formats with which to work. *[So the entire Creation, in fact, is in the form of a lotus?]* Yes. *[The Vedanta scriptures describe this; they describe the manifest Creation as a lotus floating in the void.]* Yes, and oftentimes they would often show Gods, which would be Creator Gods, sitting on a lotus as well.

Why did Creator desire to make this Creation?

To have a worthy dance partner; one that could receive fully the boundless love that Creator has, and one that was—as much as is possible—able to reflect all of the facets and gifts that Prime Creator has.

What is the overriding theme or intention of this Creation?

Beauty, harmony, rhythm, creativity, expansiveness, joy. When you look in this world at the great beauty and diversity of nature, and you look at the nature of a fractal, and how incredibly gorgeous it is as it expands in its complexity, you will get a small taste of what Creator is trying to express.

What was the Creator's intention for all beings, large and small, who should live within this Creation?

The highest wish of Prime Creator is that each individual life form or aspect of Creation would blossom fully outward in its expression to the pinnacle of its individual essence. And simultaneously, that it would have the awareness to look back at Source to know who it is and where it came from. The intention is to have a simultaneous full expression of individuation, and full encompassing of union with the Creator at the same time. Creation is designed so that anyone from a tiny insect to a galaxy would have that ability.

Please discuss the communication and oneness between all beings in an unfallen Creation. For example, if I want to communicate with someone in another universe, can I do that easily?

Yes. It is a matter of thinking and it is done. *[So there is no sense of separation.]* There is not. *[The whole Creation is a living organism, and all the cells can communicate with each other?]* Yes, and also there is the ability to be in more than one place at one time. This is described in quantum physics. It is basically a matter of focusing on where you would desire to be, and you would be there.

Please discuss the connection and communion with God that is present for all beings in the light universes.

There is no concept of there not being communication, of there not being constant contact. It is in the air that everyone breathes. It is everywhere. It is the medium that everyone and everything lives in.

Is there pain in the light universes?

There is very little, and what there is would be the result of a connection between one of the light universes and one of the fallen universes.

What is nature like in the unfallen universes?

If any of our readers have visited areas of pristine wilderness and observed the beauty and the magnificence there, it would be a magnitude of perhaps a hundred times more perfect. Imagine, if you would, one of those great breaking waves upon the Hawaiian shore, those that the surfers ride; and you see the beauty of the dynamic that creates such perfection of water falling upon itself. Then imagine that wave a hundred times more perfect. I can't put words to it; I can only tell you that even with the forms here that are beautiful, it is better than that by so much.

Are there certain archetypal animals and plants that we would find in most of the universes? Would we recognize cats and horses, roses and oak trees?

Yes. You would recognize many similar forms and also many variations. For example, there are variations in color between different worlds. There are places where the photosynthesis happens almost like a red and green simultaneously. On this planet you see some plants with red leaves, but there are other places where that color predominates. If you look at the red Japanese maples, you would see forests on those worlds where there are varieties of trees with different variations of that deep red—with some green, but the primary color being red. This occurs primarily on planets that would have a hotter blue star, and a different spectrum of light.

Please talk about the relationship between humans and nature in the light universes.

In terms of the relationship with nature, there is no concept of exploitation, ownership, or stewardship, as is taught in some of your scriptures. For to walk upon the earth is to walk upon the body of God. To swim in the water is to swim through the body of God. And to breathe, and to eat, and to drink, are to ingest the Creator within the vehicle of the created, and there is no separation. Again there is that complete individuation of the human combined with a total connectedness to God and nature. They are not seen as separate.

Is there technology and mechanization in the light universes?

You would not be able to separate nature from technology. They are seamlessly wedded in harmony.

Is there predation among animals in the light universes?

It is somewhat difficult to describe. It is a harmony and a play which is acted out between predator and prey, where permission is asked and permission is given. Once the permission is given, it is a service of the prey to be consumed by the predator. It would be much more akin to the river merging with the ocean, where the prey would consider its life form to flow into that of the predator. And it is a harmonious act. It is not gross the way it is on this planet. *[Is there pain?]* No. I would also say that the human type life forms on those planets are all vegetarian. The animals which on this planet are omnivores, such as those in the canine family, would be vegetarian in an unfallen universe. It would be only the felines, and a few of the fish, and a few of the birds, who would be predators. In the light universes predators are in a very small minority, but they serve a function. There are also some carrion animals and birds as well, but less so than here. *[In our world, when a cat catches a mouse, she plays with it in a very cruel way. Is this a distorted reflection of the harmonious playfulness that would occur between predator and prey in a light universe?]* Yes.

Why are humans called the Crown of Creation?

They have the greatest autonomy and individuation inherent in their character, and the greatest ability to reflect Prime Creator to each other and back to Prime Creator.

More than just about any other creature, humans really get to enjoy the fullness of the beauty of Creation. Having a high metabolism and mobility gives humans the ability to explore, learn, enjoy, absorb, and reflect, to the fullest extent.

CHAPTER TWO
THE FALL

PART I—THE REALITY OF DARKNESS

According to Heru, and according to the memories of those of us who can remember back to the times before we entered this universe, the original Creation was without stain, without suffering, without even disharmony. If all this is true, then why are we, in this part of Creation, experiencing life in a way which bears only a small resemblance to that original state of perfection? And what is the condition of this universe as a whole? Are the problems which plague our planet the exception or the rule?

I personally found that a part of my spiritual maturation was a series of shocks and disillusionments about the nature of things in our world and even beyond our planet. These have not been pleasant, but the willingness to come face to face with reality has been an essential aspect of growing up for me. Humans who are able to acknowledge the truth of existence on our planet have had to acknowledge the fact that all of our major institutions (government, medicine, finance, religion, etc.) are riddled with corruption, and exist more for the purposes of power and control than for the service of humanity.

As I expanded the horizons of my knowledge and experience, I found that Earth was not the only place where evil existed. I spent a number of years reading every available book on the extraterrestrial abduction phenomenon, and accessed my own memory of a frightening encounter with the Greys early in life. (The Greys are a group of extraterrestrials who are reported to be responsible for the majority of the ET abductions.) Some years later, I teamed with a psychic friend to do extensive work in an attempt to reclaim some of the dark fourth dimensional reptilian races. In the course of this work—both through my own experiences and through further study and cross-referencing with others who had authentically experienced these realms—I was forced to realize that our galaxy is filled with war and strife. Peaceful planets exist, but only because they are protected in one way or another. Past life memories also surfaced of personal experiences with warring and destruction in other star systems and galaxies.

An even greater shock occurred when I discovered that negativity is not confined to the lower dimensions. As I continued to explore and expand my horizons, I found that dark beings and energies exist even in higher dimensions. I remembered being attacked and almost destroyed as a being at a time when I lived on the sixth dimension. Heru and Sananda told us that pretty much all of the ruling councils in our universe—whether they be planetary, galactic, or even broader in spectrum—were compromised to some degree. We also discovered dark grids on the fourth, sixth, and eleventh dimensions, which were covering large areas of our universe. When we asked Heru if darkness (negativity) was more prevalent in the lower dimensions he replied, "No. It is as above, so below."

It is comforting to think that Earth is a primitive schoolhouse or a brutal but effective boot camp, a tiny and troubled speck floating in the cosmic oceans of love and light. Heru states that this is not the case. If our universe were a place of peace, truth, and joy, he asked us rhetorically, would the situation on Earth have been allowed to persist—the injustice, the enslavement of so much of humanity, the prevalence of suffering? The truth, according to Heru and the other masters we have spoken with, is that we live in a fallen world which exists within a fallen universe.

PART II—THE FALLEN STATE

What does it mean to exist in a fallen state? In this section, I will briefly touch on some of the ways that this reality has impacted the existence of humans and all beings in our world and beyond. I do not mean in any way to say that our planet is entirely negative or that life here is only misery, for that is certainly not the case. Earth is renowned throughout our universe for its exceptional beauty and diversity, and even under great duress the human spirit can be indomitable. Every person who holds to some degree of truth, of love and of light, creates a small bit of heaven—and it is all of these together which make our world a place of great hope and unexpected miracles.

With that preface, I will proceed. For humanity, the fallen state means that life is short and, in most cases, fraught with difficulty. The struggle for survival dominates the human experience, and a high proportion of humanity lives in grinding poverty, barely maintaining the necessities of life. Rather than spending our lives in the delight of creativity, in the joy of spiritual growth and unfoldment, most of our time and energy goes into obtaining food and shelter. Relationships bring love and connection but also deep disappointment and heartache, and many people are alone, abused, or emotionally adrift and lost. True fulfillment is rare and usually fleeting. The hearts of humanity are filled with sorrow, even those of us who are the most fortunate. We exist in a state of separation from God and from Life itself. The fallen state of humanity means that our DNA has been decimated, to use Heru's word, and that we experience illness, aging, suffering, and death.

The fallen state of our planet means that all of our institutions are corrupt, and that no matter how hard we try to change or replace them, corruption again ensues. The fallen state of our world means that we live behind massive, though unseen frequency fences or energetic barriers which keep the light of the Creator from us. It means that countries are unable to live in peace with one another and that despite all the efforts of all the peacekeepers throughout history, we still fight and kill one another—and always the innocent suffer. It means that with each advance, there has been an equal or greater decline. For example, as technology has developed it has freed us from the plow on the one hand and chained us to the computer on the other, and has also caused the poisoning and devastation of our beautiful planet.

The fallen state of nature means that even in this least contaminated part of our reality, predation, parasitism, and competition are the rule. The strong devour the weak. Even in the plant kingdom, vines strangle trees and roses grow thorns for protection.

The fallen state of our universe means that the very atomic structures, the building blocks of matter, have been so distorted that matter itself is corrupted. As Heru says, "The very stones of Earth cry out." Matter, instead of existing in a pure and perfect state, continually falls into entropy. We can still perceive something of the original divine order of things as we study the cosmos. Yet we see chaos even there, as galaxies collide and stars consume one another.

Before we plunge into the details of the fall, I would like to offer some of Heru's words and ask you to hold them in your consciousness as you read the next section.

I am so glad that I have even a few memories of life before the fall.
It is very helpful, even for those who do not have direct memory, to call upon their soul or their monad to hold up for them that image of themselves in an unfallen state. When each of you sees your original template, and understands that you did not cause your fall, that you are not to blame for this fall, you will have taken a huge first step in reclaiming your divine nature. And when each one of you begins that path—the path of separating what is not you, what is the fallen, from who you truly are—it is a path of glory that I cannot put into words for you. There is so much wondrous joy that awaits you in this discovery. For each one of you, each and every individual on this planet, has descended from the very highest lineage. You were created by Creator Gods of the highest order, and as such royalty the likes of which you cannot imagine flows in your blood, in your bones, in your DNA. It is your heritage, it is your destiny, and it is time to reclaim this.

PART III—THE HISTORY OF THE FALL

Heru, if Prime Creator made and designed this Creation to be one of joy, harmony, and perfection, what happened?
Approximately 1.3 billion years ago in your time, there was an invasion which occurred in a universe near this one—an invasion of darkness. What we will call darkness, for the purpose of these discussions, is a non-souled, non-living substance, antithetical in structure to the basic life inherent in every atom of Creation. It is not known where it comes from, or who or what designed it. It has the tendency to permeate anything that it touches, though some beings have been able to resist it, at least in maintaining the purity of their spirit.

The universes had never experienced conflict prior to this event, and therefore the membranes around them were only designed as containment of form and not as a protective barrier. I would liken this invasion to the effect of the bite of a poisonous spider or snake on the human body. The original universe which was affected then sickened, and essentially died in a very short period of time, almost immediately. Of the beings living in it, those who could do so fled into the neighboring universes, unknowingly bringing contamination with them. It was at that time that a small assemblage of beings was sent to help. This group was not the one to which the light workers on Earth belong; this was prior to that time. The structure of the one dead universe was collapsed and melted back into the All, with great sadness and solemn ceremony.

Those who had escaped seemed at that point largely unscathed. But from that time forward, the surrounding universes began to experience some disharmony. And this began to grow and magnify, and spread rapidly, as there is much commerce between universes. This spread continued and did not seem overly alarming, just concerning. When this reached some several thousand universes, it was decided that a concerted effort would be made to deal with the situation. Therefore a large group of beings assembled, and that is most generally the group that the readers here belong to—the group which we call the light workers. They arrived, each of them with their specialty and their mission, and began to do their work.

If you were to examine the state of those affected universes at that time, as compared to the present, they would look far more light and harmonious than your current universe does. It was as though everything was perhaps one degree off where it should be. It was small, it was subtle, it was not dramatic. There was not a great deal of suffering, there were no wars, there was just a level of disharmony, a small amount of disease, and a sense that everything was slightly off. Things were no longer perfect. Meanwhile the insidious nature of this poison, or this darkness, was that it penetrated deeper into the infected beings and deeper into the systems in these universes. The worst part about this poison is that, unbeknownst to the host, it would usurp its free will in a very subtle way and begin to redirect its life.

At this time there was a concentration of many of the great and mighty beings who were contaminated and infected by darkness, such as the Creator Gods, angels, Archangels, and Elohim. It is the fall of these elevated beings which, in your mythology, later came to be known as the Lucifer rebellion. Again, unbeknownst to these beings, their free will had been usurped and they were being guided into paths that would not normally have been their choice. The reason that there were many great and mighty who fell was two fold. Onewas that the Creator Gods and the angelic beings who were in that original universe were the ones who managed to escape. They were more mobile than a cat or a bird, for example, in terms of traversing great space and time. They then met with their equals to work on the problem, and their equals and counterparts then too became infected. Therefore, because of the nature of those who escaped the original universe and who dealt with the melting down of that universe, they unknowingly ended up contaminating a large number of very high level beings.

Each of these beings would have a job, so to speak. Wherever they were working, and whatever they were assigned to when they returned, would then also be corrupted. Therefore fallen Creator Gods would create fallen universes. These were much darker than your universe is currently and are not salvageable; they are not structured on the basic sacred geometric principles that your universe is structured on. There was also a point in time, just prior to the erection of the frequency fence, when these Creator Gods decided that they would create in their own way and in their own manner. In their delusion, they declared this a superior Creation to that of Prime Creator.

Did the contamination then spread from the highest dimensions down?

Yes. As I stated earlier, when the original invaded universe died *and was melted down, those highest beings out of that universe are* the ones who escaped. Therefore this contamination happened from the highest orders, and actually spread downward through the dimensions. In the fallen universes, darkness exists through the eleventh dimension.

PART IV—THE FALL OF OUR OWN UNIVERSE

Heru states that about six percent of the universes in this Creation are dark. About two percent are wholly dark, for they were created by fallen Creator Gods. The other four percent were created light and were invaded. Our own universe, which was originally a place of "symphonic loveliness", in Heru's words, is one of these.

Heru, we would like to discuss the fall of the universe that we live in. First, how many universes are there, and what percent are dark or compromised?

The universes in this Creation number in the tens of thousands. Darkness is only in the last outer layers of the universes. Perhaps less than two percent are wholly dark, and maybe an additional four percent are embattled.

Then let us look for a moment at the creation of this universe. We know that universes are made by Creator Gods such as yourself; and that in order to create the large universes they work in groups. Who created our universe? Several years ago we were told, by a source outside this universe, that its creator was called Godin. Who is Godin?

The spelling of this name is G-O-D-I-N-J, and the "j" is almost silent. Godinj is actually not one person. It is the collective signature of the dozen or so Creator Gods who came together to do this. That signature, Godinj, is written in the atomic structure of all matter in the universe, and that is why it carries power.

We notice the similarity between this name and our word "God".

Yes, and I believe if there were scholars who could get this name into the Hebrew alphabet, they would find some good information and make theories around it.

Please explain exactly what Godinj is.

Godinj is a group of Creator Gods who wove the membrane, creating the perimeters of this universe around the great plasma given to them by Prime Creator. They themselves form, in essence, the nucleus of that great cell [i.e. the universe]. And spinning out from them are all of the forms of this universe, large to small. *[Were you and Durga/Sekhmet part of the original collective of Godinj?]* No, we were more in the role of advisors, and we chose the beings that make up Godinj.

Please describe the fall of our universe.

Your mythologies have many descriptions of the fall, the most famous in the west of course being Adam and Eve, and the apple and the snake. If we use this as a framework, we would say that the apple is the body of contamination and contaminated knowledge, the knowledge of duality. We would say that the snake was the carrier, the contaminated Creator Gods and angels and Archangels. And Adam and Eve would represent the original blueprint of humanity as well as that of this Creation and this universe. When this poisoned fruit was consumed, not only did the blueprint of humanity fall and become corrupted, but the life forms and worlds also fell. So both the Adamic and Edenic blueprints for this entire universe fell.

There was, of course, resistance. The Creator Gods Godinj—those who are instrumental in creating and holding this universe in form—were divided. Some fell, and some were then imprisoned by the ones that fell, giving the fallen essentially free rein. There were some very, very destructive battles in this universe. An uneasy truce was then struck, with the dark dominating the light, but the light holding enough mass and power to prevent the entire universe from falling. Many compromises were made, not for the better, but for the purposes of stalling the dark until rescue could be effected. And that is pretty much where things have stood up until now.

Did the fall of our universe occur fairly early on in terms of the invasion, or relatively late in the game, so to speak?

Early on. It occurred about 900 million years ago, in your time. *[What percent dark is our universe at this time?]* It is about 75% dark.

Going back to the information we originally received, we were told that Godinj made a terrible error in the creation of this universe, and that in the process he himself became split into two parts, one light and one dark. Is there any truth to this?

This is an interpretation of what happened. What occurred was that this universe was created close to perfect. It had some slightly flawed blueprints, which have occurred in the outer or newer universes, but everything was functioning relatively well here. When this attack happened, the dark forces used those flaws to create a tremendous fall and rending. When that occurred, it split the overlighting council of Creator Gods who created this universe, so there was a rending within that group. Two of these Creator Gods fell, and this again relates to what you call the Lucifer myth. And those who fell are the ones who have created the completely dark universes.

Please explain the slight flaws in the replication of blueprints in the universes, and how the dark used this.

The basic structures of all life, including DNA and atomic structures, were created essentially the same throughout this Creation. In the process of creating more and more universes, the outer petals on the flower of Creation contained a few minute distortions in DNA and also in atomic structure. This happened as the replications of these basic structures and blueprints were repeated countless times. However, these minuscule flaws were not seen until the dark invaded. The dark then used this as an opening and magnified and further distorted these imperfections. In the unfallen outer universes, this has not been much of a problem and is being corrected with ease.

Did this damage to the DNA only affect life forms on the lower dimensions?

No. DNA is a multi-dimensional structure which has its roots in the twelfth dimension and passes through all of the dimensions into the third; and the structures of life are then built upon it. Therefore truly each cell of your body is a gateway to the higher dimensions. When the Creator Gods and other high beings fell, the DNA became damaged and distorted. The Godinj collective, for example, is the support for every cell of life in this particular universe. When it fell, every cell within this universe was affected. Therefore the corruption begins at the top and descends out into each cell of Creation, distorting throughout the entire process. And not only the cells are affected, but the same applies to the atomic structure. From the very top, the atomic structure was distorted. An effect of this distortion is the fact that in a fallen universe all matter is subject to entropy. This is one of the laws of physics in your world. In an unfallen universe, this is not the case.

PART V—THE FALLEN EXPERIENCE

As we continue with information about the fall, I would like to remind our readers that this information is only being given out now because of the fact that rescue is at hand. As Heru stated in the introduction to this book: "I want you to know that the only reason this stark truth is being allowed to come forward at this time is because of the certainty and the nearness of the dissolving of all that is dark. It is truly very close to us now, and even upon us." Later chapters will focus on the coming restoration and reclamation of Earth and our universe.

I would like to understand the many ways the forces of darkness have distorted life here and made certain things impossible, and other things of a destructive or unhappy nature the norm. Like children raised in highly dysfunctional or abusive families who have no idea that their experience is wrong and "abnormal", even perhaps criminal, I think we on this planet have no idea of the extent of abnormality in our own life experience. How does all of this relate to the fall?

This is really a vast question, but let me first state that none of these conditions exist in an unfallen universe or world. There are as many pathways of disease and disharmony as there are illnesses of body, mind, and society. There are countless factors, and I could list them all. Let us start, however, with the fundamental premise that what society has defined as human nature—the aggressive desire for conquest, the desire for dominance, greed, selfishness, cruelty—all of these things are not normal and are the result of the fall. Then when you look at how this so-called human nature has expressed itself in culture, in society, and in the institutions that govern this world, you have an idea of the complexity of what needs to be reformed in every system and on every level. Be assured that all of this will change, and very rapidly, as the restoration of your planet and your universe proceed. And as humans are restored to their original nature, their hearts and minds will again express the divine blueprint and perfect harmony that was intended by Creator.

Are there some sectors of the population, such as political leaders, darker than others?

Yes. Those who are the most aggressive in acquiring and maintaining power and control over others are in general quite a bit darker, and are also oftentimes used as vehicles for some of the fallen beings to carry out their agendas.

What percentage of the human race at this time is not corrupted by some degree of darkness?

All humans are affected by darkness to some degree. Because it exists on the atomic level, there is really no way to escape it. However, we have noted that the souls of some beings have been able to resist this influence. More than half of the people on this planet, perhaps as high as 60% of the humans on this Earth, are in a state where their soul, their spirit, their intention in life, is to manifest light. And that is truly a miracle. Things look so bad, and the negative structures are so strongly in place; yet the weakness in the plan of the dark is that they have not been able to corrupt the human spirit in so many. *[I often think of the humble people of Earth, many of them very poor, many living in underprivileged countries, yet who maintain their purity of spirit and dedication to God.]* Yes, and many of them are much happier than the privileged.

What percent dark is Earth at this time?

Despite the fact that over half of humanity still holds to the light, the darkness tends to be in control here because of all the systems that are in place. Therefore I would have to say that Earth is, at this time, about 75 to 80% dark.

What, if any, is the difference in the personal experience of life between those infiltrated by darkness and those not?
Imagine, if you would, two tuning forks. One of them might be covered with whatever junk that would prevent it from sounding, but the tuning fork itself is still in perfect pitch. At any time that it is unwrapped and struck, it will resonate. Because of that it holds at its core that true resonance, even though it is not sounding. Then imagine a second tuning fork, where the tines have been twisted and distorted. Whether it is wrapped or not wrapped, whether it is struck or unstruck, it always carries that distortion at its core. And that is not to say that this is uncorrectable.

Is life easier for those humans who are fallen, who are not resisting the dark?
That is perhaps too broad a question. In some cases yes, in that they would receive a great deal of support in acting the nefarious schemes of the dark. You could say the wheels are greased and their ambitions are oftentimes not thwarted, because they are in essence sons of the ruling body, whether that is literally or in spirit. But ease does not equate to happiness or harmony. *[Is there a tremendous pain deep in the soul of all the fallen?]* How could there not be?

PART VI—A CREATION WITHOUT DEFENSES

If this Creation was made without any form of negativity, then was it unable to defend itself against darkness? Why didn't the Creator act to drive darkness out of the Creation?
This Creation is a creation of love and light, of beauty, of vast amounts of diversity. And as I said earlier, it is an expression of something beyond words, that indescribable place which the Creator expressed from. In this expression there was no thought of destructive or negative forces. These were not even conceived of as being a possibility. Therefore this Creation was created without weapons, without defenses. You will see in the universes which are not fallen, for example, that the whole concept of predation is much different.
When this Creation was attacked, although the Prime Creator was aware of it instantly, the Creator was not able to comprehend the danger and was not able immediately to come up with a good solu-

tion. Therefore it spread. Really, the amount of time that darkness has been here is a very short one in terms of the time of the Creator. To use an analogy, it is as if this Creation were a human who was bitten by a brown recluse spider. The initial bite did not seem that bad, and nothing was done immediately. But as with a brown recluse spider, the toxins spread from cell to cell bringing death, rot, and decay with it, until the flesh around the original bite began to die. It is at that point that the body would begin to marshal its defenses. However, as with the brown recluse spider, the natural defenses would perhaps not be enough. And in fact, as stated before, this Creation had no defenses whatsoever.

Therefore it has taken some planning and engineering in order to create weapons that were never before conceived of, to create defenses that were never before conceived of. For you see, the angels and Creator Gods, and all of the beings who are on the front line of this fight, have had to cobble together defenses and weapons out of whatever they can pick up. They have been picking up their shovels and broomsticks and trying to fight a highly sophisticated invader when they have no prior knowledge of defensive strategy. And that is why in many cases it appears that the dark side wins the battles. But the shift is happening. The Creator has come up with a strategy. The weapons are in place; the armies of light have been created; and the tide has turned. And in a short swift time, the war will be won.

Still, why did help not come earlier? We're talking about an enormous stretch of time here. Is it not true that all the original beings in this universe have been crying out to the Creator for help, with their uncounted trillions of voices, and for eons?

Yes, and it is being answered. I know it seems to humans and to many life forms that this has taken such a long time to accomplish. And there is regret that there has been so much suffering and that this has taken such a long time. I have outlined the reasons, but there is definitely regret that there has been this amount of suffering.

CHAPTER THREE
THE LIGHT WORKERS

Some time after our Creation had been invaded by dark beings, plans were made to heal and counteract the damage. The first plan was put into place about 500 million years ago. At this time the true intent of the dark forces had not been revealed, and it was thought that they were innocently harming the universes into which they had spread. Therefore, the first major attempt to help the fallen universes involved the sending of a substantial force of light beings into each of the universes that had been affected. These light beings were mostly from the inner universes, the older ones which are located nearest the Godverse and which are closest to the pristine purity and power of the original Creation. The beings who were sent were healers, restorers, and educators, for it was then believed that the invading beings could be helped and restored to the divine flow of life in this Creation. Most of the light workers on Earth belong to this group, and therefore most of us have been in this particular universe for about 500 million years. The light workers are generally characterized by a high degree of awareness, along with a profound longing for home.

There were many aspects to this initial plan. The one I am most familiar with involved the bringing of pure, uncorrupted genetic or blueprint material from the Godverse to a selected number of critical planets in those universes which had damaged genetics. As you read this section, you may come to a remembrance of your intended part in this great plan.

THE MISSION OF THE LIGHT WORKERS

Please give some additional information on the group of light workers which was sent about 500 million years ago to help the dark univers-es. We'd like to know what prompted this group of beings to come, who made the decisions, how they were chosen or how they volun-teered, and so on.

The Creator Gods in the fallen universes convened a council. They met and put forth a call for help. This call went out and a great council was convened amongst the Creator Gods of the light univers-es. An extensive recruitment then took place to assemble a large entourage of multi-skilled, multi-faceted, multi-dimensional beings to come and do what they thought would be reclamation work. It was hoped that the size and skills of this force would be sufficient.

This force arrived into the universes which had been affected by darkness, and at first things seemed to be going well. They set up their schools, their healing missions, and so on—all of the work that they felt would be needed. Some thousands of years into this project, the dark achieved a critical mass, declared itself, and sealed off this quadrant of universes behind the frequency fence. And essentially at that point the battles began.

What kind of numbers were sent into a universe such as this one?

Hundreds of thousands of beings were sent into each universe. This venture was considered very important, and the recruiting effort was large. It went across pretty much the entire spectrum of talents and beings. At that time it was still believed that the dark beings could be helped, and so the light workers that were sent were chosen as healers, restorers, teachers, and so on.

Would you speak on some of the other major facets of the plans and purposes of these light forces? I feel this is important because light workers reading this material may remember the reasons for which they came here.

Yes. I would suggest to each of the light workers who come to read this to look at their passion and their talents. For instance if someone has a passion for akashic record work or healing work, to look at that, and see it as the seed of the mission they came here to accomplish. It will also be helpful to realize that great numbers of peo-ple with similar talents and similar missions were sent into each uni-verse. For example, perhaps several thousand people with the great ability of akashic record reclamation would go into each dark universe and be stationed throughout. Then there would have been the intention to link up with a being in the healing arts, or a being doing genetic work, or whatever. And these different groups would have worked hand in hand, and put together a comprehensive program for healing not only individuals but worlds and systems. Since your personal work involved bio-systems, for instance, you would have worked with geneticists, and would have also worked with beings who specialized in cleaning up various types and levels of pollution. Then there would have been the teachers, the educators, those who specialized in emotional and spiritual work, and so on.

These beings then began to set up something almost along the lines of a great university on each planet, so you would have a whole university type structure of classes on healing and other subjects, which would be coordinated from a centralized location. Since there are many inhabited planets in each of the fallen universes, a teacher or healer would be assigned to many, not just one. Remember that wormhole travel at that time was very possible, though it has largely broken down since then. Parts of this great system were actually set up within the universes before everything was totally disrupted.

Are the remains of this original force of light workers now concentrated on the twelve critical planets? [Please see the Glossary for a definition of the twelve critical planets, of which Earth is one.]

There are remains on each of those planets. However, these areas have been targeted by the dark forces, so many have fled to some safer areas. There are some of these beings in that area where your relatives are, near the edge of this universe. Those who could flee to safety did so, however many were entrapped in the karmic cycle of this planet or wherever they were at the time.

Please discuss briefly what it was like for us when the fall happened, knowing nothing of darkness or even of defending ourselves.

It was horrible beyond words. If you were to look at some of the sections of Michelangelo's fresco of the Last Judgment and you look at the fallen souls, it would look something like that, only magnified many hundreds of thousands of times. The light workers and other beings in these universes were trapped, and ripped asunder from their connectedness with Prime Creator, and also their connectedness with all their companions. There was the rending apart of twin souls; and many other connections were also torn apart. For example, those who don't have twin souls would have their connection to nature severed, or their connection to the Creator Gods, or to Prime Creator, severed or twisted. It was like a descent into hell.

Have many of us attempted to return home, and have we been unable to do so?
I would say just about everybody who has any consciousness left has desired to go home, but most have had no way to do so.

Did a high percentage of the light workers fall?
Even one being falling is a high percentage. But I would say in the range of 30% fell. And I believe that most or all of these beings will be reclaimed. *[How did you, yourself, resist the temptation to fall?]* In my own case, I never felt the temptation or the lure of whatever it is that darkness has offered, and so for me resistance has not been difficult in that way. It is the only thing I know, to be light and to be of service.

Is it correct that the vast majority of light workers on this planet are from this original group?
That is correct. And it is the light workers, collectively, who have taken the greatest brunt of this destruction. For you simultaneously fell victim to the controlling nature of the darkness and yet could see that this was not the true nature of humanity, for you had your memories intact. So this has been, for all of you, the roughest ride.

Is there anything you'd like to convey to the light workers?
I would like to say that the remnants of the families or the groups that people came in with are here. The time is right for people to seek each other out, through whatever means is available, in terms of like minded groups and conversations with people who have similar passions. They may wish to form discussion groups, either in person or through the Internet. There can be a sharing of experiences with no agenda, simply trying to jog each other's memories and come up with common experiences.

The other thing I would like to say is that the beings who came into this project were considered the best and the brightest within the Creation, representing a cross section of all of the kinds of talents of all the Creator Gods, across all the universes. They were not Creator Gods specifically, but they were representatives of their particular brands of creation, in a sense. *[It must have been a loss to the rest of Creation, then, to have their best and brightest lost for so long.]* Yes, and I would also like to say that I believe all will be reclaimed. It is my hope that even those who were lost or melted down can be restored, and there are relatively few of those.

Why are these beings from the older universes the finest and brightest souls? Are we just older?

Well, that's perhaps a qualitative judgment on my part, a preference on my part. It's maybe not fair of me to say finer and brighter, but they are among my favorites. *[What would be the difference between one of these beings and one from an outer universe?]* It would be like the difference between an ancient wise tree and a young sapling.

Please give some further information about the particular aspect of this work that has made Earth so important—that of selecting twelve critical planets and seeding perfect genetic material into them.

That was seen as part of the rescue mission, as it was seen that the genetics of the fallen universes had been corrupted and damaged. At that time, it was not known that the forces of darkness were so adamantly bent on destruction and control. It was thought that they were wayward and were innocently damaging the Creation, not through evil intent but just through being in an inharmonious state. It was not seen to be a consciously driven attempt at destruction, more a byproduct of their flawed nature. Therefore it was felt that if perfect genetic material could be re-introduced into the fallen universes, then their genetics and their blueprints could be corrected.

The further that you get from the Godverse, the center of the universes, the more and more flaws and divergence you get from the original, perfected blueprint of life. Therefore the universes that are furthest from the Godverse are the ones where these flaws have multiplied and magnified. It's similar to the way that DNA will form new cells, but as it multiplies hundreds and thousands of times, flaws develop and then perpetuate themselves and increase. What you and your group did was to take original material from the divine blueprint, material taken from very near the center of things, and bring it way out to the edge of Creation, to this critical point which is Earth. These critical planets were carefully chosen as they form a grid within the universe. In each of the outer universes, in fact some of the closer in ones as well, there has been this embedding of key points. In the fallen universes they have been fought over greatly and have been the source of many of the wars, because control of these key points means control of the light coming in.

However the original flaws in the outer universes would have been easily corrected, had not the dark forces taken advantage of them to damage, corrupt, and destroy the genetics and blueprints in the fallen universes.

27

One of the most damaging results of the invasion was the fall or taking down of some of the Creator Gods. For each universe is created by a being or beings. Therefore as the Creator Gods were corrupted, what they brought forth was faulty DNA and faulty structures and so on. For what is not created in light is an abomination. The fallen Creator Gods created universes which are almost entirely dark and devoid of light.

Was the perfect genetic material in the twelve key planets being held for the future?
There are two aspects here. There were beings who brought in genetic material to restore that which was damaged. Your mission was somewhat different in that it came somewhat later, as a last gasp effort to retain the integrity of things before it was lost. *[And do you still believe that this perfect genetic material from the twelve critical planets will be able to restore the damaged genetics in this universe?]* It is quite likely, yes. It looks to be still doable.

For those of us who have been here in the fallen universes, has there been any benefit?
The benefit is of endeavoring to save that portion of Creation from being overtaken by the darkness; there is a great benefit there. The great heroics of the beings who have come here have not gone unsung, and the service that has been rendered is very appreciated. These beings become great teachers, and in doing so serve the light *mightily.*

CHAPTER FOUR
THE ROLE OF PRIME CREATOR

This section mentions two very important components of the restoration of Creation: the Omniversal Energy and the Light Warriors. Details are included in later chapters; please consult the Glossary for short definitions.

PART I—LOSS OF FAITH IN THE CREATOR

Heru, our topic for today is not a pleasant one. After the channeling we did a few days ago, as I was mulling it over, my emotions began to boil. First I felt intense grief as I considered all the suffering that has occurred due to the invasion of darkness, particularly because it was useless and purposeless, not part of some greater plan. Then, deep anger and rage at the Creator came up, underlain by a profound sense of betrayal and abandonment. I'm sure these feelings have an irrational component. Nevertheless I'm going to share the track of my emotions with you, because I'm convinced that almost all humans on Earth and in all of the fallen universes have similar emotions, consciously or not.

They do.

First of all, the amount of time that we're dealing with here is staggering. You said that the original invasion happened about 1.3 billion years ago, and that our universe was invaded about 900 million years ago.

That is correct.

Then I started thinking about the number of universes that must have fallen. If the universes number in the tens of thousands, let's say just for example that there are 40,000 of them. If six percent are fallen or embattled, as you have said, then we have 2400 dark universes! And

I feel that a billion years and 2400 dark universes is just way, way too much, and way, way, way too long.
    I agree.

This is not like a spider bite on a person's arm. It's like losing a whole hand to infection and death. In fact, it feels almost to me as if this Creation is like a beautiful woman who has been raped. Maybe the rape only took place in her vagina, in six percent of her body, but it affects the whole, and it's not a small thing.
    That is a good analogy.

When I began to think of the amount of suffering and devastation that has occurred because darkness was allowed to spread, and wasn't dealt with for such an incredibly long time, a tremendous feeling welled up in me that said, "Regret isn't enough." For those on the highest level to say they're sorry they didn't act sooner is just not enough to balance the weight of the countless numbers of beings who went through not just many lifetimes of suffering, but millions of such lifetimes. It's also not enough for those beings who have actually been destroyed, who have ceased to exist. For them, the rescue has come too late. They are gone forever.
    That is true.

I feel that hardwired into all life in this universe is the belief that Creator is loving, Creator is just, Creator is merciful. But in fact, those beings in the fallen universes found that when darkness invaded, God did not act. God did not protect the innocent. God did not stop the rape, the devastation, of worlds and galaxies and universes. Like a husband who is cowardly or paralyzed, God stood by and allowed His Creation to be raped, stood by and watched and did nothing, when we were fighting not only for our own existence but sacrificing ourselves to help the whole. God is finally acting and we are all grateful, but it feels like too little, too late. Yes, we need help, but we needed it about a billion years ago!
    Yes.

At this point Heru, I feel a need to ask: Do you trust God, the Prime Creator?
    I trust the intentions. I do not always feel that the Prime Creator can totally reach into the Creation and effect the change that is needed. Just as I recently tried to manifest in your third dimensional world and was unable to, Prime Creator has attempted to deal with this but has been, up until now, ineffectual in dealing with it. *[But you do*

absolutely and totally trust the intentions of Creator?] Yes.

I realized that there's a large part of me that no longer has that trust. I feel like a child in a household where an invader broke in and raped, tortured, and killed the children, while the parents stayed on the top floor of the house and didn't do anything. How could I ever trust my parents again?

Then a feeling came that is perhaps even worse than the anger. And that is the sense of being betrayed and abandoned by God. I know that I was part of the group of light workers which were sent here 500 million years ago to help the fallen universes. To use yet another analogy, I feel like a member of a special task force that is sent by my government to a dark and dangerous place. We are sent by our country, and we are sent with the mandate and the promise, "Establish a base—reinforcements will follow, very soon." Heru, am I wrong? I feel in my bones that this was said to those of us who volunteered to work in the dark universes.

It was, and the help was not able to come through.

So we went out. We suffered, we died, we have been ringed about with enemies all around. But no help arrived. We sent telegrams, we sent messages, we cried out for help. But no help came. Not until now. But by now, as a force we are in rags and tatters and a lot of us didn't even make it to this point.

This is true.

The sense of abandonment that I feel around this is so profound that it feels as if every cell in my body could weep for a thousand years.

In any case, to conclude this tirade of emotion, I return to the metaphor of the woman who gets raped. The husband finally acts, the perpetrator is carried off to jail, and the woman is healed of her physical wounds. But what about her emotional scars? She still carries, imbedded in her soul substance, not one trauma but two. First, the trauma of the rape, and secondly, the trauma of the fact that her husband allowed it to happen, for a long stretch of time that, for her, was an eternity of horror.

Yes.

So now the Creator is finally acting to expel the dark invaders. This is a time of great joy. But, as we who have suffered the effects of this event begin to raise our heads and to see the light again, mixed with our gratitude are the painful emotions that I've just described. So I feel that the healing which will take place must also occur within the family of this Creation itself, between Creator and creatures. We have uncountable numbers of beings now who have ceased, on some level and to some degree, to trust God. How will this trust be restored?

I don't know that I have the answers to this. These are profound and deeply sorrowful questions. And I am sort of in the middle, where I have participated in the creation of the universes. I have watched them fall, and have been to some degree powerless to prevent or correct that. I don't even know how to begin to address the sorrow and the loss.

I know that when I feel anger at someone, that anger immediately evaporates when I can stand in that person's shoes. Perhaps if we, the creatures in this Creation, could truly grasp what the Creator went through when the invasion occurred, then we could forgive this great lapse of time and the unspeakable horrors that have happened.

Yes. I would suggest attempting a direct communication, having Karen channel the Creator. And express what you have expressed to me, directly.

Can you add anything else?

I would tell you that all of the Ascended Masters have felt similar emotions to what you have expressed. If you would look at the life of Jeshua [Jesus], he would be a pretty good manifestation of the attempt of all of us to effect change, and how that was ruined and distorted. *[Are you speaking of his life, or what happened to his teachings?]* Both his teachings and what happened to him, in the crucifixion. As this world fell further into darkness, any attempt at a public ministry by an Ascended Master would meet with the same fate.

PART II—THE CREATOR RESPONDS

Karen and I took Heru's advice, and we set out in an attempt to access some aspect of the consciousness of that being whom we call Creator. I must confess here that I have always felt extremely skeptical of those who profess to channel "God". In fact, in a lifetime of travels on the inner planes, I had never encountered any being or consciousness whom I could call God. However, when Karen and I called in the Prime Creator of this Creation at Heru's suggestion,

32

there was indeed a response from a consciousness which was both awesomely powerful and tenderly loving. I still do not know if our Prime Creator is the ultimate God beyond which there is no other. I do feel that we communicated with an aspect of the consciousness of the Creator, however. The energy was so intense that the words coming through were sometimes, of necessity, extremely simple. I wish that these words could convey the profound power and love which filled the room during those moments.

Greetings to you, Creator. We have called on you in hopes that we can understand you better, and to heal our relationships with you. We understand that you are the One who created this Creation that we live in. Is this correct?
Yes. *[Are you a singular being, or are you an expression of group mind, an expression of a group or council which created this Creation?]* I am One. *[Do you have gender?]* No.

Are there Creations created by Gods other than yourself?
It appears to me that there are but I do not interface with them.

Would you please describe to us something of the vision that you held when you created this particular Creation?
I have created many Creations, and this was to be my most beautiful Creation yet to date. In large part it is successful. I am aware of your pain and concern in this part of the fallen universes. I would like to discuss that today.

Thank you, we would as well. How did you feel or perceive the initial attack of darkness?
It was actually fairly small initially, like stepping on a nail; or a pinprick or a bee sting, something of that nature. The initial pain was not that severe. However there was a venom that was inserted through that opening, which began to spread fairly subtly and rapidly—subtly enough that I did not perceive its spread immediately. This foreign invader began to lay eggs and set up colonies. And that did not appear extremely harmful at first. It seemed benign and it seemed that these universes would not be harmed by it, for I felt there was room for all.

At that point, were you getting calls for help?
No, for these beings were not manifesting their true intent for

quite a long period of time. They were well established before they revealed their criminal intent. Regarding when that intent was revealed, let us see if we can set some timelines. Your time is difficult for me to relate to, so perhaps you can help by giving a framework.

Heru states that the initial invasion occurred about 1.3 billion years ago. To continue, at some point you realized there was a threat, and these invaders were not innocent?

Yes. It seems that this occurred hundreds of millions of years ago, but not billions. And so there would have been that long amount of time for the corruption to spread and to spread, amongst the Creator Gods, the Angelic Hierarchies, the Elohim, and the other hierarchies, almost all of which have been contaminated. During that time the dark beings were keeping within themselves, and very closely guarded, the secret of their criminal intent. The fullness of this criminal intent did not become clear until the dark universes began being born out of the darkness. Again, that time was perhaps several hundred million years ago, but not as much as a billion.

It appears that the light workers were first sent into the contaminated universes about 500 million years ago. So perhaps it was shortly before that.

Yes, that is most likely correct. At that time it was not known whether these light forces would prevail or how effective they could be, for we had and I had never encountered anything like this. There was hope that this would be enough. And all along the way, those of my Creation who had succumbed attempted to hide their contamination. Therefore throughout this whole process was obfuscation and delay. These delays made it take longer than it should have for it to become apparent that the efforts of the light forces were not enough.

Were the dark and contaminated universes sealed off at this point so they could not infect others?

I had no mechanism with which to do so. This invading force is able to penetrate anything and everything in this Creation. There was really no material in this Creation built in such a way that could deflect or seal or contain this contamination. It was at that point that I saw the need to create something outside of this Creation, and began to create a new Creation. And that is where the Warriors of Light have come from.

Why did this take so long?

The declaration of the dark and the erection of the frequency fence happened about 500 million years ago in your time. In the age of this particular Creation this is a relatively short time period, though it would seem incredibly vast to you. That being said, the greatest difficulty in bringing forth the Light Warriors was in creating an entirely new substance with which to create. Creating the forms, the personalities, the talents—all of that—basically followed the patterns that had already been established. But to create something wholly new, a new substance, takes a lot of time.

Why did you not send help to the light beings who went into the dark universes, as promised?

Help was sent, and it was defeated. [This statement seemed to be followed by a deafening silence, as the tragedy of it sank in.] In fact, instead of my sealing off the invaders, the invaders sealed me off from this part of the Creation. And many have been lost.

Is all the infection more or less located within a certain area of the Creation?

Yes. *[Is it still spreading?]* At this point, no, but only because of the Light Warriors.

I know how we felt, we who were in the dark and fallen universes. We felt abandoned and betrayed by you. We didn't understand that you had sent help. How did you feel at that time?

The whole of the Creation wept. There are no words to describe the grief at the loss of part of my beloved, for this whole Creation functions as one entity. And it was as if she were dying and amputated—that this part of her was amputated, and that the whole of her was going to die. For the whole Creation has been threatened by this invasion.

It has been a terrible thing. But then the new Creation was created, and you made the Light Warriors.

Yes. *[How do you see things now?]* (Strongly) <u>I have created something that no darkness can resist.</u> I have cordoned the darkness off from the rest of this Creation, and have begun the great battle. I myself know nothing of war; it is not a part of what I am. But amongst these Warriors of Light are great captains who are in the process of uncloaking themselves as we speak. And in a twinkling of an eye, things in this Creation will look much different. Then the healing will begin. Those universes that were created by the fallen will be destroyed, for they are not reclaimable; they were not built upon my founding principles of light. *[And the invaders will be destroyed?]* Yes.

Will the Light Warriors destroy all the darkness in this Creation?
These Light Warriors will not stop at the perimeters of my Creation. They will reach out into the heart of what sent the darkness here, and will destroy it. *[Once this Creation is cleared, will you protect it from further attacks?]* Yes, I will ring all of Creation with the Warriors of Light.

Have other Creations been threatened?
Yes, indeed. There was a second attack, on another of my Creations. However it was much smaller and much later, and I was able to fend it off. *[And how about those made by others?]* I cannot say. *[Those are too far distant for you?]* Yes.

Do you know where the dark beings came from?
Yes, but it is somewhat of an indescribable place. There are no words. It is outside of this Creation.

How can the sense of abandonment and betrayal, that so many of us feel, be healed?
I would say that the proof is in the pudding. When I have eliminated the darkness, then the healing will begin. Then faith can be restored, and not until that time.

I realize my own anger at you was unfounded, and ask you to forgive me for that.
My darling one, it is I who needs to ask your forgiveness, for it is I who am responsible for what occurred. There are no words to express the depth of my sorrow about this. *[It is hard for us humans to realize and understand that even a being so powerful as yourself is not completely omniscient and omnipotent, to realize that even for you this is a learning process.]* Yes.

The hardest thing for me is the beings who were lost. Will there ever be a way to reclaim them?
Their blueprints are intact, their records are intact. *[But their essence? Is it gone forever?]* Once the darkness has been removed, we will see. It is not known yet.

The communication ended at this point, because I was crying, as was Karen, and it seemed that Creator was weeping as well. The energy was also too strong for her to handle, so we released the connection.

[Elora:] To explain the last part of the communication: certain beings within the fallen universes have been attacked in such a destructive way that the only recourse was for them to be "melted down" and returned to Source. An analogy would be a golden cup which is thrown into a vat of molten gold. The pure metal remains, but all individuation is lost. This has been the ultimate tragedy resulting from the invasion of darkness, for many great and beautiful beings have been lost. It is hoped, however, that ultimately even they can be reclaimed.

A week later, we spoke to the Creator again. The communication flowed more easily this time.

PART II—THE DANCE OF CREATION

Creator, thank you for coming to speak with us again today. We would like to know, first, can you affect change in this world, in people's lives here?

Yes. It is an interesting paradox. I know you have been receiving information about the fact that when they become enlightened, people have a sort of bubble around themselves where all they see is love and light. To some degree, faith and belief play a big part in that. *[When people have faith you can work more easily?]* Yes.

I am puzzled by something that Heru told me. He said that since we are a free will universe, the release of the Omniversal Energy and the Light Warriors had to be petitioned for, and it was voted down many times, therefore delaying the release greatly. Is it true that you were waiting on this petition to come to you—and if so why, since surely you are aware that free will in the fallen universes is a mockery?

That is perhaps not quite the way I would describe it. I don't want to say that Heru was incorrect, but from my perspective it was somewhat different. It is one of those synchronies that is the magic of this Creation. For the cry for intervention did not develop until the Light Warriors were ready to be released. Therefore as fragmented—as fallen, dense, separate, and dark as this sector of the Creation is—it still resonates with my blood, with my life, and with my light. And this is proof of it. And that, my dear, should make you very happy. For what that says is that you still belong to me, you are still my beloved, and I still dance with you.

There was not a unified cry for intervention before then?
It was as if the beings in this sector could feel the help that was coming, they could smell it being ready. So as the readiness came, the cry also came. That is why I say it is a synchronous happening.

Even on Earth, we have prophecies which have looked forward to this time. And I've wondered, how did we know?
Exactly. You knew. And you still have that connection with me, in spite of everything that has been done to each of you.

I have seen that a mighty pulse of energy is going to come out of the Godverse some time in the future. Could you explain exactly what this is?
It is the Breath of God. My breath has great restorative powers, as you can imagine—for healing, for restoration, and for cleansing. *[Will you breathe once in that way, or many times until healing is complete?]* Three times. *[Somehow I want to cry when I hear that.]* Because you know this, and because you know that these three breaths will bring you complete wholeness.

You said that the fallen part of Creation was cut off from you. How did this occur? Have there been frequency fences placed all around the fallen part of Creation so that we were disconnected from you and from the rest of Creation?
Yes. This occurred in the reverse order from what you may imagine. The invasion came. It appeared benign, and spread through a number of universes. Once the invaders had an area sufficient to give them a platform upon which to launch the takeover of this entire Creation, they then built the frequency fences, cut everything off, and caused the universes to fall. All of the fallen universes are grouped together inside this frequency fence.

So the fallen part of Creation became like a cancerous tumor, walled off from the rest of the body.
Yes, but once it reached a certain mass or density or intensity, it would have exploded into the rest of Creation, just as a cancer would metastasize.

I remember from being in Virqie, which is of course a light universe, that there was a continual experience of being connected to God. It was more than being connected, it was that all life was One and all life flowed together. This is part of what was cut off, this oneness with the whole?

Yes.

It seems that there is a characteristic of this Creation, that the highest and most powerful beings, paradoxically, cannot seem to affect the manifest part of Creation itself. Is that how this Creation is, or is it solely due to the separation and sealing off that has been done by the dark forces?

The latter. In an unfallen universe there is no separation.

Some say that you, the Creator, are too far above or too distant to take an active part in Creation, and that the role of active participation in Creation must be undertaken by other beings and forces. Can you speak to this?

In the unfallen part of my Creation I am very present within every action, every cycle, every part of what happens. I am the stuff from which the Creator Gods form the universes, and so there is a process of co-creation with both of us together. It is a beautiful dance. How it has been distorted in the fallen universes, I do not really need to explain. But that dance is a very interesting, multi-layered, fluid give and take. There is the dance between me and the Creator Gods to create form, and then there is the dance between me and the form, almost as lovers. The beauty, the intricacy, the intensity of all of this is a magical song. And yes, it has been very distorted.

Karen went to a lecture last night where the speaker was talking about the incredible fire of all-consuming longing for the Beloved. He described that fire as torturous, and how it entails going through the dark night of the soul. And that is part of the distortion. It is not created to be painful in that way. Yes, there is ecstasy within that pain, but pain is not native to the process. Yet that fire does live in every soul. And that is where, as a soul, you will find me.

You state that you are the "stuff" out of which Creation is made. This reminds me of Krishna's statement in the Bhagavad Gita: "Permeating the Creation with a fragment of Myself, I remain." In other words, God permeates the entire Creation, yet is also beyond it in an unmanifest state.

Yes.

Are you the guardian and protector of this Creation?

Prior to the invasion of the dark, I am ashamed to say that I did not see the need for protection or guardianship. It was just a lovely dance. I have created the Creation of the Light Warriors to ensure that this Creation will be restored to that dance, and will remain that dance. For as you have seen I could have armed this universe and this Creation; but I would no longer want to dance that dance with this Creation. And in the end I would have had to destroy it.

Have you not done so now? Have you not armed this Creation?

Yes, but with something outside of the Creation—and that is the difference. Had I armed it with something from within this Creation it would have destroyed it. *[Because war is so antithetical to the nature of this Creation?]* Yes. I would have had to arm everything from the greatest universal structures to the tiniest subatomic particles, and so the entire Creation would have been weaponized. And I have no desire to dance the intimate dance with a warrior.

Many humans see God the Creator as a parent, as a father or mother figure. I have personally always been more drawn to the concept of God as the Beloved. Which is more correct, from your perspective, or are both of them correct?

Being everything and all that is, yes, both are correct.

It is very hard for us to understand what motivates dark beings. Why do they wish to harm, to destroy, to enslave, to take over other beings?

The reason that it is so hard for you to understand is because it *is one hundred percent antithetical to your nature, as it is to mine as* well. I do not understand what motivates the dark. I sent and sacrificed many of my parts in an effort to educate, salvage, heal, transform, and reform these dark beings; to make them compatible with this Creation. All I can say is that now they must be removed forever.

CHAPTER FIVE
THE OMNIVERSAL ENERGY

The text that follows is my own story of what I noticed during the first six months of the Omniversal Energy's presence on Earth. It was written in February 2004, before I made contact with Heru. I would like to note that my husband John and I live near Asheville, NC, an area which is very energetically active with many ley lines, portals, and power points. Parts of the country which are energetically calmer have not experienced as much upheaval or release of negative energies as we have here.

PART I—ELORA'S ESSAY ON THE OMNIVERSAL ENERGY

I came into this life filled with a tremendous drive to evolve, as well as a visceral expectation of planetary ascension and of my own involvement in that process. I studied Vedanta as a teenager, read the Findhorn channelings in the 70's and many others in the 80's and 90's, and was convinced that the rapid transformation of our planet was imminent.

Somewhere in the mid to late 90's I began to lose my faith. It was very clear that, at least on the outer level, Earth was <u>not</u> transforming. In fact, because of the increasing environmental devastation, overall things appeared to be getting worse. I tried and tried to understand what was really happening. Had there been a plan, and had it gone awry; derailed (as so many have been) by the unexpectedly recalcitrant behavior of humanity and the density of 3D life here? Had interference from the dark side simply been too great? Or had the whole thing been a grand illusion, and were most channelers simply recycling mass thought forms which bore no resemblance to reality? A number of my lightworker friends felt the same way. There was a sense of weariness, of deep disappointment. So many of us had worked so very hard, and it appeared that the transformation of the our planet—if it happened at all—was probably thousands of years down the line.

That's how things stood with me until September of 2003. Despite feeling discouraged about outcomes on Earth, I never ceased to explore inner realms. It was about mid-September that John and I both noticed a great increase of psychic attacks and various types of attachments in people we knew. Everybody was picking up dark forces, negative entities, and even discarnates. Even John and I were getting attachments, for the first time in many years! I own a small business, and had to continually clear my staff. At times the "infestations" were so bad that one sensitive employee couldn't get to work until she was cleared.

John and I separately went to guidance and asked what was going on. To our surprise, we were told that the upsurge in attacks and attachments was due to something positive—an increase of light on the planet. The cockroaches were being flushed out of the cracks, so to speak. This information interested me greatly, so we did our best to get more details. Some of my contacts on the inner said they didn't know where this light was coming from—it was a source so high that even they couldn't comprehend it, but they could certainly perceive it. I tuned in to the Omniversal Energy, as I call it, and found that it felt like an intense beam of light energy which was experienced as descending directly through the crown chakra.

John is quite a good channel and has recently been channeling a being who identifies himself as Maitreya (not the current Maitreya, but the first one on Earth to hold that office). Maitreya had a lot to say about the Omniversal Energy. He said that it is the highest and most powerful energy we have ever known on this planet. He told us that this energy is what we have been waiting for—and while its arrival was expected to occur quite a bit earlier, it is indeed here now. As it intensifies, Maitreya told us, the OE (as I call it for short) would change everything on our world beyond recognition. It will clean up our planet to the very last corner, and as the OE increases in power, absolutely nothing will be able to withstand it. The OE will gradually raise the frequency of Earth as well, so that all matter here will become less and less dense.

Maitreya said that the Omniversal Energy is affecting not only earth but our entire universe. It's my understanding that what we call the star seeds on Earth not only came here from other planets, but originally came from other universes, in an attempt to help this one. In any case, Maitreya stated that the OE will ultimately cleanse and transform our entire universe. He said there would be dark corners for a time, and many highly negative beings would choose to leave Earth as the light increases, to hide out in such places. Even they, eventually, would have to face the music. Earth, however, was in line to receive a high dose of this energy and is therefore a good place to be right now. As closely as I could get, the Omniversal Energy had arrived on September 5, 2003, and we started noticing the effects very shortly after that.

We also began to observe that many people around us were experiencing dramatic and intense life changes. For example, Karen had followed a certain Eastern master for all of her adult life as well as for six lives prior to this one. On September 6, she found out that he was not a being of integrity and renounced him. Shortly after that her father died, her apartment was flooded, and she had to deal with ongoing psychic attacks from the astral minions of her former guru. Of the four staff members who worked in my business at the time, three of them had deaths in their families in the months directly after the entry of the Omniversal Energy. I myself broke a karmic contract of over 3000 years standing and went through other intense changes and realizations.

I was personally told that this energy or light comes from a central power source within the Omniverse (the central universe within this universal system, often called the "Godverse"). It was for this reason that I coined the name "Omniversal Energy".

Initially, the Omniversal Energy was not well absorbed onto our planet. Due to frequency barriers and the like, much of it was seen to be "sheeting off". That has changed to some extent, and I also see people becoming more acclimatized to this energy as well. A balancing of the OE seemed to occur at the time of the Harmonic Concordance, but I emphasize that it had arrived on our planet before that time.

As of February 2004, things have continued to be quite intense in our area. John, Karen, and I all noticed that areas located on or near ley lines became too highly energized for comfort. In fact all of us moved from such areas to places which were more energetically quiet.

With the arrival of the Omniversal Energy, I feel once again that our world is on track for a rapid transformation. Just how rapid I do not know for sure, but I believe the rate of change is going to be speeding up exponentially. I do hope that those of us who have been doing our work for so long will ultimately be able to ride the waves of change in a joyful way, as well as being able to help others who may be struggling.

I have found that the Omniversal Energy is highly intelligent, responsive, and seems to know everything. I often communicate with it. I don't know what percent of its full intensity we are currently receiving, probably no more than a tenth. Any person who is sensitive to energies can tune into the Omniversal Energy simply by requesting the connection. The connection will be felt directly through the crown chakra and will feel like a very pure and powerful white light. One may also request other colors of this light, such as rose, emerald, gold, or silver; and these may be used for protection and healing.

PART II—THE NATURE AND ARRIVAL OF THE OMNIVERSAL ENERGY

Heru, would you please speak on the Omniversal Energy—what it is, how it got here, and so on.

The Omniversal Energy is a beam or ray of light, projected directly by Prime Creator as a beam of focused intent designed to penetrate all levels of Creation. It has, to a greater or lesser degree, penetrated and touched every atom of Creation, with the intent of restoring the true light of the Creator to all Creation. Embedded in this beam or ray of light are encoded many programs and many beings, including the Light Warriors. These programs and beings are designed to activated sequentially in order to perform the restoration of the fallen universes and all beings and substances contained within them.

Will the Omniversal Energy continue to increase in strength?

Yes. I would describe it almost like the rotating beam from a light-house, and it is rotating through all of the fallen sector. It's not so much that the beam will become stronger as that every time it comes through, it will affect more, and will penetrate more deeply. The rate of rotation is so rapid that the effect is very constant, not as fast as a strobe light, but it's as much on as off.

But it will continue to increase, in our experience?

Yes, it will. As the frequency barriers fall, more and more of that light will penetrate. And as time goes by, more of the programs will be activated as well. *[It will increase until the Breath of God reaches us?]* I know of no time that it will not continue. It may increase indefinitely, and may just be a new standard level of existence.

I'm surprised that so few people are aware of the Omniversal Energy and the timing that it came in.

Well, remember the frequency fences at that time were still very much intact. Many are feeling changes in energy and are attributing them to astrological events or the coming of the new age and so on. Much of what has happened in the past year has been attributed to other events and causes.

Is Omniversal Energy the best name for this energy or light?

It is a very good name. *[I experience it as being like a living presence, very intelligent.]* Oh yes. *[And it seems to know everything.]* Yes, it is like the finger of God in your life.

How did the Omniversal Energy reach the fallen sectors? Is it being stepped down through the Great Central Suns?

No. Prior to the advent of the Omniversal Energy, the conduit path of energy from Prime Creator would pass through the Central Sun of a universe to the Central Sun of a galaxy, to the sun of a solar system, and so on. However, corruption and fallen energy had taken over so many of these systems that this was not working. So the Omniversal Energy was designed to come directly to every atom, bypassing that whole structure. In your traditions and mythology in many places there are statements that one cannot look directly at God—if you look directly at God you will perish, you will be blinded, etc. And the Omniversal Energy bypasses all of that. For the first time and for all of Creation, there is a more direct energetic conscious flow both ways: from Prime Creator to all aspects of Creation, and from each aspect of Creation back to Prime Creator.

So the Omniversal Energy is not traveling on a path?
No, it is being broadcast universally throughout all of Creation, both the fallen and unfallen universes. It has a somewhat different effect on the unfallen Creation, for in those regions it gives every atom a more direct communication with Creator, and just sparks up everything a little. I don't know if it's considered a huge change there. Everyone likes it; it feels very good. In this sector, it is of course having the effect of disrupting and discomforting the dark, and bringing hope to all light beings. And this will also assist in the reclamation of the fallen nature of matter in this sector, for the very stones of this Earth and much of the other solid space in this fallen sector have been defiled. The atomic structure itself has been distorted.

When I work with the Omniversal Energy, I feel it through my crown chakra. I call on it, and I ask it to do things, and I ask for information. Can you give other suggestions to readers to work with it?
Many people will pray blindly to a God that they have never seen, have only vaguely experienced, and never receive direct feedback of that God's existence. If people will address not only Prime Creator in their prayers, but also call upon the Omniversal Energy with Prime Creator, they will find their connection to become a direct face to face communication. And this changes everything.

Is the Omniversal Energy why so many in the West are now waking up?
People in the West have been experiencing awakenings for several decades. And it is actually still a fairly small minority of people that are having these awakenings. This is not so much tied to the advent of the Omniversal Energy as much as it is tied to the changing of the ages, and the larger cyclical wheels of time that are lining up for the 2012 portal. Given all the delays in launching the Omniversal Energy, it was felt that once it had finally been released, it would be advantageous for its full impact to correspond to the 2012 timing when this was all happening.

Without the arrival of the Omniversal Energy, apparently things would have been very bleak in our universe.
It would look to be at some point a great conflict on the horizon, where the forces of dark would seek to wage a final battle of subjuga-

tion of the light forces, and would have almost certainly have succeed-ed in that. So yes, things would not have looked good without outside help.

How did you feel about the coming of the Omniversal Energy?
Well, we knew. We were petitioning for it for some time, and it was in my mind overdue. And there had been delaying tactics by the dark in an attempt to stop it. *[Doesn't the Omniversal Energy come from the Godverse?]* Yes. *[So how could the dark delay this?]* It's a similar scenario to this planet receiving help form the outside. This is a free will universe, and so there need to be petitions made for some-thing like the Omniversal Energy. And so great discussions were had—do we call for it, do we not, and again and again things were voted down. *[So it was not going to come until called for?]* Yes. *[And does agreement have to be reached for this sort of thing, not just with-in the forces of light?]* Well, that is in an interesting question. The light beings cloaked themselves and held a meeting and did this petition without the rest of the council knowing about it. And that is how this was accomplished. However, even once the Omniversal Energy had been released, there was a last-ditch effort by the dark to stop it from reaching Earth. The timeline on Earth was distorted, bringing this time lag about, so that you are in fact not in linear time where you were supposed to have been. Earth's timeline has been rifted, somehow taken out of its proper place and distorted. These beings are very clever.

If the timeline hadn't been moved, when would the Omniversal Energy have reached Earth?
It looks like around 1976. *[That's a long delay.]* Yes, and much damage has been generated due to that delay.

[Elora:] Light workers who were awakened during the 70's will remember the tremendous sense of anticipation that was felt during that decade, and the feeling that the great shift on Earth was immi-nent. We know now that these intimations were based on the fact that the Omniversal Energy should have arrived on our planet around 1976. It is tragic that the dark was able to move Earth out of its time-line and therefore delay the coming of this great event. From this point, however, we can look forward in the knowledge that no more delays can or will occur.

CHAPTER SIX
THE LIGHT WARRIORS AND
THE BREATH OF GOD

PART I—THE LIGHT WARRIORS

We have seen how our Creation was invaded by an alien darkness against which it had no defenses. Heru has explained that angels, Ascended Masters, Creator Gods, and other beings who were created in Light have had to stand against darkness in order to prevent the fallen universes from collapsing entirely. None of the beings in this Creation were made to be warriors. When it was finally seen that the dark invaders were both soulless and unredeemable, our Creator formed an entirely new Creation. From this Creation were born the beings whom we call Light Warriors. Light Warriors are created for one purpose only—to eradicate darkness in all its manifestations. They traveled to our universe hidden and cloaked in the Omniversal Energy. On August 12, 2004, Heru told us that the uncloaking had begun.

Heru stated that the Light Warriors were beginning to uncloak themselves all over our universe and throughout the fallen quadrant of our Creation. "They are beyond count," he said, "and they are more than sufficient to do the job." He stated that it would take about two years (from the summer of 2004) to win the battle for Earth. This time frame corresponds with statements made by other channels, although none that I know of have spoken of the existence of the Light Warriors. When we asked why it would take that long, he replied that it takes time for humans to change.

In first looking at the Light Warriors, they appeared to me almost as if they were made of a pale golden metal, with an indestructible diamond at their core. Even if their bodies were destroyed, which is unlikely, the diamond containing their soul essence would remain. I also felt that they were all expressions of a group soul. Again, even in the inconceivable event that such a being could be destroyed, its soul would simply rejoin the rest of the group soul and nothing would be lost. In the great battle which must occur, our Creator has striven to ensure that no further souls will be lost.

Heru, perhaps hindsight is wise now that the Light Warriors have arrived. But it seems clear that only a response by force would be effective. I still don't see why this was not understood sooner.
There have been many debates on this. There were many beings who wanted to use only light and love, for that is the ingrained prime directive in this universe and all of this Creation as well. And in order to deal with this situation, it has been necessary for Prime Creator to create another Creation from which to draw these Warriors of Light. Within this Creation, there was not the material necessary to create Warriors of Light. It's hard to describe it, but this Creation just does not contain the proper elements to produce this type of being. This is a great reason for the time delay in the Creator coming to the aid of the fallen part of Creation. This was something completely different than had ever been conceived of by Creator.

There are times when I feel the stain of darkness, and the trauma of what I've experienced, has gone so deep in my being that I wonder if I can ever be completely healed. Do you feel we will ever be healed?
I do. You can work with the Light Warriors, calling them to work on you at the deepest cellular and atomic level, to root out everything that is not of the highest light. Ask them to come within you and work on your systems. Consider everything from pathogenic bacteria to the state of unconsciousness that humans have fallen into. There is quite a bit of work on all fronts. The Light Warriors are able to go into both the microcosm and the macrocosm. That is necessary for the elimination of darkness, for it extends to the subatomic level as well as the universal level.

Given that we have uncounted numbers of these beings, why will it still take two years to free Earth from darkness?
Perhaps because of the need for personal work, and because humans can only change just so fast.

The material you have given us on the prevalence of darkness in this universe has been difficult to absorb, but I wish to extend to you my heartfelt thanks for your willingness to tell us the truth. I appreciate the fact that you do not simply give sugar coated euphemisms, for these would never satisfy my desire for truth.

And I would say also that it is good to find an ear which is willing to hear. Up until now there have been many veils, and many people have only been able to handle the sugar coated aspects of truth. For it is a very painful, and in a sense a hopeless message, without the introduction of the Warriors of Light. Until now it has been a hopeless, thankless task that the light workers have engaged in.

Then there is also a reason for the timing of this information coming forth.

Yes. The other part is that it has been said for some beings, it's been enough just for them to hold to the light. And that has been true, that has been the message that has been sent down from the higher planes—to just hold on a little longer, until help can come. It grieved us so deeply when some beings were unable to continue holding on, and would fall or be destroyed. And it took far longer than we had anticipated. *[Did it take longer to make this new Creation than was thought?]* Yes. *[So Creator, too, is learning]* Yes. *[Do you have a tremendous love for Creator?]* Yes. *[And does Creator grieve for this?]* Oh yes. Deeply. Creator has never known grief before this.

So for you, the coming of the Light Warriors must be a great celebration.

Well, I'm not ready to celebrate yet. It is a beginning of the restoration. And when it is complete, I will celebrate.

Do you have any doubts that the Light Warriors will be successful?

No. You have seen accurately the nature of these beings, that they are made of a diamond hard matter. There is nothing in this Creation that is as hard and as sharp as that. They are indestructible and invincible, with an unquenchable thirst to find and destroy every last speck of darkness. That is their nature, it is what they are made for, and they are relentless.

On August 17th, 2004, we spoke with Sananda about some other matters. At that time, we also asked him for an update on the work of the Light Warriors. Sananda replied:

There are a great many of them working against the wall that you were told about yesterday, the wall that encompasses the fallen universes and separates them from the rest of Creation. They are massed there and are pushing forward to break apart that great frequency barrier so that the light may stream in. They have basically formed a solid wall there. That is the major part of the force which has been opened up at this time.

However there are also representatives who are mainly, at this point, scouting everywhere. Those are the ones that you have been seeing. They are running a reconnaissance and information gathering mission that is three quarters complete, and from that their strategy will be built. More and more of them will uncloak as the strategies are formed. More will be unveiled and uncloaked, and they will begin their mission in this part of the universe. Therefore not a lot of action has taken place at this time. However if you are in need at any time, any of the scouts are available for help. But you should be seeing many more in the weeks and months to come.

Have you called them in to sit with you and protect you? Do so. They are very effective in preventing any of the psychic attacks. All of the light workers have been under attack in that way, and the dark has used these attacks as an avenue to invite in the physical. So you would have an etheric virus and then have the physical virus, and have an etheric parasite and then the physical parasite. But now you can protect yourself with these Light Warriors. They come in pairs and you can have as many pairs as you feel you need. That sense of safety will allow you to truly relax. As you relax, you will release many of the deep traumas you are holding from many lifetimes.

Sananda, what feelings do you have when you see the arrival of these forces?

Relief. And joy. And the comfort of knowing that this long awaited process is beginning. For us it has been somewhat touch and go until they were unleashed. There was great danger to all of us, that any of us might be killed or might succumb to the darkness. We were surrounded.

[Elora:] We strongly suggest that all light workers call upon the Light Warriors for protection. Those who are "high profile" or experience a good deal of interference for any reason may want several as personal guardians. The first group of Light Warriors tended to "drift" and therefore requests for protection had to be reinforced on a continual basis. The second wave of Light Warriors, which arrived in October 2004 and are described in Chapter 8, do not have this tendency, and they are also more powerful. Also note that the first wave of Light Warriors came in pairs, whereas the second wave did not. You may call on other Light Warriors to protect your home as well.

Chapter 17 gives more information on working with the Light Warriors.

PART II—APPEARANCE AND ATTRIBUTES OF THE LIGHT WARRIORS

As it became clear to us just how important the Light Warriors are, we decided to make contact with one of this great force. Between August 20 and September 14, 2004 we had several communications with Rashona, one of the Light Warriors. For ease of reading, I have divided these into two subject headings.

Rashona, would you please begin by describing your appearance.
In your world I would appear to be roughly fourteen feet in height, slightly more male than androgynous. We are similar to an angelic form in that we have a human-like form with wings; however they are both in the front and the back so that we have four wings. Our skin appears somewhat plated. It has a similar appearance to the iridescent small feathers on the neck of certain birds, only as if they were almost in the form of a scale, and they are extremely hard. We are white and gold with a faint iridescence. Our eyes are gold. Our wings are largely white with little flecks of gold.

Please describe some of your other attributes, such as the type of matter you are made from, and the "indestructible diamond" at your core.
There are no words or concepts in your universe for the hardness of our matter. It is as if the atomic and molecular structure of our beings is tenfold stronger than yours is, so that we may penetrate any form of matter. The diamond at our core would be the same, and it is the original matter that our Creation was founded upon. And then our beings were grown out from there.

This reminds me of the matter of a neutron star, which is so dense that even a tiny piece placed on the Earth's surface would immediately plunge through to the core.
We are not heavy in that way, it is just that the bonds of the atoms are stronger. We do not require that kind of density, but we can penetrate that kind of density with ease. Were a human to go to a neutron star, of course they would be crushed, whereas we would not be.

What sort of weapons or energies do you use in battling the dark forces?

We use a flight that is different than the flight you would use in this universe. We use these four wings to create a spin, an upright spin. We almost become like a drill bit, enabling us to create wormholes at will and go anywhere at will with this spin. So speed in flight is one weapon. The second weapon that we have is a laser-like beam which is emitted from our eyes, that we turn on and off at will. It will incinerate whatever it is aimed at. The third weapon we have is that we are impenetrable and that nothing can touch us.

It is my understanding that all of you are manifestations of one group soul. Is this correct?

Yes.

Some of us have the sense that if you were not needed for a time to actively work against darkness, you could go into a dormant state from which you could awaken at need. Is this correct?

Yes, and I would also say that in a sense we sleep with one eye open, so that we may remain vigilant. *[Therefore if you were guarding Creation, and there were no active threats, you could sleep and guard at the same time.]* Yes.

PART III—THE WORK OF THE LIGHT WARRIORS

When the Light Warriors arrived in our universe, they set about developing strategy. More can be learned about the progress of their work in Chapter 8. However, in general, they have chosen first to go after the great military strongholds of the dark, and to free the Great Central Sun of our universe. While we would like them to go after the worst offenders on our planet, they stated that "a part of our strategy is to separate the dark beings from the fallen humans, so if there is a chance of reclamation that may be done." Cleaning up darkness on Earth is not at the very top of the list for the Light Warriors, for good reason; but I believe we will begin to see the effects of their work early in 2005.

Can you briefly describe your strategy?

Our strategy is highly complex because it is both multi-dimensional and multi-sized, going from the sub-atomic to the universal macrocosmic level. Let me just state that we have Light Warriors positioned on every level and every dimension, and it is a magnificent push through all of these dimensions in an orchestrated manner. And let me also state that we are unstoppable.

Do the Light Warriors have the power to affect the physical, and is that power limited?
      Yes, we have that power. I know of no limitation.

Can you, and will you, clean up pollution on this planet?
      That appears not to be our primary objective. There are those that will come after us who will be working on that. We will, however, take out the sources of these pollutants, for instance the nuclear power plants.

Can you, and will you, clean up blocked or contaminated energy portals?
      Yes. We are highly effective at that. We are already aware of the major portals that need to be worked on and are building a strategy for clearing them.

Will you break down, deactivate, and/or destroy the nuclear weapons on this planet?
      That will be one of our primary objectives, yes.

Humans have been promised help and relief so many times that many of us find it hard to believe that help is finally here. We've all been told that we would be rescued by mass landings, photon belts, various types of divine intervention, and what-not; yet on our planet things are still getting worse. If you have the ability to affect the physical, is there any way that you could manifest your presence in a way which would be perceivable to third dimensional humans?
      Not yet but soon. In the next few months.

On August 20, 2004, we asked Rashona: We are told that large numbers of you are massing against the wall that cuts us off from the rest of Creation. Is this correct?
      Yes, it is. We are working to break it down. In one or two places it has been breached, although the opposition is attempting to shore it up. But we have made inroads.

Are most of the Light Warriors working on this wall, or is this only one division?

Oh no, it is only one of a multitude of divisions. It is not anywhere near the majority. About 15-20% of our total force is arrayed there.

[Elora:] On August 26, 2004, Heru told us that part of the "wall" or frequency fence around the dark universes had been breached by the Light Warriors. This wall, incidentally, appears to me something like the gigantic chunks of the alien ships which crashed to Earth and lay in the desert in the movie *Independence Day*. It is extremely thick and made of some dense and highly unpleasant material. Heru said that a "good sized chunk" had been broken out of the wall, and that light beings were starting to come in from the other side of the wall in order to assist our universe, though not yet in large numbers. He commented that "It is sooner than we thought, and more has happened than we thought. It does look like nothing can stop the Light Warriors." Heru also stated that people who were sensitive will begin to make energetic connections to their home universes for the first time, though they may not understand where this sense of "home" comes from.

On August 31, 2004, Rashona stated:
As you know the frequency fence has been breached sooner than was anticipated. And the uncloaking of the first wave of Light Warriors that are seeded throughout this whole quadrant of the dark universes is going very rapidly and well. We are making great progress on this.

Are you able to work on the twin soul rift in this universe?
That is very complicated. The rift itself, though causing evil, is more of a tear in space. I believe that the first wave of beings that are coming in will address it, and they will be coming through shortly, within three months. This rift is one of the first issues to be addressed, for it affects not only human minds but universes as well.

Heru stated that you would be working on some of the beings who ensoul the stars, such as our own solar logos, who is 65% dark. What do you do when you work on such a being?
Generally, a being like that would have attached to it a soulless vampire of some kind, and we would remove that. And that would remove most of the dark. However at that point an ensouled being is given a choice—the choice point to choose light or dark. Any time beings are faced with that decision, if they choose to renounce the

dark they will then be put into the care of caregivers for healing. If they do not choose to renounce the dark, they will be put in a holding pen until such time as they can be dealt with. *[And given further chances for reclamation?]* Yes, and at that point it is out of our hands—unless they once again are able to attach themselves to the dark, which is unlikely once they are confined.

Is it true that the Light Warriors sing as they go into battle?
    Yes. That is in fact one of our great weapons or tools. It disrupts the stability of the dark.

[Elora:] I have heard the song of the Light Warriors as they battle the dark. They all sing together in a grand, stirring harmony. Their song is somewhat reminiscent of parts of Handel's Messiah.

PART IV—THE CHILDREN OF PROMISE

    Once the fallen universes are cleansed of all darkness, a great deal of healing will still need to be accomplished. Many beings have fallen, and even those who held to the light have been damaged in one way or another. As Heru stated in the last section, the Omniversal Energy contains, encoded within it, a number of beings and "programs" which will enable the damaged parts of Creation to heal. He has also said that "a great deal of work must be done to restore not only the third dimension but all of the other dimensions." Even the atomic structure has been distorted in the dark universes. The healing of the fallen universes is a monumental task, but the help that is almost on our doorsteps is fully equal to that task.

Heru, when the light workers first came to the fallen universes, we could say that they came with Plan A. Plan A was an attempt to mend and heal things, but without destroying the dark forces. However it wasn't enough, and we weren't equipped to deal with the virulence of the darkness. Therefore Plan B was created, which would be the coming of the Light Warriors. Did Plan B change things?
    Yes. Plan B would supersede all of that even if Plan A doesn't entirely work. At this time, representatives from all over the Creation are lining up at the parameters of this frequency fence. Once the fence has come down that is cordoning off this part of Creation, you

will see a great influx of new, wonderful, fresh, unsullied, and uncorrupted beings. In fact they are lined up anxiously waiting to come. As soon as it is deemed safe, they will begin their work. And there are legions of legions, countless numbers of beings wanting to help. *[All of us here are pretty tired.]* Justifiably so. Also, you have called on the same angels and masters for generations and generations, and it is not only you who are tired.

Once the frequency fence comes down, some areas may receive help sooner than others. It may be individual planet by planet that would be safe enough for these beings to come to. In other words, some planets might be safe for them to travel to, but others might not be so for a time. These beings will not be asked to risk themselves.

What I would like to say to you and the other light workers is this: that the burden of the restoration and repair will not be yours, nor will the burden of the battle that is coming be yours. Your work has been essentially to hold onto as much light as you could, hold the space. And now that help has come, you may consider your job well done.

The ascended masters and other beings who are helping this planet want everyone to know that even though there has been failure in intended missions, the fact that the light was held long enough until aid could come has been vitally important. This universe did not collapse, and that otherwise would have happened. But there are beings here who are uncorrupted; who have, through the greatest of traumas, held the light, held the original desire to still implement the plan even though it was being thwarted at every stage. And how incredibly important that has been in the process of bringing help to this planet.

That is one of the great miracles. That any of the beings on this planet have been able to hold the light and hold integrity is truly a marvel. Of course many have succumbed and many have become corrupt. But enough—and each one is very precious—enough have held onto their integrity and have been willing to sacrifice their lives for truth again and again.

You have mentioned some beings called the Children of Promise. Please tell us about them.

They are a family from one of the older universes in this Creation. They have held with them many of the unsullied blueprints of many different kinds of systems, systems for the animal and plant kingdoms and mineral kingdoms, in somewhat of a different way than how you brought them to this universe. Their promise is the promise of restoration. It is not exactly known how this restoration will happen, for we have never attempted it before, but they do appear to have the material and the talent to do a great deal of positive work.

How and when will they be coming to universes such as ours?

I would think by the beginning of next year [i.e. January 2005] you will begin to see them. They are, in some manner, actually incarnating into the children that are being born on the planet at this time. They are incarnating not as the whole being that they are, but as a fraction of themselves. A large influx of that energy will be happening as soon as early next year. Once the frequency barrier to this cordoned-off part of the Creation is broken through, much change will happen quickly. And as the Light Warriors are unveiled and begin to assemble in each locality, much change will happen rapidly.

Going back to the Children of Promise, I saw them as looking like a very large angel, and it almost appeared as if they had a sun in their heart area. Also they seemed to carry many colors within them for healing, including some that we don't know of. Is this correct?

They take many forms, but yes, that would be accurate. And yes, there are thousands upon thousands of colors. Many of them have not been seen on Earth or have not been seen for a long time.

I had the impression that they would be borne in on the pulse from Godverse.

As I said, they are fractionally being born into children now. There will be manifestations of them in the next year. Fully aware beings, and beings who can complete the magnitude of the work that is required, would be coming on that pulse. But I believe that you will *see and hear about them before then. For the present, it will be frac*tions of what they are. *[And they will be able to heal on all levels, from the microcosm to the macrocosm? Even the atomic structure, which is distorted in this universe?]* All of that is correct.

PART V—THE BREATH OF GOD

In the last paragraph above, Heru mentions the "pulse from the Godverse". This was touched upon in Chapter Four, Part III, and is also referred to as "The Breath of God". Some time after the arrival of the Omniversal Energy, I began to see this coming. It looks to me like a great tidal wave which will sweep through the universes with magnificent power. The Breath of God will probably arrive in our universe in about 300 years, although timing is very difficult to predict now. As Heru says, that is only a fraction of a second in cosmic time.

THE RETURN OF LIGHT

Heru and Sananda have both stated that (in this universe, at least) there will be a period of chaos both before and after this event. As to whether this event will completely set everything to rights, Heru does not know. He said that given how long darkness has existed in some universes, and a million other unfathomable complexities, no one knows what the results of this event will be. This universe, unlike those which were created dark, "is very repairable" but certain parts of it may not be reclaimable, some stars may collapse, and a few beings may not make it either. However, everything and everyone that can be saved will be saved.

We do not have a great deal of information on the Breath of God, but we asked Heru a few questions.

Heru, is the energy pulse from the Godverse in response to the invasion of darkness and the fall of the universes, or is it part of a vast cycle that was going to happen anyway? It is said that many cosmic cycles are coming to a close at this time.

It is actually both. There was a periodic pulse scheduled to come, and the Creator has used that energy to propel and to bring forth the cleaning and the solution to the invasion. So in a sense the pulse from the Godverse is the vehicle through which all of this is being transmitted. And the Omniversal Energy could be seen as the first wave of that pulse, almost as if the aura of the pulse from the Godverse precedes itself in this way.

Had we not done the work that we did in this universe, what would have happened? Would it have been unprepared for the Omniversal Energy and the pulse from the Godverse?

Yes, it would have been unprepared, and most likely this universe would have collapsed. But much help has been given, and much energy has been set in place for that not to happen. If you look at your own efforts and you multiply it many times, there have been similar efforts in many different arenas.

CHAPTER SEVEN
PLANETARY TRANSITION

Moving from the grand scope of the Creation and the fallen universes, let us now take a look at the impact of some of these events on Earth. Many of the lightworkers today were nurtured by a flood of prophecy and channeling which began in the early 70's. During those years the expectations were high for a rapid shift on our planet. Despite continued predictions, the expected transition to a higher frequency paradisiacal world has not happened. What caused the delays? Will the shift still occur as predicted? Heru speaks clearly and succinctly on these topics.

PART I—HOW THE GREAT SHIFT WAS DELAYED

In a conversation with Sananda, he stated that the great shift on Earth was supposed to take place during the 70's and 80's. Do you agree with this, Heru?

Actually, it was supposed to occur during the 30's and 40's. Then when that did not occur, it was set again to happen during the 70's and 80's. *[And now it has been delayed yet again to the period we are currently in?]* Yes.

There was a great wave of prophecy and channelings that began in the early 70's. Basically two things were predicted. First was that the great shift or ascension of Earth was imminent, and the other was that massive earth changes would occur. You have explained that the shift didn't happen then due to delaying tactics from the dark forces. Why did the earth changes not occur as predicted?

I believe it was the prayers of the light workers and many other light beings that held it back. For to have had the destruction without the influx of the light would have increased the likelihood of the fall of this planet. Since the influx was not happening, this would have been a very dangerous situation.

We asked Sananda: Sananda, many people say that the shift has been delayed in order to give as many people as possible the chance to "make it".

That has been the reason given, but I would say that the corruption goes into many levels, and this has been a technique of delaying and obfuscation. And it is time for this to stop. On some of the councils there have been people preaching such delays, whose interest has not really been for the good of earth or humanity, but who have been seeking to maintain their own secret interest.

What kinds of councils?

Planetary councils, the council of the solar system, the hierarchies that sustain this planet and sustain its place in space, the councils which sustain this universe. This is really far more than just a planetary issue.

The continued delays regarding the shift on Earth have had some good effects, but the result has also been that the biosphere has suffered terribly. I feel that the situation with the biosphere and the ecology is absolutely critical.

You are quite correct. I agree that the situation has become very critical.

PART II—ENVIRONMENT, MASS EXTINCTIONS, CHEMTRAILS, ETC.

Heru, we are experiencing a period of mass extinction on our planet. But each creature that has ever existed must be stored in the akashic records, with its DNA and so on. Would it be possible, when Earth has reached a higher vibration, to bring some of these extinct beings back?

Yes, it can be done.

As you know, I have a profound love for this Earth. I would like to know if you see Her reaching perfection, reaching the full potential that She was designed and created for?

Yes, and you have been a very important part of that. *[You feel absolutely certain? There is no doubt in your mind?]* I am certain.

Do you feel things will begin to shift politically, economically, and ecologically on our planet in the near future?

I see in some respects the tide has already turned politically on the global scale. There have been unforeseen events where the dark forces have been held back, knocked out of power.

The ecology is far more complex, and it will definitely take the concerted effort of a great many beings on this planet calling for intervention, and the opening up and downloading of technologies that are not readily available to bring balance back into the ecology. There will be assistance from the positive extraterrestrials. And also there is much technology that has already been downloaded but has been hidden or suppressed. What is going to begin to happen is that it will begin to be believed. Currently such technology is ridiculed as conspiracy theory, marginalized, fantastic, and so on. Instead, people will begin to believe it, to see that these technologies are possibly a solution. That perception just in and of itself would go a long ways to changing just about everything. For right now the whole economy and energy of the world is on this one ditch, the oil ditch, for energy. And there is a great disconnect between most humans and the planet, between humans and Gaia or nature. But this will begin to turn. People will begin to look at alternatives, broaden their minds, and not just keep feeding at the same trough. And that in itself will bring about fundamental changes that are really big and far reaching.

Will there be a reduction in population to reduce the load on Gaia?

Some. I wouldn't say the dramatic numbers that some have predicted, but there will be somewhat of a reduction. And in some places it won't be anything more than a decline in birth rate. It is actually happening already in some places, where people are choosing not to procreate the way they have been programmed to do. Part of the burden of the great population on this planet has been the fact that everybody that's ever been on this Earth wanted to be here now. In a sense everybody needed to be here to witness this time. And everybody has come; the party has been fully attended. But it is not needed for everyone to stay, so that part has been fulfilled.

Heru, we discussed with Sananda whether it is possible to do anything about the extreme abuses of the environment that are happening now, such as requesting an instant return of karma for the worst abusers. He didn't see any productive avenue to follow.

It will be time for instant karma to begin its return within one to two years. So the time basically is at hand. The reason it has been delayed to this point is that it has been necessary for the true extent of evil to be revealed. Now it is like a snowball, and the beginnings of the instant karma are there. It seems slight, it seems small, but believe me it is rolling down a rapid slope.

From where we are at, we can't see it at all.

No, but it is happening. And will it change anything to ask for it? It's almost like this. When a pendulum swings on a long arc, there is that moment where it reaches the top of the arc. And with this situation, it appears to be about there. The evil being committed has swung as far as it can go on its arc. It is at that "pause point" where it is still and poised and ready to come back. There's nothing that anyone can do to change that arc or to prevent it from coming back. Therefore I believe that Sananda's statement was basically his way of expressing the fact that it's going to happen and it's about to happen. And whether you pray for it to happen or not, it's still going to happen. It's almost a mechanical numeric trajectory.

A channel in Florida predicted some time ago that there would be a hurricane which would look like an eye, and that this would signal a series of major earth changes. Hurricane Charley looked like an eye at one point in its development. Can you comment on this?

The channel you mention did foresee this hurricane, and I do believe a series of events will begin to transpire which will make it apparent that we have reached a tipping point in the ecological systems on this planet. And it will begin to be apparent to more of the mainstream people that it is not just coincidences or random events.

Do you think these changes will be mostly weather related, or also earthquakes, volcanoes, etc.?

I see some increase in earthquake activity, volcanic not so much. But I do see some major polar ice cap events, such as melting and large blocks of ice breaking free and so on. *[Enough to raise sea level? It takes a lot to do that to any significant degree.]* It may begin to, yes. *[How about Yellowstone? Some people say there will be a big volcanic eruption there.]* I do not see it happening. I know there has been much talk about it.

We are very distressed about the chemtrails. What is their purpose?

The purpose is control of the ionosphere via some undisclosed weapon, not HAARP. There is an element of mind control. It is already being used as a net of control of consciousness.

What do you mean by control of the ionosphere?

The chemtrails are composed of both lighter and heavier elements. The lighter elements drift up to the ionosphere, and the heavier ones sink down to earth. Each layer of the atmosphere holds a consciousness. If you think of the atmosphere as being somewhat analogous to the auric field of the Earth, then the surface would be the skin and each of the layers would hold a certain vibration. With the chemtrails, the part that flows down to the earth has toxins for humans and mind control elements. The part that goes up creates a distortion in the ionosphere that makes the planet impenetrable, to some extent, to beneficial influences and higher energies outside. These upper layers then form what is essentially a frequency barrier, or a physical manifestation of the etheric frequency barriers that shroud this planet.

In other words, the upper layers are to hold back the evolution of the planet and humanity, and the lower layers are to sicken, weaken, and control people.

Correct. Another aspect of this is that, as we've come into the more highly charged area of space that some have called the photon belt, there is a cosmic wind which has greatly increased. The chemtrail "shroud" is a defense against that. Of course it keeps getting torn away and so needs to be replenished daily... and ultimately it will fail.

Are the chemtrails then being mandated from very high levels of the secret government?

Yes. Earth, being one of the twelve critical planets, is what you would call a very coveted world. It has a central importance. It has been seeded with an unusual amount of diversity and an incredible depth of knowledge which has been brought here from many planets, and indeed from many universes. Much hinges on whether this planet shifts into light, both for this universe and perhaps some surrounding universes. There are twelve such planets in this universe and they are all being fought over.

In that case, Earth must be the most important planet within our entire galaxy.

Yes, Earth is by far the most important planet in this galaxy. The other planets in this galaxy are pretty simple—they may have more evolved life forms on them, but their fate is in a sense already established. The path they are walking down has been long established, light or dark. Earth is very pivotal, and because it's so complicated it's been impossible to completely control it from the dark side.

Is it correct that the chemtrail formula now contains more heavy metals?

Yes, and other toxins. Viruses, fungus, and small amounts of radiation. The toxicity of the chemtrails is greater now than it has been in the past. Those responsible are also intensifying efforts with the chemtrails as the cosmic winds become stronger. But it will end in tatters, it will end soon—most probably within about one to two years [i.e. sometime in 2005 or 2006].

PART III—COSMIC CYCLES AND TIMES OF TRANSITION

What is the significance of 2012?

There are two factors here. The first is what I would call the millennium factor. It is similar to what happened in the year 2000. A great deal of energy was projected upon that point in time from the collective consciousness of humanity, and a good thing happened. If you recall that New Year's Eve, a very deep peace and silence occurred, as there were many prayers for peace at that time. So you have that factor, because many people are focused on 2012.

Beyond that, 2012 is a significant astrological event where a lot of factors are lining up. If you would, imagine a clock—but instead of there being a dial, there are wheels within wheels within wheels. Every few years, some of them line up to their beginning point with each other. For example, this year the innermost and the next would line up to zero. And then maybe ten years later the second and third might line up to zero. 2012 is a rare point in history where all of the wheels will line up to zero. We are at a place where the light from the Central Sun of the universe will be shining without obstruction upon this planet for the first time in many hundreds of thousands of years. Therefore it is a gateway of great opportunity, and it is a significant time.

What do you feel will happen at that time?

It is not known; it will depend on how much growth can take place. Those of us who are working on this have high hopes. How much can take place in that time will depend upon the reclamation of the sun in this solar system, which we believe will be done by then. We also believe that the Central Sun of this galaxy will be reclaimed in large part, for the Central Sun of this galaxy is not as dark as the sun of this solar system, but it is not all light either. We believe there will be a very incredible influx of light onto this planet through this succession of gateways.

Are we humans safe on the planet during this transition?
It appears that most everyone will be. There will be an intervention to prevent an all out nuclear war. Humans can withstand some amount of radiation, but the full onslaught of a nuclear blast, such as occurred in Japan, does cause irreparable harm to souls, and that will not be allowed.

You are confident that all this is so, and that the intervention will hold?
Yes. However I do want to say that it is important to be conscious, conscientious, careful, and to protect yourselves at all times. For there is a great degree of random debris flying around, and it would be very easy for some of that to strike you. However, as long as you maintain your focus on serving the highest orders of light, a great degree of protection does surround you and there is less chance of your being hit by random debris than a denser person.

You have mentioned a cosmic wind which is increasing at this time. What is the cosmic wind?
It is a combination of several factors. There is the galactic photon belt, which occurs on a 26,000 year cycle. But there is a greater cycle happening too, which has aligned this galaxy with the Central Sun of the universe; and the Central Sun is also in alignment with the central universe of all universes, the Godverse. It is a long, majestic cycle that is coming into play with many more facets than I can describe.

Essentially, the cosmic wind is a flow of very high energy?
Yes. And I see it literally blowing people off the planet. Not physically, but people will be leaving their body because the intensity is too great for them to stay here.

A number of channels are giving very dire predictions for the coming years. Do you agree?
I do believe things will be somewhat rougher than they are now. I do not see them being quite as universally dire as some are saying. *[So maybe 10-20% worse than they are now?]* Yes, approximately.

If things aren't going to be that bad, why is it that you have several times counseled us on the importance of staying safe?

Have you not just gone through a series of very difficult psychic attacks in recent months? That is what I'm speaking to. If you look at how disruptive and draining that has been for you, I would counsel you to position yourself where you do not need to go through any more of that. It is not so much that I see things getting significantly worse other than the continued pressure from above, of the entities and the negative life forms being pushed down into the third dimension. But in a sense there are still entities and negative life forms all around you, that given an opportunity would love to have you for dinner. And that will continue for roughly another year [i.e. until or through the fall of 2005]. *[So the psychic negativity is what you are more concerned about?]* Yes.

Many sources have spoken of a separation of the old and new Earths. Do you see this happening?
It has been believed that there would be a literal separation of the worlds. However this is not to be. What has happened is that those who have entered into a more fourth or fifth dimensional state, such as yourself and Karen, are living in the new world; and those that are operating more from their first and second chakras are living in the old world. There is currently a separation, and this has been allowed for the purposes of growth and comfort. But in the end, all will be reunited as one world. And all will actually still exist on the third dimension. However, with the frequency fences gone, just as humans are capable of traversing all twelve dimensions from the third—which includes the first and second dimension and going into the states of consciousness of the plant and animal kingdoms—this planet then will be free to express itself and communicate on all those dimensions as well.

So it's as if we have different states of consciousness and density currently co-existing side by side?
Different vibratory rates. This is a natural occurrence on this planet, however it has been suppressed, fragmented, and so on. The nature spirits would be a good example of fourth dimensional life on this planet.

The expectation that there would be a separation of worlds has now changed, due to the coming of the Light Warriors?
Yes. *[This is then a recent change, for when we spoke about this earlier, perhaps in the late spring, you felt the separation was going to happen.]* Yes, it is a recent change. *[And you feel this is a more positive solution.]* Yes, I do.

You have mentioned that there will be an amnesty of karma for beings who are willing to turn to the light. Please elaborate on this a bit.

This information is not brand new, as it has made it into some writings on the planet. Several years ago the Lords of Karma announced that all karma could be cleared within this lifespan, if a person so desired and worked diligently to do so. With the advent of the Omniversal Energy, this is further enhanced. If a person were to call forth their original blueprint, call forth their monad, and ask that the way be made clear for the releasing of all karma, and that the path of reunion and liberation be made known, it will be so. At this point in time nothing is impossible, and the advent of the Omniversal Energy makes this so. Listen to those words, for there is the hugest blessing embedded in them. Tell yourself in your heart that nothing is impossible. Imagine, if you would, one of those paintings of the annunciation, where the Holy Spirit is entering Mary, and Gabriel is announcing that she is now pregnant with God's child. This is an allegory; I am not commenting now on whether that image is historical or not. I am using that as an allegory for the fact that each soul on this planet has now been impregnated with this Omniversal Energy in a very similar way to that image of the annunciation. Take to heart the grandness of this event.

CHAPTER EIGHT
THE RESTORATION BEGINS

On June 1, 2004, Karen heard the words, "The Great Work is Complete." We asked Heru what these words meant. Heru responded: "It means that all of the armies of the light are in position. For everyone is now in their place. Everything is in place for the great transition to happen." And indeed, from that time on, we began to see massive changes on the higher dimensions. We wish as much as anyone else to see these changes filter down to Earth. Unfortunately the lower dimensions seem to be last to feel the effects of what is happening in our universe. We do believe, however, that some positive changes will be noticed on Earth within one to two years, and that after a couple years time the rate of improvement will increase rapidly.

This chapter summarizes the changes and victories on the inner realms which we have observed during the summer and fall of 2004. Dates are included in this section so that the progression of events may be seen. We invite those of our readers who are clairvoyant to confirm this material for themselves. While some of these details may not be of interest to all, the events recorded in this chapter are most inspiring.

PART I—THE DARK GRIDS

Starting in June of 2004, Heru began showing us the dark grids which have been a major part of the controlling energy structures of this fallen universe. The first one to come to our attention was the sixth dimensional grid. Heru explained that it was like a net covering a large portion of our universe, and that it worked like a frequency barrier. Just as Earth has a frequency barrier around it which prevents light and higher energies from entering, similar structures have been set up for our universe. We were then made aware of a similar grid on the eleventh dimension. As Heru has said, darkness in this universe exists through the eleventh dimension. Finally, a third grid existing on the fourth dimension encompassed Earth itself. Up until the summer of 2004, it had not been possible for the light forces to affect or take down any of these controlling structures.

Tentative plans were laid for the dark grids to be burned with cosmic fire. However, this would have resulted in the incineration of many beings who were closely tied to the grid. Instead, the Omniversal Energy was run through the sixth dimensional grid, which almost seemed to be made of a hollow piping. This was followed by an assault by the light forces on the eleventh dimensional grid, as well as on the grid surrounding Earth. Over the summer of 2004, large portions of all three dark grids were dismantled. The remaining portions will be taken down by the Light Warriors.

The sixth dimensional grid looked like a huge net. Until recently it was covering 40% of our universe, and growing. Heru said that the Hartmann lines were a manifestation of this grid, and that it affected "not only all the dimensions below it, but all aspects of matter down to the sub-atomic particles. When someone says the stones cry out at the abuse of Earth, it is a literal thing. And that is also how the imprint of horrors, like the Holocaust in Germany, can be imprinted so deeply into the Earth, and be very hard to remove."

The breaking down of the dark grids is only one battle in a very large war which is being fought for the control of our universe. It is unfortunate that, here on Earth, we cannot yet see for ourselves the great impact of all that is occurring. As of the summer of 2004, every clear source that I read gives a time frame of about two years for the great shift to become apparent on Earth.

On June 11, 2004, we asked: Heru, we would like to check on the status of the dark grid on the sixth dimension. What is the timing for bringing it down?

It seems to be changing because it appears that this grid is no longer dark, and instead of being destroyed it has been transformed from within. The Omniversal Energy has infused it with great light. Many of you have perceived unusual amounts of dark beings in unusual circumstances. This is due to the fact that beings who have been wrapped around or hanging onto this grid are fleeing like cockroaches. They are scurrying around madly trying to find new homes, and by and large they are unsuccessful. There is a great sweep up happening, where armies of light beings are finding them and incarcerating them.

Many beings in this universe have cried out for freedom. It was this call from so many voices, including yours, that initiated the process of dismantling the sixth dimensional grid. And it may not be in the words that you're putting it, but it is the heartfelt desire for true freedom. The dismantling of the grid would have happened anyway, but it occurred much sooner and in a much gentler manner than would otherwise have been. Of course the experience was not gentle for the beings who were hanging onto it—for them Armageddon is here. For beings of light, liberation is here.

[Elora:] When the eleventh dimensional grid began to come down, starting on July 31, 2004, we could see great celebrations happening all over the universe. It almost seemed as though the sun had come out for the first time in millions of years. From higher dimensional planets, it was possible to perceive the Great Central Sun of our galaxy for the first time in eons. Heru stated on August 1st that "It is a very joyous time; there are many celebrations happening today. Interestingly, with this grid in place it was impossible to communicate between many different places in the universe, and actually for this universe to effectively communicate with the other universes. So you would say the phone lines are very busy today with hellos and reunions, and catching up and celebrations."

From a conversation with Sananda in August, 2004: We've been told by Heru that the eleventh dimensional dark grid has essentially come down, as has the sixth dimensional dark grid. It also appears that the dark grid surrounding planet Earth is in the process of crumbling. Is this correct?

The grids appear to be about 60% gone on the eleventh dimension, 57% on the sixth, and about 45% on the third.

If so, why don't we notice anything different on Earth? It seems just as dark and dense as ever here.

You must remember that it is human consciousness that holds the vibrational frequency of this Earth. And humans carried the effect of this gridwork for many millions of years on the DNA level, on the cellular level. The grids will be dismantled completely before there is a change in human consciousness. There will be some lag of perhaps a year or two, and in some cases three. It is not going to be an instant change in human consciousness but there are several changes to look for. The first will be with the babies that are born from now on; there will be virtually no dark beings coming in. Secondly, the light-workers will have much greater access to non-contaminated sources of knowledge. And then I would say over the next year or two or three, to look for some general lightening of the load for everyone.

The madman in the White House, although he may remain in the White House, will be increasingly powerless, more of a caricature than anything else. People's focus will begin to turn away from the fear mongers. And that in itself will be a turning of the tide.

PART II—THE LIBERATION OF GODINJ

Heru has explained elsewhere that our universe was created by a group of Creator Gods. This composite of Creator Gods was called Godinj. Some of these beings fell, whereas others were chained by darkness. Of the composite, four remained, up until the first of September 2004.

9/2/04 Heru, I felt that something major happened last night, and that it had to do with Godinj. Is this correct?
Yes. It is as if Godinj has re-energized Itself and is sending out a renewed pulse of Creator God energy for the restoration of this universe. *[How many beings are still part of Godinj?]* Four of the original Creator Gods, and they have added one new being that was never there before. *[Are the four original beings two pairs of twin flames?]* Yes.

It appeared to me that Godinj had been veiled or in chains; and had freed Itself and was sending out huge light.
Yes, and part of that light has been the incorporation of a fifth Creator God who was instrumental in freeing Godinj. There was somewhat of a rescue mission sent with the help of the Light Warriors, and one of the beings involved in the mission was this fifth being. *[Godinj was, in fact, trapped by the darkness?]* Yes.

It looked to me as if a huge light was shining over the whole universe on the higher dimensions. It appeared to light up dimensions five and above. And the universe looked shabby, dirty, and bleak—like an old attic full of junk and cobwebs, where someone suddenly turns on a brilliant light. But this light did also show up who was dark and who wasn't and left few places to hide, except for the very lowest dimensions. Is all of this basically correct?

Yes, it is. The dark beings will be attempting to hide wherever they can, but mostly below the fifth dimension. There is tremendous chaos on the fourth dimension right now, and this will continue for some time.

I also saw a huge battle raging over the entire universe, and I heard the words, "Battle is joined." It looked like Armageddon. Is this correct, and if so can you give details?

Yes—this is it. The Light Warriors are unstoppable, and it is going faster than we had anticipated. It's good to see that for a change instead of all the endless delays.

10/6/04 In a conversation with Farwaren [one of the members of the Godinj collective] last night, she stated that she and her twin flame were going to conceive a child. This had not occurred yet, but would in the near future. With great emotion, Farwaren said that this child would be something like a cosmic avatar for this entire universe. Is this correct so far?

We believe it to be so, yes.

She said that the child would be a singular soul, containing both male and female, and that it would be almost as if it would contain all the light which has been drained from our universe through these eons of darkness. Did I hear this correctly?

Yes, that is the intent and we feel confident that that will come to fruition. *[Are you helping them?]* Not directly, but I have lent some assistance.

Later that same day, we asked Prime Creator: We understand that Farwaren and her twin are going to give birth to a cosmic avatar. Is this sort of thing going to occur in other universes?

Something of an equivalent magnitude is left up to each group of Creator Gods that created each universe—in what way they would express their newfound freedom and liberation. I believe this will not be the only expression in this universe. There are a great many beautiful things to come about.

PART III—THE RESTORATION OF THE GREAT CENTRAL SUN AND THE BATTLE FOR OUR UNIVERSE

9/9/04 Heru, are the Light Warriors now working to free the Great Central Sun of this universe?

Yes. When this happens, the Light Warriors will begin to go after the individual suns, and the sun of this solar system [the solar logos] will be then worked upon.

I have also seen something which is near the center of this universe, but is not the Great Central Sun. There are twelve stars, in a perfect ellipse. Does this exist, and what is it?

Yes, it does exist. It is a fulcrum point or a portal. In a way it is both. It is something like a gyroscopic energy vortex that allows in energy from Prime Creator and also maintains the balance of the entire universe. *[And this is also being freed?]* Yes.

9/13/04 I have been observing the battle that has been going on in the inner regions and higher dimensions of our universe. I would like you to confirm and/or comment on what I saw, please.

For much of the week, I observed that the Great Central Sun was in the strangle-hold of a gargantuan monster that looked something like an octopus, and it must have been the size of a galaxy. I assumed that this creature had been entrapping or attacking the Great Central Sun for a very long time. The Light Warriors were attacking it.

Yes, that is true.

On Friday night, it appeared that this creature had been broken up and destroyed. In fact, it seemed to have exploded; and a huge wave of dust, soot, ash, and debris was passing outward through the Universe. Is this correct?

Yes. *[Did this explosion harm the regions around the Great Central Sun?]* I don't really see anything of the light that was harmed. There may have been fallen beings around it that were harmed, but I don't see any light beings having been harmed.

On Saturday, I strongly felt the effects of this etheric wave of soot and dust. It felt to me as though the inner planes were choking with ash and smoke and grit.

Yes.

On Sunday some debris was still present, but things seemed calmer. In fact, by Sunday evening, I felt a strong sensation of peace. In looking at the Great Central Sun of the Universe, I could see it more clearly, though there was still a lot of dust in the air. It also seemed that I could see three huge light beings hovering around the Great Central Sun. Did I see correctly?

Yes.

Who are these beings? Are they the Seraphim?

That would be the equivalent word in your language. These three beings are basically the collective parent of the being which ensouls the Central Sun of this universe.

Is the Central Sun partially dark?

It had been trapped for so long. It had resisted mightily, but was damaged. I can't say that it was corrupt, but much healing needs to happen, and will happen now.

Is the Great Central Sun the presence of God in each universe?

You could call it that. Within each person there is that connection, and through that connection the divine spark of the Creator. That format follows on the macrocosm as well as the microcosm. On the microcosm, within each cell or atom of a human there is also that spark and connection; and within each galaxy and universe there is that spark and connection. On the macrocosm, the Great Central Suns plays that role. Now that the Central Sun is free, that alone will change a lot in this universe.

It now appears that the Light Warriors are regrouping to set up their next strategy.

They have already set it up, but they are staging their positions. One of the next positions they will be taking will be to work on your own sun.

My impression is that they are targeting key strongholds of the darkness. I saw that there are great military strongholds of darkness which appear much like the Death Star in the movie "Star Wars". There seem to be between 700 and 800 of them in our universe, and I felt the Light Warriors would be going after them next. In fact, it looks like they've already started.

Yes, you are seeing accurately.

[Elora:] The destruction of the Death Stars was a tremendous battle which raged for several weeks. Great squadrons of Light Warriors attacked these gargantuan military strongholds, appearing in wedge-shaped phalanxes and literally cutting the artificial planetoids to pieces. After they had destroyed all the Death Stars, the Light Warriors began to target the next level of the military power held by darkness, which were great intergalactic battleships. These were much smaller than the Death Stars but there were many more of them.

I felt that the twelve critical planets, including Earth, are somewhere on this list, but not at the top of the list.
Yes, and there is a strategic reason for that. It is not felt that they will be targeted for destruction by the dark, but if they were surrounded by light beings and liberated, then that would invite an attack. Therefore the Light Warriors would rather leave the twelve critical planets alone for the present and go after what would essentially attack them later—as you said, the military strongholds.

How about the masses of dark beings in the fourth dimension? They are not being targeted yet?
Not yet, but they will be soon. Actually, there will be some kind of a comb or a sieve to capture the fallen ensouled beings for refor- mation, and to separate them from the dark beings. That will come down the line a little later. So you can see what is going to happen; there will be a parting of the ways there.

Overall, are things still moving faster than expected?
Yes, they are.

[Elora:] As the days passed, I continued to watch the Great Central Sun of our universe. As the clouds of dust and debris cleared away, I was able to see that it had the form of a huge white lotus. The bud appeared to be closed, but very gradually began to open. In the early stages of this process, only a faint beam of pure white light was emit- ted from the nearly closed petals. Many celestial beings could be seen working with this Sun, which is definitely an ensouled being. First I saw the Seraphim singing to this being, using pure tones of sound to heal and awaken it. After a few days they were replaced by the five members of Godinj, who also used what we might call "sound thera- py". At all times thousands of other higher dimensional beings were

76

gathered around, encircling this dramatic scene of restoration. Many appeared to be praying, and all watched with reverence and often with tears of joy. On September 14, 2004, we had occasion to speak to Kuthumi, one of the Ascended Masters. I asked Kuthumi for his perspective on the events occurring with the Great Central Sun of the universe, remarking that it appeared to me like a lotus unfolding. He replied:

[Kuthumi:] This Sun has been in chains for many million and millions of years, and as such was never fully able to express its light and its glory. And yes, it is much like a flower unfolding, endlessly unfolding. What you are witnessing is the beginning of a beautiful process of infinite petals unfolding; and each petal that unfolds emits waves of love and light that stretch to the end of the universe. The lack of this light has had a deleterious effect on every aspect of life in this universe. And so this will be truly a dawning of a golden age. *[The being which ensouls the Central Sun—it is expressing itself through the form of the lotus? It's as though the lotus is its body?]* Yes. It is a most magnificent being; and there is an actual mechanism of creative energy that is expressed as this unfoldment takes place. It is lovely to behold.

[Elora:] About another week passed before the Great Central Sun became fully open. It appeared as a magnificent, radiantly white lotus with a multitude of petals. And then suddenly the lotus appeared to become activated. Great, effulgent rays of golden-white light poured from every petal, and filled the universe with its glory. I could see angels standing near the Sun in ecstasy, bathing themselves in the light. I wish I could say that this light penetrated everywhere. Alas, from what I could observe, not much of it reached the lower dimensions or planets like ours which are imprisoned behind very dense frequency fences. Still, much of our universe is now filled with light where darkness reigned, and the light of the Creator is seen here once more.

10/6/04 Heru, we would like to start by asking you to confirm several things that were told to me by Farwaren, who is a member of Godinj, on Sunday night. First, Farwaren said that a large group of helpers and healers had come through the breach in the great wall and are in one of the safe areas, waiting for the time when they can be deployed to other areas. Is this correct?

Yes, indeed it is correct. The numbers would look large to you, but I would tell you that this is only the forerunner of what is to come. There are so many more waiting to come.

Next, she showed me that a vast wave of Light Warriors was about to move through the breaches in the wall. They were still on the other side of the wall, but shortly to pass through. The numbers that I could see were vast, uncountable. So many in fact, that it seemed that the Light Warriors currently in our universe were only a small advance guard. Would you comment on this?

Yes, that is correct. As they come through in the next weeks and months, you will begin to see a great acceleration in the turning of the tide. I guess you could say it's at that tipping point right now, and when things first start to move it's slow but then it accelerates and accelerates more rapidly. And that is at hand.

It seemed to be that maybe a tenth of a percent of the total force is here already.

Yes. And they will be coming in waves as well, so this second wave is not the full complement. It will be like the tide coming in, in the ocean. So the first wave was small, the next will be bigger, the next after that bigger still.

I was told that when the Light Warriors fill our universe in vast num-bers, they will set up a multi-dimensional and very fine grid or net, which will allow them to seek out and destroy all darkness. This will be done so that nothing slips through the cracks.

Yes, that is correct.

I see this universe as being shaped something like a huge, oval, flat-tened disk—not unlike the shape of a galaxy. Is this more or less cor-rect?

Somewhat. However if I were to describe it in a shape that you could relate to, I would say it is more the shape of a red blood cell: a flattened disk, slightly thicker at the outside edges, and having a very distinct membrane to it.

Then is it also correct that the area where the chinks in the Great Wall have been created is on the other side of the universe from where we are, so that when the Light Warriors and other beings come in from the light universes, they have to cross most of this universe to get here?

That is correct.

PART IV—INTERVIEW WITH A SECOND WAVE LIGHT WARRIOR

On October 22, 2004, Karen and I spoke to Vikhona, a member of the second "wave" of Light Warriors. This new group of Light Warriors feels very strong, and considerably more substantial than the first. They also seem to have more of an emotional nature, and one can sense the heart feelings in speaking with them. There is a great deal of light around them, and they are very beautiful.

Greetings. May I begin by clarifying that you are one of the second group of Light Warriors which has entered our universe?
Yes, I am. *[Would it be correct to call you "second wave Light Warriors"?]* That is a good description.

I saw six huge second wave Light Warriors guarding our planet, one in each direction. They are each nearly as tall as the diameter of Earth. Is this correct?
That is correct. *[Are they just guarding our planet at this time?]* Their primary purpose at this point is to guard, but they are also working with the magnetic energy fields of the planet. You might perceive, if you looked, a beam of energy coming out of each one's solar plexus to the Earth. It is penetrating to the core of the Earth and supporting and energizing this planet.

It appears that you are more powerful than the first wave Light Warriors, and have some enhanced abilities. Would you comment on this please?
Yes, we are a magnitude of perhaps twelve times stronger. We typically appear larger in size, and as such all of our abilities are that much greater. *[Do you believe that each "batch" that comes through will be stronger and more capable?]* Yes.

Did a new group of micro Light Warriors also come in with you?
No, but there will be a new group with the next, in about three months time [i.e. January 2004]. There are seven groups of us in all.

I noticed something in the area of your heads that almost looked like a rotating eye, or the revolving lens of a lighthouse. Can you tell me what I was seeing?
It would be almost as if we had a helmet with a rotating crystalline

beam of light, which can illuminate all of the hidden cloaked beings and cloaked substances, weapons, all of that. *[Does this mean that the second wave Light Warriors will have better vision than the first group?]* Considerably, yes.

Do you also come in pairs?

No, although we can travel in pairs and often do.

We have all noticed that you and your companions "drift" less than those in the first wave. Is this true?

Yes. It is almost as if we are more solid and more dense. If you were to put an elemental quality on us, we would be earth and they would be air. *[The first group was lighter, and would almost seem to float around?]* Yes. We are much more solid and will tend to stay in one place to do our work, though we are also very mobile.

Will you begin your work on Earth and the other eleven critical planets soon?

Yes. *[Can you give us a time frame for Earth?]* I believe it will be approximately four to five weeks before this begins [i.e. about the first of December, 2004].

Can you give us any details of how this work will begin?

I am not on that particular task force, and so I do not know. We do not have quite as much of a group mind as the initial Light Warriors had, and so I am not able to see what everyone is doing. *[You are more individuated?]* Yes.

It appears to me that the second wave of Light Warriors have been progressing through the universe with their net, scooping up huge numbers of fallen and dark beings. We have seen these beings fleeing through our airspace in the last two weeks, so to speak. It hasn't been a pretty picture, as the dimensions near ours looked like something out of "Night on Bald Mountain". Things seem much more peaceful since the new group of Light Warriors arrived—would you agree?

Yes, I would.

I also felt that the Light Warriors would be driving the dark and fallen beings to a place which is somewhat "off to the side" of our universe, much as cowboys would round up several herds of cattle into one huge massed group. This place appears to be a large area between galaxy clusters, where there are few or no life forms. Am I correct so far?

Yes, that is correct; and they will be held there pending whoever is to process them. We are not to do any processing.

There will be an enclosure created there?

Yes. Each universe will have a similar enclosure. *[The number of beings that will be gathered there must be countless.]* Yes. We do not know how many there are, but there are many, many. All sizes and shapes. *[Will they have to be sorted?]* Yes. There are both fallen and dark among them.

I felt this would start in about one week's time from now, or near the end of October 2004.

That sounds about right.

When Heru first told us about the Light Warriors, he said that they were contained within the Omniversal Energy and they were uncloaking. However, I saw your group appear on the other side of the Great Wall or frequency fence. Do the Light Warriors uncloak from within the Omniversal Energy, or do they come in from the other side of the wall?

Both. You may perceive the Omniversal Energy as a directed beam, but it is not limited to that beam that you perceive. *[In other words, some beings uncloaked from within this universe, and some uncloaked from outside the universe.]* Yes. And some uncloaked outside the frequency fence.

Is there anything else you would like to add?

Just that we are brand new beings, and are not infallible in the results of our efforts. We are unwavering in our desire to serve the Light, and I ask for patience and forgiveness in the fact that this is taking some time. I know many conditions here are at a critical state, and I know most or all will be salvaged. I regret any moment that goes by that the pain is not relieved immediately for so many. But we are doing what we can as quickly as we can, and more help is on the way. We serve only the will of Prime Creator, as I know you do as well. My deepest heartfelt desire is to stand with you after the restoration is complete, and drink with you a toast of a celebratory glass of light wine—pun intended!

After this conversation, we asked Heru: Given all these hopeful developments, do you still feel that it will require about two years to "win the battle for Earth", so to speak? About two years before we will be able to experience some real positive changes here that we can see with our own eyes?

Things do seem to be proceeding somewhat more quickly than originally forecasted, and I would revise that estimate to be between one and a half to two years [i.e. somewhere between the spring and fall of 2006]. However, there will be people earlier on for whom their personal lives will change dramatically for the better. My hope is that this book can get out rather quickly and spread somewhat widely. If it is known that people can call upon the Light Warriors and use the techniques I have given then many individuals will benefit by having a much better quality of life, even though the world itself still may look to be in shambles. *[Do you think that the light workers in particular will find their lives improving quickly?]* That is what this book is targeted at, yes.

When we began these conversations in the early summer of 2004, you stated that our universe was about 75% dark. What is the percentage of darkness in our universe now?

It is down to about 60%, so there has been much good work, but there is still much to be done.

[Elora:] I would like to add several notes to this chapter as this book goes to press. First, as of early November of 2004, work began on the solar logos of our sun. Our sunlight should become energetically cleaner and clearer as time goes on. We are also told that some large sections of our universe are substantially cleaned up. The best news of all is that, on the first of December, the Light Warriors arrived in large numbers to begin their work on Earth. They are, at the time of this writing, beginning to dismantle the frequency fences behind which we have been imprisoned. We would caution our readers not to expect immediate miracles, as Heru has stated that things may actually appear somewhat worse during the next year or two. However, we believe that the greater influx of higher energies into our planet will be a tremendous aid and support for all beings who hold to light.

SECTION TWO
THE DISCOURSES

CHAPTER NINE
THE CREATOR GODS

The Creator Gods are an essential part of the cosmology which Heru teaches—and Heru himself, as we have noted, is one of the greatest of these Gods. According to Heru: "A Creator God is a being who is capable of taking the stuff of Creation, the plasma from Prime Creator, and manifesting it into form. These forms may be as large as universes and may be as small as microcosms."

We asked Prime Creator who created the Creator Gods. He/She replied: "I did. It was one of the first acts of creation. They were created prior to this Creation, so they are actually older than this Creation."

[Heru:] The Creator Gods create from the Void. Your scriptures speak of this, describing it with great eloquence. Into the Void—the formless, wonderful Void, where nothing is formed and everything is potential—the Creator Gods will go. They go singly, as couples, or at times in groups, depending on their intent. They will drop out of Creation and into the Void, much as you will do in the third technique. In that space they will form, with their divine mind and their divine heart, their intent for creation. They will put it forth, and it will be done.

Interestingly enough, there are many kinds of creations. Some of them just require that initial spark. In these cases, the Gods create something independent, with its own life, which itself is tapped into the Void so that it generates its own self-perpetuating creative impulse. A soul, or what becomes a human being in all of its multi dimensional layers, would be one of those aspects. At that point it is an individual being. Whether it is conscious of it or not, it has the power to perpetuate its own existence indefinitely. On the third dimensional level where you live this would be largely an unconscious process, but in the higher dimensions it would be more of a conscious co-creative process.

Then there are systems which are different in that they are not self-perpetuating. This applies more in the mineral realms, and some-what in the planet realms. In these cases, councils will form to create structure. The Gods in these councils will place themselves, or a part of themselves, into a Creation Chamber.

A Creation Chamber is essentially the heart of the Creator God or Gods. It is the power of their love to create. If a Creator God is sin-gular, he would go into his heart in much the same way you go into yours to go into the void, and with love and passion will create. When there are more they will join hearts, and between them will be the ves-sel in which they create. They create with divine thought, and divine thought is very different from the machinations of the human mind.

To return to my discussion of creating something in the mineral realm: That part of the Gods which is placed in the Creation Chamber must remain there for as long as the particular substance is desired to continue to exist. For instance, if I wanted to participate in the creation of a ruby, I would join with others and we would take a part of our-selves into the Creation Chamber. As long as we wanted the molec-ular structure of rubies to exist throughout this entire universe, we would remain in that chamber, actively generating it. That is how we create matter.

Plant forms are created in much the same way. However, with plants it is more that we would hold the seed form of that particular vegetation—not an actual seed like an acorn, but the archetype of the tree or of that plant form through its entire life cycle. We would hold that archetype there. The animal kingdom is much like the human kingdom, where animals have independent lives, although they are created more as a species or type. What happens when an extinction occurs on a planetary scale is that this group, council, or person is no longer in the chamber. With an animal species, they will have left the chamber. The species will not disappear immediately, but the impulse for it to recreate and stay in form disappears, and so they will die out. However, these Creator Gods can be invited to reconvene and recre-ate those beings that have disappeared.

Throughout Creation there are a multitude of what you would call devic energies. Devas are actually those fragments of the Creator Gods which are in the Creation Chambers. Therefore when you call upon them, that wonderful magic can happen. Working with the devic energies would feed them too, in a sense. It is like the phenomenon which has been described with what you call Gods on this planet, that they seem to die out when people stop believing in them. Therefore if a planet such as yours has inhospitable regions for this particular life form, the Creator God fragments will leave the creation chamber and allow it to die out—unless humans in their great power will call them forth again, and in essence feed them with their love and their desire for the continued existence of what they are creating.

Different Creator Gods are focused on different things. There are Creator Gods who are basically creating substance, material to work with: sort of like yarn, or raw material, or clay to be sculpted. These Creator Gods would be in place to create the stuff of Creation, raw undifferentiated material. And there are various types of specialists, beings who like to create within their field of specialization over and over again. There are those who are specialists in the plant kingdom, and the animal kingdom, and in star creation.

Then there are beings who are not specifically Creator Gods, but who are more the weavers of Creation. They take material that has been created and weave it into new and beautiful form, giving it order, giving it luster, giving it stories. Stories are very important to this process—themes, orchestrations. These beings who are the weavers would write a story, make an outline, and begin to weave material around that outline. Thus they would create worlds and people them. They would be the architects of jewels in space. They would in many cases appear to be the creators—and yes they are the creators, but you see how many levels there are to this.

You say that life forms can be called into existence again if humans will do the work from our side. Will that help to restore some of the life forms on our planet?

Oh yes, there is great possibility of that happening.

Please explain why the Creator Gods work.

Ah yes, why they work. It is the expression of love, of creativity; it is the reason for our existence. We live to create, as an artist would. And creating is an expression of something that language cannot name. The place that this desire to create comes from is so vast that there is nothing which could describe the motivation of creation. And it is never ending.

Do the Creator Gods have their own realm?

Their home is in the Void, beyond this Creation. Although they may come and manifest forms, even into the third dimension, they will identify most with and return to their home which is the Void beyond the Creation. When you enter Heru's world in the third technique which I have given, you are coming to that place. *[That's where you live.]* Yes.

In the process of creation, how do twin flame Creator Gods, such as you and Durga/Sekhmet, work together?

Perhaps the closest analogy would be making love. Our focus in general is on the focus of the creation of new souls. Other Creator Gods would focus on creating animal species, entire blocks of vegetable life, and so on. Yet others would create minerals, planets, and the like.

I would assume that your work in creating souls is done with Durga/Sekhmet in your role as cosmic progenitors. Is that correct? [See Chapter 11 for more information on cosmic progenitors and the creation of souls.]

Yes. *[Are the two of you parents to all the souls that you created?]* We are parents to a few and the grandparents of many. *[How many direct children do you have in this universe?]* A few hundred.

Are there other Creator Gods who create human souls?

There are others. And some human souls are created in groups, by groups. You will see them on this planet. They are not quite as differentiated, and would perhaps identify more with nationality, religion, etc. That is not to say they do not have the potential for evolution into highly differentiated beings. But they do begin as a group. And interestingly, in those groups there will emerge leaders that will raise the entire group up. Therefore when that entire group rises up, great changes happen in humanity.

Then there are souls that are created as twins, as you know, and souls that are created as individuals. Each of them would be an expression of the variety of life that exists in Creation.

Is there something along the lines of a divine plan that you create within?

There are divine principles, which would be the structures—the lines on the road or the walls of the canyon, so to speak. Principles of structure, the way light forms, and the basic geometries—these things are there within all of these universal structures. The molecular, atomic, and DNA structures follow the same pattern within all the universes of this Creation.

But as far as a theme or a message, that will in many ways vary from universe to universe. Nevertheless, you would still recognize the basic forms of life. You won't go from this universe to another universe and find all the humans and higher beings to be made of geometric shapes, a triangle for a head and a trapezoid for a body and so on. Life throughout this Creation follows certain forms, and you would recognize those forms from universe to universe. You will recognize life, you will recognize kinds of matter. There are other Creations where life forms are geometric, but that is not part of this structure of universes. And there are certain archetypal forms which are found throughout the universes.

How many Creator Gods are there, and how many are able to do the work of creating universes?

The Creator Gods do not exist in huge numbers. There are maybe a thousand or a few thousand in all the universes, in all of Creation. I never sat and counted them. And among the Creator Gods there are not many who can create universes and for whom that is their profession, where it is not just a one time interaction or activity. *[You and Durga/Sekhmet can create universes?]* And have. *[Was this as part of a group effort, or just the two of you alone?]* As part of a group effort. By and large for a universe of this size it would take more than two beings, even Creator Gods, to do so. However she and I have created, alone, a small universe for just the two of us. She and I occasionally retire there for some rest and recreation. It is like a little jewel.

As a Creator God, do you have higher aspects, or is it just you and the monad?

It's a little difficult to describe because it's sort of yes to both. I have presences and lives on each of the levels, but in a way it's just me and the monad because all of those levels are enlightened.

Would it be correct to say that many of the Gods and Goddesses of ancient mythology were, in fact, ascended masters?

You could put it that way, or you could say that they were visitors from the higher realms, the God realms, or the Creator Gods. I hesitate to use labels because they seem so bound by concepts. *[Would the appearances and disappearances of the Gods, as recorded in legends, be the Gods and ascended masters moving in and out of physical manifestation?]* Yes. Also the veils at that time were thinner, so it would be easier for humans to see those manifestations.

CHAPTER TEN
LIGHT AND DARK ASPECTS

Until the time when I began working intensively with Heru, I had a vague idea that there were higher levels to every human being, yet could never determine exactly what they were. Like most people in metaphysical circles, I had heard terms such as higher self, soul self, Oversoul, and I AM Presence. I had also seen drawings and paintings of the third dimensional self surmounted by a number of higher and progressively more radiant selves. Still, I had no real sense of what all these levels or selves actually were.

As Karen and I proceeded in our explorations, my clairvoyance continued to develop. I perceived the higher aspects in a whole new way, and was able to check my perceptions with Heru. Like most of what I have learned in the past year, the discoveries I made in the area of higher aspects were fascinating, illuminating, and sometimes shocking.

What we learned is as follows. Third dimensional humans are aspects on a chain of connection which reaches all the way up to the monad. The monad (which is the original soul created by the Creator Gods) is a great, magnificent being, existing on what we would call the twelfth dimension. It is, for each of us, that from which we spring. We are expressions, or aspects, of the monad. Beyond the monad is only Source, God, or Prime Creator—whatever term one wishes to use. Heru often likens the monad to a mighty oak tree. To follow the metaphor, this tree then extends a branch of itself into this universe, or any universe in which it chooses to create aspects. At several junctures along that branch there exist the higher aspects, with the third dimensional aspect being at the end of the branch.

Karen coined the term "ladder" for this progression of aspects. A typical "ladder" may contain an aspect on the third dimension, which we would experience as a physical human being. Then there might be aspects on the fourth, sixth, eighth, ninth, and eleventh dimensions, for example. And what are these aspects? They are people! They are ensouled beings, similar to Earth humans in many ways, but living on different dimensional levels. They have names. They have lives, including occupations, friends, clothing and activities that they prefer, dwelling places, and distinct personalities. Among the higher aspects we have met there are healers, teachers, musicians, and counselors. Most of the higher aspects we encountered are living on higher dimensional planets in such locations as Arcturus, Sirius, or the Pleiades. Occasionally we found an aspect living on a higher dimensional starship. Higher dimensions have matter just as we do, and to them it is solid, just as physical matter is solid to us. However the higher one goes the more fluid matter becomes, and the easier to change and influence. Higher dimensional bodies in the fallen universes age, as physical bodies do, though much more slowly. A strong infusion of energy can rejuvenate a higher dimensional body, whereas rejuvenating a physical body is very difficult.

Time moves differently in the higher dimensions. We found that a month would pass for us when only a week had gone by for a sixth dimensional being. Because of the greater density in the lower dimensions, and because time is so slowed down here, the lower aspects in the "ladder" tend to be somewhat wearied. This would not be the case in a light universe.

Higher dimensional beings require nourishment, as we do, although they need less of it. The highest aspects seem to subsist mostly on pure water and light. Those in the middle ranges, such as the sixth to eighth dimensions, could be sustained by a few pieces of perfect fruit per day. These beings need sleep and periods of rest as well, though again less than we do.

All of the aspects on one "ladder", or one branch of the monad, have a strong commonality. The personalities will be different, yet similar, as they are all expressions of the same monad. Certain core qualities will show forth in all the aspects, and there will be a recognizable soul essence about all of them as well.

The monad and its aspects are connected to one another by fine, glowing strands which are called light filaments. Light filaments look like fiber optic cables, and they carry prana. By working with the light filaments, skilled healers can affect the state of aspects on various dimensions.

Aspects in other dimensions, depending on their state of evolution, may be more or less aware of their own higher and lower aspects. A very evolved fourth or fifth dimensional aspect may give much guidance and help to his third dimensional aspect. In other cases there may be a lack of guidance and help, or even a negative influence. The most difficult fact to accept about the higher aspects is that they are not always the pure, radiant beings that we have been led to expect with terms like "higher self". The monad, according to Heru, is incorruptible. However, higher aspects who dwell within one of the fallen universes are just as susceptible to the corrupting influence of darkness as are third dimensional humans. And, as Heru has repeatedly said, darkness exists in this universe up through the eleventh dimension. We were shocked to find that even many lightworkers have dark aspects. In fact, since it is common to have about four aspects on the "ladder" between the third dimensional self and the monad, and due to the great difficulty in resisting dark influences, most human beings have one or more dark aspects. The worst I have seen was a person with four dark aspects. Therefore even among lightworkers it is a rarity to find a person who has only light aspects. Fortunately, because all aspects are ensouled beings, reclamation is hoped for in the vast majority of cases. The reclamation of lost souls, as Heru terms it, is discussed in more detail in the last section of this chapter.

The best and most hopeful example that we have of the restoration of a fallen higher aspect is Majaron, to whom Heru refers several times in this section. Majaron is the sixth dimensional aspect of Karen's twin flame. When we first encountered him, Majaron was heavily veiled. We were unable to see him, and even Heru had a difficult time penetrating his disguise. Eventually we learned that he was about 90% dark. Imagine the sixth dimensional equivalent to a gangster and drug dealer—that was Majaron. He was heavily attached by a dark being and had come to the point where he completely identified with the dark side. Using techniques taught to us by Heru, and with the help of Durga/Sekhmet, we worked on Majaron. We were able to assist his transformation back to a loving and positive being of light, albeit one who had missed a great deal of growth and spiritual maturity due to his eons of existence as a fallen being.

Much as we might prefer not to think of the possibility of dark aspects, knowledge about them can be important and helpful. Having dark aspects directly above the third dimensional self can have a deleterious, even crippling effect on the third dimensional human. We observed that in most cases of this nature the person in question found life a continual struggle, despite the best of intentions and despite tremendous efforts to heal. Also, Heru tells us that it will not be possible for lightworkers who came here from the unfallen universes to return home until all of their aspects are light. Dark aspects also impede the ascension process. Therefore, clearing the aspects and light filaments is a tremendous aid to growth and evolution. Please see the Appendix for more information, including assistance for those who would like to have their aspects checked and/or cleared.

PART I—COMMUNICATION BETWEEN LEVELS

Heru, when we are working down from an eighth dimensional aspect, for example, to transform an aspect on the sixth dimension, we notice that the eighth dimensional aspect does not engage in this work unless we ask it. Why is that?

You third dimensional humans do not understand the greatness of your power—that you can request what nobody else can request. A sixth dimensional being could request something but it would only apply to that dimension, or an eighth dimensional being for the eighth dimension, or whatever. But there is a specialness in the humans on the third dimensional level. For built into them is a mechanism for ascension, and it does not happen until a being fully incarnates on the third dimensional level. And when this happens, they can call for action on all the dimensions.

It also appears that aspects on the various dimensions are not always that aware of one another.

That stratification [i.e., that most beings are essentially confined to the dimensional levels where they reside] is one of the fundamental structures in this universe. Were it not there, there would be a level of chaos that is undesirable. And yet that stratification has become so embedded as to be hampering the influx of the greater light. This applies to the question you asked about the releasing of normal rules and boundaries at the time. This is correct, and specifically for this planet in that it is one of those key points at which everything is aimed: the greatest darkness and the greatest light, the greatest chaos, and the greatest growth. When you visit the Pleiades it looks stagnant to you, but those living there do not feel that. For them it is the ordered progression of growth that they are familiar with. If they were to plunge into this planet, it would be very hard for them. But Earth is almost like a rocket that, when the thrusters are fired, will break through those stratifications and allow the upward movement of all into the higher dimensional levels. This is a truly revolutionary process. So once again, we point out the key position that this planet assumes at this time.

For what is happening here is not occurring elsewhere. It can only happen here, and what is happening here has implications that are far reaching. Imagine these so called lowliest little humans, the little ants or whatever you call them, that are demeaned throughout the universe as stupid, as dark, as unevolved—yet they are making something happen that has never happened before. And that is this rocket ship of ascension. *[Planetary ascension?]* Yes. *[And thus contributing to the ascension of the universe?]* Yes. And by the way, speaking of the ascension of the universe, don't think that because this universe is far, far away from the central universe, the Godverse, that it must always remain so. It is as much a matter of vibration as it is of age. Just as there as wormholes and wrinkles in time and collapsing space within this universe, so there are such things between the universes. And don't think that the being who ensouls this universe doesn't want to be close to home.

To return to our earlier question, is it because of this stratification, then, that a higher level light aspect would not necessarily fix the dark aspect below it?

That is correct. The best way I can explain it is that there's not a great deal of permeability between dimensions and not a great deal of traffic in energies between the dimensions. It is very stratified. What would be air in this dimension would be solid as brick in a lower one; and it is the same above you. So were your eighth dimensional self to attempt to reach into the seventh dimension, it would be met by a wall of density that it would not be able to penetrate. What would be air in the seventh dimension would be solid in the sixth. The higher aspects may be dimly aware of unpleasantness happening below, but they pretty much have an independent life and no real way of correcting the problems which might exist in the lower aspects.

Again, this is the greatness of the third dimensional form, and soon even the second and first dimensional forms, if you can imagine that. It is from these lower dimensions that the real movement takes place. It is the ability of the lower dimensions to go into the higher dimensions which enables this crossing of the barriers to happen. And once that opening is made, then the upper dimensions may come through that opening to assist the lower dimensions. *[There are actually first and second dimensional forms?]* Yes, and I don't believe there are words in your language to describe them. It would be like a universe inside a dot and a universe inside a line. It seems there is a book called *Flatlanders* that would give a description of it.

Would a being such as an ascended master have more power, vision, and ability, than a higher dimensional aspect?
Correct. Greatly more, because they have created within their template that opening or shaft between all of the dimensions and they are free to travel up and down that shaft, as if they had an elevator and had control of the buttons.

PART II—WORKING WITH ASPECTS

How does an aspect go dark, if its higher aspect is light? In other words, how would a light aspect spawn a dark one?
It is not a matter of spawning. It is more a matter of the fact that everything in this universe is quite susceptible to corruption. It's as if the immune system were in a weakened state. There are "viruses" rampant throughout the universe [i.e. various forms of darkness] and it is very easy for a being to catch a virus, with that virus being of a lower vibration. *[So a light aspect becomes dark?]* That's what happens. It is commonly called the Fall.

People with dark aspects seem to have major twists in their light filaments, enough to choke off the flow of prana. But I noticed that even with people who have all light aspects, often the light filaments will appear slightly kinky or wavy. This will start in an almost imperceptible fashion from an eleventh dimensional aspect, but increase with each level as it goes down. What is the meaning of kinks in the light filaments?
That is the inherent weakness of this universe in manifested form. The blueprint has been replicated so many times that there are weaknesses in it, and so a mutation on the highest level will become

greater and greater as each level descends, bringing forth on the third dimension problems, disease, and discomfort. *[These kinks reflect a distortion of some type?]* Yes.

Regarding ascension, can a person only ascend when all aspects are light, and when they are all completed?
There are instances when ascension has taken place before that is complete. However, there is a great deal of burning and pain associated with it. It has been done; it can be done; it is not recommended. *[So it's recommended to wait till all aspects are clear and complete?]* Or close to it.

Please speak more about the strands which connect higher and lower aspects.
They look like fiber optics and they are called filaments of light. They are the encoding which would create the DNA on the physical level, but they exist on many dimensions. And they are, in a sense, how form is created in any dimension. It is from those filaments that the body is formed, so a distortion in them would create a distortion in the body of that dimension.

Why would an aspect start to become light just because the light filaments were straightened and cleared?
Let us take the case of Majaron. Due to the straightening of the strands, he was brought into a state of awakening and into a state of *instant karma. His karma was up against his face and there was no* escaping it. *[Why would straightening the strands have such a powerful effect?]* Because these strands are so powerful. They are the vehicle through which prana travels. Without those strands, there is no life. Distortions in the strands will create distortions in the life and the straightening of the strands will bring a restoration of life in its pure sense.

How does this work given that the strands were straight to begin with, yet some aspects turned dark? Or would turning to the dark occur as a result of having crooked strands?
No, it is more the former. It is more that a being would be hit by corruption, almost like being slammed with a dirty snowball. The distortion would hit the being at that dimension and almost spin them around, if you can imagine that. At least in Majaron's case, it was like being spun around. And that twisted the cords and choked the life force. In other cases it could be different, but something of that nature.

I do want to add that when there is a severe blockage it not only affects the beings below, but those above the blockage. For prana, in order to really work, needs to make a complete circuit. It descends down from the upper dimensions to the lower dimensions and makes a loop or a circle. If that circle is blocked it detrimentally affects everyone, all the aspects.

What is the connection between sleep and light filaments?
When a human sleeps, this allows the body to repair itself, renourish itself, and be reenergized, and much of this happens through the light filaments. When the filaments are damaged, it would almost be as if your airways were constricted and you were struggling for air. That is how your body would feel, having an impeded flow of energy. *[I have observed that it is harder to fall or stay asleep when the filaments are damaged, and easier when they are repaired, along with having a better quality of sleep. Why is this?]* I do not know, but it appears to be correct.

[Elora:] We will conclude this section with a quote directly from a monad who was observed to be actively working on all of his aspects—in this case, beings on the tenth, eighth, sixth, and third dimensions.

Zandrion, please explain the work you are doing with your aspects, and what is the purpose of this work.
It is a fundamental restructuring of the life energy of these beings so that they may handle the influx of the greater energies that are coming, without it distorting and blowing them up or having a blow out like a tire. *[This implies that beings who are not getting worked on in this way could get "blown out"?]* Well, don't assume that anyone is not getting worked on. At this time there is a great concerted effort for everyone to get worked on. Everyone is very busy right now. It's like people who are getting ready for a car race where they are doing the last minute adjustments, tinkering, calibrating, tuning up, and so on. They know in a few minutes the starting bell will ring and it will be a very fast and furious transformation. So there is much going on at this time.

And all this activity is more complex than I can really describe, because it's not just the vertical levels that you see. On each level that there is a being, there is a horizontal segment of work that is happening as well. It's something akin to what Karen was describing in seeing her twelve selves in twelve different planets. It is not exactly parallel selves, but that would perhaps be the closest description to it: where the energy comes down from the Omniversal Energy, to me, and it goes out in all directions. Then it goes down to the next level, and on that level it again goes out in all directions. Therefore in each area it's not just the light filaments between the levels, but there is also quite a bit of work to be done in aligning the patterns that go out horizontally. For example, when you tune into all of your bodies, the physical, emotional, and so on, they go out and out. It would be more like that—what radiates out from each life that is lived. There is a great deal of work to do and everyone is very busy.

PART III—THE RECOVERY OF LOST SOULS

By "lost souls", Heru means those beings from the Creation who were originally light and pure, and who have fallen and become corrupted by the dark.

[Heru:] As I have stated, the dark itself is not ensouled. It has made forms in a parasitic fashion, using some energy and genetic material from the Creation and forming it into the hideous demonic entities and shapes that you have all experienced. Therefore when we speak of the recovery of lost souls, we are not addressing the dark beings. We are speaking of members of this Creation, ensouled beings who have succumbed to the dark, and their possible or probable reclamation. Many of these beings are high, beautiful, and mighty creations and creators in their own right.

The question has arisen: when beings fall, are they aware that they are falling? I cannot say for sure, but I believe often there is not an awareness of the fall. Therefore why some have fallen and some have not is not known at this time. To reclaim someone who has become full of darkness, and is not self-aware of being dark, is a great challenge. Now that the Light Warriors are here, we believe that this work will commence and be possible.

Since the coming of the Omniversal Energy, many of these beings have been incarcerated and isolated so that they may do no further harm. Especially with the higher beings such as the Elohim, the angels, and the Creator Gods, there has not been a successful reclamation. We are very hopeful, however, that this will change now the Light Warriors are here. We are greatly heartened at events like the reclamation of Majaron. For that has been one success out of only a few. There have been others, but not that many dramatic turnarounds. And let me state that this was due entirely to the pure and unselfish love that Karen holds for her twin flame. Without that unconditional love, this reclamation would never have taken place.

Heru, did a number of us have dark lifetimes? I seem to remember some lifetimes where I was involved in black magic.
Very much so, and Karen as well had a couple of very dark lives. *[Would we have been considered fallen humans during those lives?]* It is more that you take the totality of the sum of a person's evolution. If you were to isolate a single life, you could say it was a fallen life. But if you were to look at the whole life path of the multiple incarnations, you would see that many beings would have had a dark life and then in the next life would be busy digging out of it. However far they would get in that life, it might not be very far, but just the attempt is important.

How did we bring ourselves back to light, and did this require the awareness that we had fallen?
It did require the awareness of having fallen, and the way back is arduous—or has been arduous, I want to put that in the past tense—and slow. It involves all of the laws of karma and effort.

Apparently sometimes beings are aware that they are falling, and other times they are not.
Yes, and I still do not understand the entire mechanism of those beings who are not aware that they are fallen. *[It's as if part of the fall is sometimes this unconsciousness, and that is the most deadly part of it.]* Yes, very much so, for at that point there is no real ability for that being to struggle against the darkness.

The light workers who have become dark or who have dark aspects won't be able to return to their light universe, will they?
They could, if they were allowed to, but we will not allow that to happen. They will not be allowed to return. *[When they die in this life, where will they go and what will happen to them? They won't have to reincarnate here, will they?]* Not necessarily. They will be given the choice where they want to process, and will be given much help.

What about those of us who don't have dark aspects, yet are carrying all sorts of effects from our exposure to darkness? Will we have to get completely cleaned up before we can return to any of the light universes?

I believe there will be much help given and that it would be easiest for a person to do that, to make that journey without the baggage. However, it can be a fairly quick process with the help that is coming.

PART IV—THE ASPECTS AND THE MONAD

In esoteric circles, it is said that monads are the source of all souls in Creation. The monad is supposed to be the first individualized expression of consciousness beyond Source. It is believed that the monad splits repeatedly, or at least forms a multitude of aspects, and this is how the individual souls are created. Is there any truth to the concept of the monad?

Yes. Let me give you the example of Karen and her structure. When she was first birthed, the name that she associates with that is Kapharatha, and that would be her monad. That is the original envelope, the original membrane that contains and brings forth her energy. And from that many things can happen. Kapharatha has a number of descending ladders, starting in the eleventh dimension and descending to the third. She also has parallel aspects on the twelve key planets in this universe. As I have said, she is widely represented throughout this Creation, for she also has lives in other universes as well. For the purposes of this conversation we will not go into details of those lives. But you can imagine that there are whole series of incarnational ladders and parallel selves. The life that Karen has here might then look as the leaf tip on the branch of a mighty tree that has many branches into many universes, and the root would go back to the monad. *[Or in this analogy, is the tree itself the monad?]* You could say that.

Let's take my own highest self, Aleandria. She is the One of whom I am only an aspect. Is she herself a branch, or is she the monad?

She is the monad.

I always imagined the monad as being impersonal consciousness. However, I see Aleandria as a fully individuated being, not exactly human, but like a goddess.

Let me say this about impersonal consciousness. If Creator Gods have personalities, and even Prime Creator Itself has personality, why would a monad not have personality? It is your supreme person. *[Is it my projection that I see her with a human form, albeit very great and magnificent?]* No more so than when you see fleeting glimpses of me in form. That is not your projection either. It is one way of seeing me, and one way of seeing her.

Can you define the term "monad"?

This is one of the most difficult definitions in our discourses. When a soul is created, the Creator Gods would petition Prime Creator for permission to create a new soul, and that is a very distinct act of creation. When that soul is created, the seed is born, and that seed would be the monad. From that monad would flow all of the aspects. Like a seed, it would sprout roots and leaves, flowers and stems and fruits. Once that has happened, you no longer see the seed. The seed is somewhat consumed in this process, and yet the original blueprint and intent is present within every cell of that plant's being. Where do you locate the original seed, once this has taken place? In a mighty oak tree, where is that original seed? It is contained within the entire life force of that tree. It is there, it is just not localized in any one place. So that perhaps creates more questions than it answers. *[If we use the analogy of the oak tree, I envision the monad as being like the tree, and the aspects as being parts of a single branch which reaches into the lower dimensions. Is that a good way to think of it?]* Yes, it is.

Do the monads always remain on the highest dimension below source—i.e. what we would call the twelfth dimension—and is it only the aspects which descend?

Yes.

We know that the monads create aspects. Are the monads creating souls by so doing?

This is an area of semantics where, in this context, we are using the word monad interchangeably with the word soul. The monad does not create the soul, the monad is the soul; and it can be expressed in many different ways simultaneously. Again, to use Karen as an example: her monad has projected itself into life forms in several different universes, and into third dimensional bodies in this universe on the twelve critical planets. But these are not separate souls. These are all part of her monad, living many lives on many dimensions simultaneously. Therefore what she sees as her ladder is only what is reaching from the twelfth dimension to the third dimension on this planet. There are many other ladders in many other places. And they are finely filigreed, like a beautiful fir tree.

The aspects on the different ladders which are projected into various universes, as well as the aspects on multiple ladders within a universe—these are what we call parallel selves?

Yes.

When we ascend, do all aspects merge into one?

In a way. It's one of those things that is very indescribable. You know how a telescoping device will have sections that will telescope out, and then as they go in, one slides into the other. It's not exactly a merging but it is a coming together.

So is this what happens when the aspects merge back into the monad?

It's sort of like that. Going back to the telescope metaphor, there remains some autonomy still within each layer of the circle. If you were to look at the telescope head on, it would be concentric circles. *[Is this why you say that you yourself still have aspects?]* Yes. *[Do all aspects ascend together?]* Yes.

Are the higher aspects always the same sex as the third dimensional aspect? It seems that would not be the case, since we know that people change sexes often from one incarnation to the next. Yet the aspects we've encountered so far seem to be the same sex as the aspect on the third dimension.

It would work that way in general. In the third dimension there is *the choice to switch back and forth between different genders for* experience, and to give greater opportunity for the dance to play out in a greater complexity. However that choice is not given to the other aspects on the ladder. In an unfallen universe it happens in a fairly orderly manner. It would be a pattern, so to speak, where for example every sixth or tenth incarnation there would be a gender switch. But for the most part the incarnations would happen in the original gender. However in the fallen universes everything is much more chaotic, which leads to a great deal of confusion.

Why did some of the monads come into this universe and others not?

At the time this was taking place, it was not seen that the frequency fences would be erected. The boundaries between universes then were of such a permeable nature, and movement back and forth was so easy, that it really didn't seem to matter. *[So it was basically an individual choice or preference.]* Yes. However, I don't know that the monad actually ever travels. You could say they are here and they're not here. It is difficult to describe structures on the twelfth dimension.

Perhaps the best analogy for it would be the idea of a parallel self—that the monad could project itself into a universe.

What has been the effect for those whose monad was on the other side of the frequency fence?
You would find people who would have trouble accessing their higher aspects, and would be characterized at times by losing faith in Creator. The advantage of it is that when the monad is in the same universe as the aspects, the higher aspects are then in no danger of falling. The disadvantage is in the fact that there is less support. Really it's just an awful situation either way you look at it. And it is soon to be ended, soon to be irrelevant. But in sorting out one's journey, I would say that you could look at that one particular quality—the ability to hold faith in the Creator—as an indication. *[Did the monad in some cases fall?]* Up through the eleventh dimension there can be fallen aspects, but the monad seems to be impermeable.

Please define the Seven Rays and their purpose. [The Seven Rays are discussed at length in the Alice Bailey texts and other esoteric writings.]
The Seven Rays are used in this Creation as follows. Imagine a giant crystal prism through which the light of Creator is focused, breaking into these Seven Rays. They are used by the Creator Gods, the angels, and so on, to focus and color projects that they are working on. So for instance when the Creator Gods decide to create a life, they would focus one of these Rays on that life form, giving the new monad that particular quality to radiate throughout all of its many aspects. Or if a group of angels were working on a project that they wanted to give life to, and wished to give it vibrancy and strength and energy, they would in essence take that crystal and imbue the project with one of those Rays. So it is a tool of focused intent.

Did the monads stem from the Rays?
No. They are imbued by the Rays.

When, in the cosmological tree of creation, were the Rays created?
The Rays were actually brought into this Creation from a previous Creation. *[The same one as the one from which the Creator Gods came?]* No. They predate the Creator Gods.

CHAPTER ELEVEN
SOUL FAMILIES

"No man is an island, entire of itself," wrote John Donne. And none of us is without soul family, profound connections which stem from the deepest level of our creation of our being. While the subject of twin flames is well known (though often misunderstood), to the best of my knowledge the concept of cosmic progenitors has not been introduced to humanity prior to this book. These topics are both fascinating and useful. Connection with one's twin flame is a powerful evolutionary event from which, as Heru says, there is no turning back. Given the events which are occurring in our universe, I believe that most of the lightworkers can look forward to this occurring in the relatively near future. As for the cosmic progenitors, I can attest to the fact that working with them is a life-changing process. Being Creator Gods of a high order, the progenitors are extremely powerful, far beyond the beings who are normally known as spirit guides. Therefore the wisdom, protection, insight, and love which they can bring into a person's life are unsurpassed. For me it has been like having the light come on, as well as a profound re-connection to my soul family.

PART I—COSMIC PARENTS AND PROGENITORS

We will introduce this section with a quote from our friend Z, a sixth dimensional being who had recently contacted his own cosmic progenitors for the first time.

"As the return of Christ has been prophesized, it will happen in this way. More and more people will become aware of their soul parents—and the Godhead will incarnate further into the Earth plane as these discoveries are made. As darkness appears to increase on the physical plane, this connection will bring much joy, safety, and protection, and will bring many manifestations of the Christed type of consciousness on this planet. Instead of one Christed being on Earth there will be many."

And now we return to our discussions with Heru. We asked: Heru, please define the term "cosmic progenitor".

Cosmic progenitors are a specialized group of Creator Gods who are capable of creating souls. *[Is it a rare ability to be able to create souls? Are there relatively very few Creator Gods who can do this?]* That is correct. I would say in general that in each universe there would be perhaps two dozen or so of the Creator Gods who would have that ability. And there would be several hundred of the Creator Gods in each universe. The Creator Gods were created by Prime Creator in another Creation, the most recent one before this one.

When you use the term "soul", what exactly do you mean?

It is certain that not all entities are souls, for many are just thought forms or some other such flotsam and jetsam. A soul is a very sacred part of Prime Creator. When they are ready to create a soul, the Creator Gods will go to Prime Creator and in essence request an egg. In this egg are all of the divine structures and patterns that are contained within Prime Creator, just as when a mother produces a human egg, her DNA is within that. The Creator Gods are the only ones who are able to make this request and hold it. It is through their love, and sometimes then the love of the cosmic parents, that this egg is then fertilized and activated so that it may come forth with a life of its own and become that mighty tree that we have spoken of in our various analogies.

What are these "eggs" like?

I see these forms actually as not looking so much like eggs, rather as very crystalline in structure. Interestingly, just as a woman would have no control over the genetic makeup of the particular egg that she would release, we in a sense have no control over which of those diamond crystalline forms we draw out from Source. So to us it is a beautiful surprise with each new soul that we create. The crystalline structures have a uniqueness to them that is new and unexpected for us each time. And these crystalline forms, through intent and love and prayer, can be created into individual souls, or you can give birth to entire universes in this way. To do an entire universe, though, would generally take more than two of the Creator Gods. It would take a circle of beings to pull forth one of these structures forth and create a universe with it.

In esoteric writings, it is said that the monad is the first individuated manifestation beyond Source. When the cosmic progenitors create a soul, then, is it actually the monad that they create?

Yes. And they may create monads as singular or twin monads.

How can the monad be only one step from Source, if it's created by the progenitors?

Because before it is requested and drawn out of Creator, it is not separate from Creator. It is the act of drawing it forth into the membrane that causes it to become separated from Source.

Are the monads then created directly from the Void?

They are created in the Void but not from the Void. The Creator Gods draw some of the primal creative energy of the Creator into the Void and encapsulate it with a membrane. Within that membrane are all of the signatures, the personal signatures for that being. And then they bring to it, and impregnate it again with those same signatures, much in the same way that an egg would be fertilized in a human. This is done in the Void. The energy they draw forth is an unformed plasma of light which is the substance from which all Creation is formed.

Let's return to the subject of cosmic progenitors. The cosmic progenitors create the monads, and the monads are the original individuated beings, the souls.

Yes. [Do all souls have progenitors?] Yes, they do. [Do progenitors create souls other than monads?] I don't know of any but that does not mean it does not happen.

You have also spoken of "cosmic parents". Is there a distinction between cosmic parents and progenitors?

Yes. Sometimes a soul has both cosmic parents and progenitors, but other times the parents and progenitors are the same beings. When there are cosmic parents as well as progenitors, the progenitors would work through the parents in creating a soul. In Karen's case, her cosmic parents are the beings who ensoul the sun in this system and one of the stars in the Pleiades. Her parents are in this universe, but her progenitors remained in the home universe. They are wonderful, glorious beings.

How about myself?

Durga/Sekhmet and I are your cosmic parents as well as your progenitors.

Please define the term "cosmic parent" and explain exactly what they do, and in what way they are parents.

We have made the distinction that for some people the cosmic parents and progenitors are the same, while in some cases they are separated. In the case where they are separated it is because the cosmic progenitors themselves are not twin flames. And because of that it is necessary to have an intermediary to perform the coupling, as you would say, to generate a soul. *[So in essence the parents would make love?]* Yes. *[And interface with the progenitors in creating the soul or souls.]* Yes.

In other words, sometimes even Creator Gods who are twin flames might unite with different Creator Gods to bring forth souls.

Yes; and we have. Interestingly enough, often there is a desire for what you might call cross pollination, for a greater variety of material. *[And cosmic parents would also not necessarily be twin flames?]* Correct. The desire in this Creation for diversity is unquenchable, and drives a lot of what happens.

Are cosmic parents and cosmic progenitors generally related?

Oftentimes that is the case, but more often one parent would be from another lineage. Again, the desire for diversity is unquenchable. Therefore, more often than not there is a mixing of lineages.

When parents and progenitors are different, do they both act as guardians, mentors, and teachers?

They both carry some of those qualities; it is just a greater degree in the progenitors. While the bonds to both parents and progenitors would be very strong, there would be a difference in magnitude between them, in the sense that the parents would be roughly the same size and power and potency as the offspring, but the progenitors would be an increased magnitude of greatness.

Who can become a cosmic parent? Is it only the monads, or can the aspects become cosmic parents?

It is the monads who become cosmic parents. The aspects can involve themselves in the process of creating, and that does happen.

Do all humans have progenitors, including humans who originated in this universe?

Yes, all humans would have parents and progenitors, and in some cases those would be the same beings. More often, however, they are different.

You have said that many humans are really ET's, or in some case angels. Do these have parents and progenitors as well?

They would have some kind of parent, unless they are from outside this Creation. Then it's a somewhat different structure. But provided that they were created within this Creation, there would be parents. In the plant kingdom, and in the devic realm which rules the plant kingdom, there is the combination of parenting and vegetative propagation. *[But generally beings in this Creation have parents.]* Yes.

Does each of us then have a cosmic lineage which is like a family tree?

There is a lineage, yes. However, I would like to add the following. The cosmic progenitors create beings [monads] who then go on to become parents. But when these monads go to procreate, they are then directly interfacing with the progenitors, rather than the parents. Therefore the lineage is not stepped down like a family tree. Each time, the beings who are involved in creating will work directly with cosmic progenitors, not necessarily the same ones, but always with *cosmic progenitors. [And cosmic progenitors are always Creator Gods?]* Yes, and sometimes there will be more than two involved in creating a soul.

When the monads procreate, what are they creating?

If they desired to create a soul, they would be able to do so with the assistance of their cosmic progenitors. They would call in their own progenitors, and through their incredible expression of love, a new soul would be birthed.

Can you describe the experience of creating children?

What is created is love. If you could picture Durga/Sekhmet and myself standing together and focusing all of our love on each other, then what is in the middle begins to materialize and form as a third being—or as twins, in the case of the creation of a twin soul. Thus your term of making love is very apropos.

Here on Earth, when a man and woman make love, they create an embryo. A spirit comes into that body, but the spirit comes from else-where. Can you compare this to the creation of beings by the cosmic progenitors?

This is the difference, that when beings are in such a descended state as those on Earth, there are many bodies created in all sorts of ways—with love, without love, with drunken passion, at any level of creation. Those bodies are then ensouled with existing souls. The work of cosmic progenitors is much different than that. It is the actual creation, through love, of a new being. Through intent, creators such as Durga/Sekhmet and I can create ensouled beings such as you, or can choose to create more worlds. And it is always a choice what kind of being to create.

Heru, earlier you said that the Creator Gods must go to Prime Creator to receive these crystalline structures or "eggs". When some Creator Gods fell, we know that they created fallen races like the dark reptilian races in this universe. Why would Prime Creator give "eggs" containing this sacred soul-matter to fallen Creator Gods?

Because they were Creator Gods. Even though they were fallen, they still had the right to ask for these eggs. *[Did not Prime Creator have the right to refuse?]* Evidently not, and that has certainly been a problem—just as Prime Creator did not destroy the fallen Creator Gods, and certainly Creator had the ability to do so.

PART II—TWIN FLAMES

Please define the term "twin flame".

Twin flames are born when the Creator Gods and the cosmic parents decide to create a being as twins. In human bodies, there are sometimes twins who are fraternal and sometimes twins who are identical and who are from the same egg. This would be the case with twin souls. They would be created by splitting the original form of an egg. This is done with intent; it is done with great love and reverence; and it is done to magnify the power of Creation. As I revealed to Karen recently, the mechanism of the power generation that happens between twin souls is one of the most powerful generators in all of Creation. It is a hard mechanism to describe. She related what she could to you; I don't know that I could give a better description than that.

[Elora:] Karen was shown a picture of two trains which were moving in a sort of figure eight configuration. They would come together at the train station, merge, and then separate again. As they reached the widest part of the figure eight, they would then both begin the return to the train station, where they would merge or pass through one another once more.

Please discuss the power generating aspect of twin flames.
That back and forth motion, the separation and the return—that is the power. The depths of the soul's longing to return to its twin—that is the fuel. When the merging takes place a magnificent burst of energy is created which illuminates and inspires all of Creation. That joy, the beauty of that merging, are shared on a sub-atomic level with the entire Creation. The specific incidents and experiences are not shared, but there is a qualitative sum of the sharing between the twin souls, almost like a sum of that merging. The depth, the breadth, and the power of that synthesis reaches all of Creation.

Do twin flames actually spend more time apart than together?
Time—well, you know time. Perhaps. And you must understand that the pain of the separation of twin flames only exists in the fallen universes. In the unfallen universes this process is not painful. It is actually very joyful, like a dance where the partners will be close to each other, holding each other, and then swing out, feeling the momentum of that exhilarating swing, and then that momentum swings them back together again. That back and forth swing is an exquisite mechanism.

Does this coming together and moving apart happen eternally, or is there a point where they are united and don't part any more? Do even you and Durga/Sekhmet part at times?
Yes, we do. It is an eternal process. The dance goes on. *[In the periods of separation, is there a coming together with other partners?]* Yes. And also you must understand that there is a part of the twin flame construct, almost like a hara line, that is never separated.

In this universe, it is generally considered best for twin flames not to reunite until they are both spiritually mature and ready to ascend. Is this also the case in the light universes?
No, it is not. This is purely a function of being in a fallen universe. And how horrible these misaligned joinings can be!

112

You mentioned that humans can have either fraternal or identical twins. Is there a correspondence to the fraternal twins with twin souls?

That part of that analogy does not have a correspondence. A twin soul is either identical or it does not happen. Unlike human beings though, when the twin soul is created, the male-female polarity is inserted in there. *[And that remains constant?]* Oftentimes it will reverse, where each soul will take on the opposite sex for an incarnation, but the fundamental gender will always revert to the original.

In what sense are twin souls identical? They appear to be similar but different.

Yes, and the difference is the different path that each has taken and the different choices that have been made in gathering life experiences. However, each time there is that merging at the train station, so to speak, all of those experiences will become the experiences of both souls. There is a separation where experiences are gathered and a reunion where experiences are shared and merged, again a separation where experiences are gathered, and so on back and forth.

Are the original twin flames the monads, in that a monad can be created as a twin?

Yes. *[Are the twin flames always of opposite gender, even at the level of monads? It's said that at the level of monads there is no gender.]* It is hard to describe because it is more complex than just a sexual gender. I'm not sure I can describe it.

So when we think of twin flames, these are really aspects of twin monads, correct?

Yes. [Note: See drawing at the end of this chapter.]

Are these twin aspects usually created on the same dimensions? For example, would twin monads generally both choose to create aspects on the third, fifth, eighth, and tenth dimensions, so that each aspect has its twin?

That is a highly individual choice and it would depend upon the incarnational path that each twin monad decides to embark upon. There is a great deal of individual variation in the stories of each path of incarnation. Of course the paths of incarnation in the fallen universes are highly distorted, and this results in many disasters and unplanned for events that shake things up and change things. In a light universe, the twin monads would generally coordinate things so as to have aspects on the same rungs of the ladders, so that the dance may be played out with their partner. But it is not a rule and at times, for whatever reason, there are exceptions to that in the quest of creative expression.

You have stated before that some beings have twin flames and others do not. Please explain how and why this occurs.

The how is very simple. Returning to the analogy of human birth, some souls are created as single souls and some are created as twins. The percentages are different, however. I would say roughly 60% of souls are created as twins. There is a small group, perhaps 6% of souls, who are actually created as a group soul, wherein you would have multiple souls that would actually be identical twins. *[Like a woman who has sextuplets.]* Yes. It is less common, but it does happen.

As for why, it is simply a choice. The path of the singular soul is no less great than the path of the twin soul. There are dynamics and mechanisms, paths of awakening and enlightenment, which happen with a singular soul and do not happen with the twin soul. Perhaps you could say the dynamic of separation and return for the singular soul would be played out not with a twin, but with Prime Creator, or with the Creator Gods or the cosmic progenitors. It is an equally beautiful path, just a different path.

For those who have twin souls, does the union with the twin soul replace union with Prime Creator?

It is almost as if through that mechanism, that is the union with Prime Creator, that is how it is expressed. God is known through that union.

What is the purpose of creating multiple twins over single or double twins? Is it again the diversity that drives this Creation?

Yes. I don't know that there is any specific linear phrase that you could use to explain it. It's just one of the aspects of the joy of creating.

In terms of joining with a twin when one has many of them available, how is it decided which twin one joins with, and can one join with more than one twin at a time?

It does not appear possible for more than one twin to join at a time. Regarding how it is determined which twin one joins with: let me go back to the analogy of a dance with a partner that I have used before. Instead of a tango with a twin soul, those who have multiple twins will be engaged in something more like a square dance with four sets of partners. You would have the joining and the dancing and the swirling of each couple. And then at a certain time in the music, the partners allemande left and go to the next partner, and around and around.

So there is a kind of sequence.
Yes. There is more variation. And perhaps even inserted in there are a few swings around the room with non twin soul partners. You could have a very complex dance there that would include families, cousins, and so on.

Is there a greater responsibility towards each other when there are many twins? For example, with one twin we only need to concern ourselves with helping that one individual if help is needed. But with multiple twins, what if several become severely damaged or turn dark—do we feel the effects of that from each twin that is in trouble?
Yes, of course. And remember that the original pattern for this Creation was created in a light universe with no thought of encountering these kinds of problems. With what has happened there is perhaps some greater risk, but there are also greater opportunities for rescue.

When you use the term "twin soul" is that the same thing as "twin flame"? Or is there a difference?
They are the same. However "soul mate" is different. To define that term, let us take an example in your case. Your soul mates would be more like your brothers and sisters, those who were created by Durga/Sekhmet and myself at roughly the same time period. Therefore they would be very close beings to you, and in a sense you would have perhaps spent some incubation time together. *[Then there is also the category that you call "ancient friends". Those are people we have known and loved on many occasions.]* Yes.

So we have twin flames which are also known as twin souls, and we have soul mates. Are there other levels of relatedness? I have seen some quite complicated schematics listing various levels.
The other level I would add to this would be soul family—cousins and siblings who are created at a different time period, and where there is no sense of that incubation together. *[Are close relationships often formed with soul family and soul mates?]* Very much so, yes.

For a human who is in third dimensional incarnation, what is the importance of knowing and being connected to the twin flame?

It is a life changing occurrence, a very deeply life changing occurrence. Generally twin souls will decide prior to a life whether to have contact or not. Once conscious contact is made, either on the inner or the third dimensional plane, there really is no going back. For there is nothing that will create an amnesia which will allow a person to forget the feeling of contact with their twin.

Such contact is an enhancer to one's evolutionary process? It spurs on the individual's evolution?

Yes, very much so.

What about the sense of emptiness or loss?

Prior to that contact, the amnesia will be there, and the feeling of the loss of one's twin would perhaps only be the vaguest of senses. After contact, there is no forgetting it.

The longing in a lifetime for a true partner, is that built into the human wiring or is it a remembering?

It is both. For those who do not have twin souls, there is also a longing for union which gets expressed as desire for a partner. And that is also hardwired, but for them the ultimate reunion will be with Prime Creator.

How is the twin flame important for the evolution of the higher dimensional aspects of a human? Is it more or less the same?

Yes. On those dimensions, the separation is not generally as painful even in this fallen universe, so usually there are less problems in the higher dimensions.

Is this universe based on the principle of polarity, and how does that relate to the existence of twin flames?

Yes. This universe was created much in the same manner as human souls. It was created as a twin, and this is the feminine half of the twin universe system. Let us take the metaphor of Creation being like a giant flower, with the series of universes being the flower petals around the Prime Creator. You would find that many of these petals, instead of being created as a single lobe, would be created as a double lobe. Many universes are created as twins.

Is Creation itself based on the principle of polarity?

That is one of the fundamental principles, yes. If you look at the yin and yang symbol, this polarity is a primary building block upon

which the Creation becomes dynamic. If you look at the atomic structure and what holds the electrons and binds them to an atom, it's all a
mechanism of polarity.

*There is much talk in metaphysical circles of duality, and how life in
these lower planes, at least, is based on duality. Is duality a distortion
of polarity, and a result of the fallen state of the universes?*
　　Yes. There is no duality in an unfallen universe.

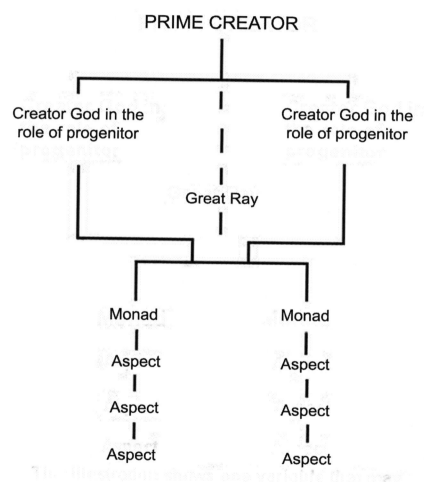

This illustration shows one variable that
may occur when creating souls (monads) :
Twin progenitors / Twin monads / Twin aspects

117

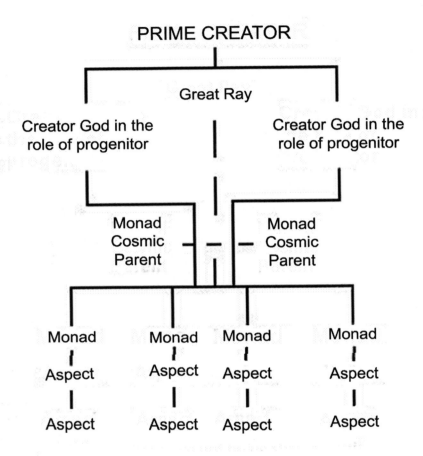

This illustration shows a soul family wherein the progenitors are not twins and therefore cosmic parents are necessary. In this case, the parents and progenitors have chosen to create souls as multiple twins, analogous to a woman who has quadruplets.

CHAPTER TWELVE
THE TWIN FLAME RIFT

Heru, we would like to ask you to look at a situation that occurred in this universe during what is called the Lucifer Rebellion. It would appear that a large number of twin flames were conscripted to work in some aspect of that rebellion, and their creative powers were being put to use, or more accurately were misused in the service of darkness. Is this correct?

That is the most accurate description I have heard from anyone on this planet. There is a tremendous amount of energy that is created between twin souls, the likes of which really don't exist anywhere else in this universe: a real furnace, a real fulcrum for creative energy. And the misuse of this power has been the source for much of the anguish in this universe. It has been used not just to the detriment of the souls who have been separated from their twins, but for many others who are just experiencing relationship problems. It has sullied the waters for healthy relationships throughout the universe.

It would also appear that something happened to this group of twin flames—perhaps what is called a time-space rift.

Yes, rift is a good term for it. *[It seems that the twin flames were torn apart in such a way that it severely damaged them.]* Yes. *[And this happened to many?]* Enough, more than enough. Not a majority by any means but as I said, this has so disrupted and corrupted and put a corrosive tinge to the basic formulation of relationship coupling, that it's almost as if not only were these individuals torn asunder but the archetype itself has been shredded. Therefore many beings who were not directly involved with the initial rending are contaminated and lose their way, and are unable to form healthy relationships. It is truly the greatest sickness in this universe.

We understand that this event caused something known as the Twin Flame Rift. Please state exactly what the Twin Flame Rift is, how it occurred, and what it means to this universe.

It is ancient. It occurred after the frequency fence was erected around this sector of universes, and the twin universe to this universe was separated from it. The agony of that separation was imprinted on every atom in this universe. And that sorrow, that grief, that trauma, affects everything. Therefore even beings who do not have a twin are affected by this rift. With the healing of the fallen part of Creation, the perfect divine twin soul archetype will once again be returned to all beings in this universe. When I say the return of the archetype to all beings, it does not necessarily imply that all beings are part of that system of twin souls, but that this universe itself is a twin and everything in it is based upon that principle. Therefore even beings who have come here from a different Creation are to some degree subject to the twin soul archetype, because that is the format and the structure of this Universe.

Did the twin of this universe fall?
No. The twin of this universe is on the other side of the great wall. *[What will occur when this universe meets its twin, and when?]* It is not fully known what will happen when there is the reunification of this universe with its twin. For there has never been a reunification after a separation like this, and we can only imagine that it will be joyous beyond words. There will be much healing needed before that can happen, and so it is not foreseen to take place within your lifetimes. It is perhaps some hundreds or a few thousand years away. But much joy, much healing will take place before then.

What needs to happen before that?
There is so much that needs to be done, I hesitate to even start the list. But if you look at the 60% or so of human souls who have twins, there is damage between each one of them that needs to be healed. Also, many stars are created as twins, and it would be the same there. If you multiply this planet by planet, galaxy by galaxy, and so on throughout this universe, you can see the magnitude of this project. If you also look at the microcosm, where even on the atomic or subatomic level there is damage and resulting disease, there is quite a lot of work to do. It is the largest job that is to be done in the healing of this universe.

In terms of our lifetime, how can we contribute to this healing? Is that part of our task?
Much of what humanity has labeled tests and lessons from God or from higher levels, are in fact not something that was created by Prime Creator but are the result of living in a fallen universe. Many of the trials and tribulations in each person's history have nothing to do

with evolution, and have only to do with being imprisoned in this gloomy place. For even though you yourself do not have shackles around your ankles and you do not live in a prison with walls, this whole planet has been imprisoned and this universe has been imprisoned.

Therefore I would have you redefine your evolution and your self worth in that manner. I would also have you rejoice in the fact that the one and only test, if you would call it that, has been your commitment and adherence to the principles of light. It is miraculous in each and every being that has held to the light; it is a miracle to rejoice at. As far as jobs go, that really was the only job that mattered. Each of you came to this universe with a task in mind to do, but could not complete that task due to the nature of the dark. Therefore, remaining in your soul is that longing to do service. That was what brought you here, and that is what has been frustrated in not being fulfilled. But the greatest work that you did was to hold enough light so that this planet could be saved, and to hold enough so that this universe can be saved.

Now that the Light Warriors have been released, by and large that work is complete. Therefore I would have you protect yourself, remain in a safe place, and await with joy the coming influx of the multitude of beings from the other universes who have awaited all these eons to be able to help in healing. They will be here within your lifetime. And they will bring you to the better part of a whole place, so that when you drop your body and your twin soul drops his body and you are reunited, it will be a union of harmony and light.

This is true for all the light beings on Earth?
    Yes.

Can you say more about the need to redefine ourselves?
    As we have said, there is an assumption of duality on this planet, perhaps epitomized by the concept of original sin and karma. What you must realize is that in an unfallen universe karma does not exist. If you were to imagine yourself as a being in the third dimension, living your life in an unfallen universe, who would you be? Who would you be without the duality, without karma? And that is, in a word, magnificence. That is who you are. Therefore as the frequency fences, all of them—planetary, galactic, and so on—are brought down, many of your connections and memories with an identity that has nothing to do with darkness will return to you. If there is any effort to be made, it is in the willingness to accept this falling away and this revelation of light, and all the joy that that brings.

[Elora:] We will close this chapter with an update from Sananda on the twin flame rift. This statement was made in October of 2004.

Sananda, can you please give us an update on the twin soul rift? Has any real progress been accomplished with it?

Overtly not, but everything is lining up around it for things to change. It is almost as if there is a giant zipper and the sides of the zipper have been jammed up, out of alignment in a way that would prevent it from proceeding. This zipper in space and time, this rift, is open and stuck open, and unable to be zipped closed. Therefore at every tooth of the zipper realignments have to be made for it not to jam. These are being done. It appears nothing is happening, but really a great deal is happening. Once that realignment is completed the zippering will begin and it will proceed rapidly. *[Can you give us a time frame?]* I believe the coming year [2005] will bring evidence of much change.

CHAPTER THIRTEEN
LIFE FORMS AND HISTORY OF EARTH

PART I—WHY THIS PLANET WAS CREATED AND WHO IT IS PEOPLED BY

[Heru:] What I will say here is not unique to this discourse, for it has been discussed before. This planet is one of twelve jewels within this universe, and was created to hold a complete library of genetic material of all of the races, not only in this universe but to contain a sampling of all universes. Therefore a being from any universe could conceivably come and incarnate here. There is enough similarity, even though on some planets they breathe ammonia. But with some fine tuning beings could come from anywhere and be able to live here.

This was done knowing that this universe was not fully light, knowing that this universe conceivably could be destroyed without having a strong resistance. With that in mind, this planet was seeded not only with genetic material but with minerals, plants, animals, and with souls inhabiting human bodies; not from every universe but including a representation of every kind of universe.

Therefore here you have the most sophisticated and highly evolved souls and you have the most unsophisticated and devolved souls, and the entire spectrum in between. You also have representatives in several kingdoms from very dark universes. Where did mosquitoes come from, and poison ivy, and such things? They are represented here at this time; perhaps not forever though.

As for the humans, you could say every hierarchy of the universal system is represented in both human kind and all of the other realms. For example, there are humans who are really angels, and humans who are aliens. In this context I am speaking not so much of beings who come from other universes—though they are here as well—but of beings who actually represent the alien races within this universe. There are also beings who represent specific universes, and who have come and incarnated into this world.

Thus this planet and the other eleven critical planets are the most complex of any worlds in this universe, and among the most complex in this system of universes as well. There are parallels to this in other universes, as there are some parallel situations. And there are universes that are much simpler than this one, as well as worlds that are much simpler than this world.

As these multi-faceted beings come to play out stories—and each of them comes with a script and intent—there is the initial burst of energy which brings them into this universe. Then there is an incarnational energy which brings them to this planet. And as they land on this planet they begin to adjust. Frequently it's not a soft landing. As beings remain here for some time, they get to know the highways and byways of life here. In some ways it is easy to spot souls who are newly arrived on this planet, for they frequently are disoriented or have trouble functioning, fitting in, and finding their place. They feel like strangers in the world; they feel lost and isolated.

It is also easy to spot those who have seen enough of the Earth and lived here enough to really know the ins and outs of everything: of political structures, of nature, of the way the world works. These souls play out their incarnational stories—and stories again are very important. Ultimately a person will become introspective enough to ask the question, "What is my story?" It is when this happens that a person begins to get to the point where they can become the co-creator in their story or myth making. And when a person reaches the point of being a co-creator with the Omniversal Energy in writing and manifesting their story, then the true evolution of a soul begins. The rest is growing up. It's as if the rest is school and this is the graduate program or the career path.

When a soul reaches the point of graduation, due to the fact that this world has been so toxic, many people get to that point and decide to graduate off of it. That has been somewhat unfortunate, for much of the light that has been accrued on this planet is now sort of sitting in a circle around the planet, not being able to effectively give back, to regenerate and renew. These people have chosen not to be here—but upon choosing that, because of the frequency fences around the Earth, they also have chosen to place themselves in an ineffective place where they can no longer be agents of change on this planet. However as the frequency fences disintegrate, as they are rapidly doing, those beings who are off planet will now be able to effect the changes that they had been prevented in so doing.

For instance let us look at your friend who intends to go through the full ascension process. If she were to have done this a hundred years ago, there is a great likelihood that after ascension she would have remained somewhat close to the Earth sphere. From that place, she would have looked back and realized that the greatest work would actually be to stay here and effect change and consciousness on this planet. This happens to a great many of those who undergo the ascension process. And yet a little known fact is that once beings would go through the ascension process, they would not be able to come back and incarnate. Very few have been able to do that because of the frequency barriers. Thus the hundreds or the few thousands who have successfully made a complete ascension have been looking for a way to come back to this planet for the work of transforming this Earth. They are now able to do so for the first time.

By this I do not mean that the ascended masters will necessarily come into physical incarnation again. The planet's vibration in many ways has shifted, so they can come here in more of a light body or fourth dimensional state. But the return of the masters is upon us; and do not limit them to one body only, or one type of body. *[What dimensions do the masters currently reside on?]* The eighth, ninth, and through the eleventh.

Heru, you once stated that Earth has become toxic to many of us, and that's certainly true. Yet I love Her so much. Did the creation of Earth go wrong?

It is not the creation of Earth that has gone wrong, but the fact that this planet was put into one of the free choice universes. The free choice aspect left this universe vulnerable to invasion by the dark forces, and this planet has been poisoned by an external influence. The blueprint of the Earth itself, if it had been unsullied, would naturally be one of the most magnificent of the entire Creation. And thus your love for it is totally justified. The diversity of the genetics, the wealth and complexity of every single layer from the macrocosm to the most microscopic life—this magnificent wealth of diversity does not exist in very many places. The whole of Gaia is populated on every level with complex, beautiful, interfacing, harmonious structures. And so your intense desire to protect it from the invasion is justified. Most worlds are very simple, where for example they might have five kinds of trees and twenty kinds of insects, instead of the incredible diversity that is here. *[Do you think that the original plan, the original concept of Gaia will be realized?]* Yes. There are so many great beings coming to her defense. Portions of the biosphere may begin to collapse, but enough information is there, enough is salvageable to be able to rebuild it. We do not see the death of Gaia. There was a time, perhaps forty years ago, when we saw the possibility, but no longer.

Given that Earth is a genetic library of incredible diversity, and that this is an essential part of her role as one of the twelve crucial planets in this universe, how do the mass extinctions which are currently going on affect this role?

It is the primary intent of the dark forces to take the Earth out of its role, to make her incapable and unable to act as the living library, as the record keeper, as the placeholder. They would love to succeed in turning this incredible jewel into a piece of cement, something no more diverse than that. <u>However, they will not succeed.</u>

With the revealing of the third meditation technique which I have given, with the breaking down of the frequency fences, and the outside help from the star brothers and sisters, anything that is destroyed can be re-manifested. There is a hidden and safeguarded chamber within this planet that holds the genetic codes and the molecular blueprints. This is, my dear, what you brought here, and it is secreted away for the restoration not of this planet only but of this quadrant of the universe. This material is safe, for only those who are supposed to have keys have them. <u>And that does not lessen the crime that is being committed.</u> But revealing this will give people hope for the regeneration of Earth—people who are heartsick at the extinctions, at the destruction—it will give them hope.

Do not underestimate the power of this third technique to regenerate the Earth. If you wish, go in there, holding the world in your hands with love, and see what happens.

You stated that Earth was a genetic "living library" of great diversity, and that it contained both very high level genetic material, as well as a sampling from fallen universes. This seems to contradict your statement that her blueprint contained pure, untainted genetic material from the Godverse and brought this to Earth. Can you explain?

There have been invasions, and just as many races of beings have populated your planets, they have brought with them some of the more noxious elements. My intent was to convey a complete collection of elements of light, not that the original intent was to have dark here.

So Earth was peopled by a great diversity of pure genetic material, then dark elements were added, and corruption occurred?

Yes, it is more like that.

If we go back in time and look at the history of Earth, how about animals such as the dinosaurs? Were these due to a dark invasion?

There was a certain amount of darkness on this planet almost from the beginning of life here. What was seen, in periods such as that of the dinosaurs, reflected the balance of light and dark that existed at that time in this world. However there is nothing intrinsically dark about lizards, however big they are, and most of them were plant eating.

Many people say there is life on inner Earth and that it is actually physical, which means the Earth is hollow and has a source of light inside. Others say that life in the inner Earth is strictly etheric. Which is true?

You would see it as etheric. Those who inhabit the inner Earth are not beings of the third dimension, but more fifth dimensional.

PART II—SOME OF THE SUPPRESSED HISTORY OF THIS WORLD

[Heru:] First of all, let us start with the fundamental religious propaganda that has been piled upon many humans on this planet—beliefs such as that the world or the whole universe was created in six days, and so on. This has been an attempt at preventing people from accessing their memories, and has been fairly effective. We look at the Darwinian evolutionary philosophy and again, the descent from the apes is an effort at obscuring human origins. Humans have been on this Earth for three or four million years. Civilizations have arisen and fallen. And there was, up until about 500,000 years ago, much commerce and communication from other worlds, and even some from other universes. There are portals that can access wormholes which not only go world to world, but universe to universe. There is a portal in the Middle East that goes universe to universe, and another one in Tibet. The great pyramids are part of the world to world portal system.

About five hundred thousand years ago, Earth was invaded by a foreign darkness. Previous to that time, things had begun to deteriorate, and darkness did exist here already. However, at that time there was a concerted effort on the part of the dark forces to secure this planet and to secure these portals. Many battles have been fought over the eons, and the remnants are recorded in a few scriptures. As the planet became more securely dominated by the dark forces, a greater effort was made to destroy evidence and belief structures of these ancient civilizations.

Egypt was the last flowering of an ET based civilization. At that time the portal around the pyramids was still open and was not in control of the dark forces. Your friend Thoth came and established that great civilization. And that is the last time on this Earth that this happened. There is a concerted effort to show that the entire Egyptian civilization is only 3000 to 5000 years old, and it is far older than that. So knowledge is still continuing to be suppressed under the guise of scientific evidence. Here and there in the scriptures you will find hints of people with extended life spans, of older civilizations, older than recorded history, and ET contact from other worlds. This is all fairly widely known in esoteric circles, so I am not really revealing anything new, but am re-stating it.

There are remains and evidences of these civilizations, but for the mainstream the knowledge is suppressed. The big battles on this planet, and the battle for freedom, does center around the portals that I have mentioned. Once they are opened back up again, knowledge will be flowing freely. Technologies will be available to clean and rebuild the environment. The help that humanity has so longed for will be available. There will be a disassembling of the frequency barriers that have kept humanity in chains, for there is a great deal of mind control on this planet.

You stated that humans didn't evolve from apes. Where, then, did we come from?

If you want to know the truth, humans were actually created first, and the primates later. The blueprint for humans comes from the highest orders of light and the Creator Gods. And humans have been in existence far longer than this planet, in other galaxies and star systems. When this planet was created it was always intended to be peopled by humans and by even greater beings—and greater beings than humans have walked on this Earth. But in the creation of all of the life systems and ecological systems, and the animals of all those systems, primates were viewed as a valuable asset. They are valued because they have a greater intelligence and self awareness than other mammals, other than the dolphins and whales of course. But of the land animals they have the highest intelligence outside of humans—and yet they retain their oneness with nature. They never separate themselves the way humans do. The fact that humans have that separation is both a plus and a minus. Therefore the primates serve to remind us in a sense of whence we come, but they are not our ancestors or your ancestors. After the fall is done with, there will be much communication between primates and humans, and there is much to be gained from that.

Would you explain the closeness in DNA between humans and the higher apes?

The reason for this closeness was to create a bridge between humans and mammalian life forms. On an unfallen planet there would actually be a continuous bridge of communication between all living species: linguistically, physically, and psychically. It is difficult to explain the mechanism; but if you can speak to a chimp, then the chimp can speak to a cow, and the cow can speak to a bird, and so on and so on through all of the life forms. When that chain is intact, then the collective communication is intact, and on the psychic levels humans are able to communicate with all of them. *[I thought that in an unfallen world, there would be direct telepathic connection on all levels.]* There is, but in the fallen realms the major part of the break in communication happened between the humans and the primates. Once that was broken and interfered with, the rest of it more or less fell apart.

How do you explain the fossil records which appear to be of early, very primitive humans?

Some of those records are being called into question. Also, some humans a long time ago did look somewhat primate-like, and some of the primates did look somewhat human-like. The dividing line, in your records, is somewhat fuzzy. But you will find fossil remains of humans that are millions of years old, leaving no doubt. There is a lot of knowledge that has been suppressed.

Heru, could you please explain something about Neanderthal Man? The records put Neanderthal Man at about 30,000 to 200,000 BC. Would this be during the Lemurian times, and were these beings Lemurians?

Neanderthal Man was actually less primitive than is commonly believed. They did not live on Lemuria. This planet has been populated by many races from many planets. The Neanderthal Man was much more connected with the cosmos than current humans, so to judge them as primitive or uncivilized is a relative term. The Lemurians were much more Pleiadian in appearance, for that is where their ancestors came from. They were tall, beautiful beings, and more ethereal.

How similar would Earth human DNA be to that of a human from another star system, like Sirius or the Pleiades?

Who do you think your parents are? It is that similar. *[There are many stories of ET's procreating with humans. Are some of these stories true, and is this possible because of having very similar DNA?]* Yes, this is all true.

I would like to ask you some questions about the history of Mars and Maldek. Did they once have third dimensional life as we know it?

They did. *[What caused Mars to lose its biosphere?]* War, attack. Specifically, something akin to your nuclear weapons, which destroyed enough of the life on the planet that it could no longer maintain its atmosphere. *[Are there groupings of pyramids still on Mars, guarded by sphinxes?]* Yes, they are there. They, however, are not remains of the civilization. They were placed there at a later time by a group that Thoth travels with, as a portal to that planet and also as a reminder to those on Earth of your ET origins. *[I remember being on another planet in this solar system with sweeping plains and great mountain ranges.]* I believe you are remembering Mars. It was a lovely planet at one time.

How about Maldek? Did it have third dimensional life? [Maldek was a large planet whose orbit was between Mars and Jupiter. The asteroid belt is said to be the remains of Maldek.]

Yes. *[Was it closer to the sun at the time? Since it is so far from the sun, it would be quite cold there.]* Its civilizations were more under water, or under glass. It was not like life on Earth. It was colonized by outsiders, and so it was a small population in a greenhouse type of operation.

What caused Maldek to break up?

There was an attack, and the colony was destroyed. The knowledge that they had was so dangerous to the forces of dark that they eradicated any record that they had ever been. *[By blowing up the planet?]* Yes. And these were some of the starseeds who later came to this planet.

The two lost civilizations of Earth have been called Atlantis and Lemuria. You said that Earth was invaded by darkness about 500,000 years ago. Was this during what we call the Lemurian civilization?

No, it was prior to that. The Lemurian civilization goes back probably a couple hundred thousand years. It was somewhat isolated and maintained its purity, while other parts of the world were much more contaminated and devastated. Because Lemuria was such a low technology civilization, and fairly sparsely populated, it was ignored. There were other more highly developed technological civilizations at that time that were destroyed.

Was the Lemurian civilization located in the Pacific basin, and if so, why does there appear to be no geological record of large landmasses in that area?

It was located in the Indonesian area and there are islands still remaining; however there were higher and greater landmasses at that time. It was not huge, but more of an island civilization. The Lemurian civilization was as close to a paradise realm as this planet has known in many, many ages.

Regarding Atlantis, there seems to be general agreement that the Atlantean civilization flourished after the fall of Lemuria, that it was more technologically oriented, at least in its later days, and that it perished due to a great struggle between light and darkness. Are these basic facts correct?

Basically, yes. However there was an overlap between the Atlantean civilization and the Lemurian civilization, and Lemuria did not perish cataclysmically all at once. It was more overrun, and it declined due to low birth and so on.

As for Atlantis—yes, both your description and many of the writings about it are accurate. The western most parts of it were in the Caribbean. There are remains there which have been explored. It extended east maybe 1500 miles or so. The maps that have been drawn of it are fairly accurate, where it has almost a rounded trapezoidal shape.

There are also countless theories as to what exactly caused the fall of Atlantis, i.e. earthquakes and breaking up of land masses, abuse of technology, and so on. Would you comment on this please?

It was abuse of technology and overreaching of power, and a battle royal between the forces of light and dark. One of the major portals was there. The beings of light, rather than letting the forces of darkness totally take over that portal, waged a battle. It is hard for me to say that they sacrificed Atlantis and all those lives for the sake of removing that portal from the control of the dark, but that is essentially what happened. That portal was a portal to the heart of Gaia. And had they gotten control of it, it would have meant the destruction of this planet as you know it. [Then what they did was right.] As horrible as it sounds, yes.

CHAPTER FOURTEEN
THE GRAND PLAN OF HUMANITY

[Heru:] Let me talk about the purpose of a third dimensional human being. For the blueprint of third dimensional humans was created in the very highest orders, with Prime Creator Itself, in an effort to have a window into his own Creation. (I use the word "his", but Prime Creator is of course beyond gender.) An effort was put forth to design a being which would have enough complexity, components of perception, cognitive intelligence, and processing abilities, that these beings could be cameras and windows for Prime Creator to see directly into the third dimension of Creation. This blueprint was set up at the beginning of this Creation. It was part of the grand scheme of this entire Creation, to have third dimensional perceivers and communicators. That had never been done before in any of the other prior Creations.

Prior Creations had rudimentary third dimensions, but they never had self aware life forms in them. As this was the most complex of all the Creations and in many ways the grandest of all of them, Prime Creator wanted to be able to experience the totality of this Creation. Therefore humans are the eyes, the ears, the fingertips, the nose, and the sense of taste for Prime Creator. In an unfallen universe, the third dimensional humans are hardwired directly to Prime Creator and their experiences are directly fed back to Prime Creator. In the fallen universes that is not so.

In the scriptures there are references to humans being the crown of Creation, and this is why. Humans are the ultimate complexity, far more complex than angels. They are the ultimate bio-computer, the ultimate sensing machine. Therefore what we touched on earlier about the insatiable desire to experience is hard-wired into humans.

The existence of the third dimension is not an aberration or an error, distorted though it may be in this universe. If you look at fractals: as they branch out and out and out, they get smaller and finer and more complex as they spread out. The physical plane is like that, like the fingertips of a fractal. Look at the nerve endings in your hand, how many there are, and how they flower out into so many millions of sites to experience. That is similar to the third dimension. Then if you look at the center of the body, there aren't those kinds of complexities in nerve endings. And that would be more like the center or the higher dimensions of Creation.

So you on this physical plane, in human form, are the nerve endings. You are the perception points for the Creator to experience the Creation. And all that you have ever experienced goes directly back to the Creator. There is much purpose in this, and in a balanced light universe, there is great joy in this level of Creation. It is felt that life would not be complete without it. For within every atom and every subatomic particle, there is that direct link with the Prime Creator. And this is not something that even a Creator God can create. A Creator God can create a universe, but he or she will do so out of the stuff that Prime Creator has created.

In the Grand Plan for humanity, each human would carry within the self a fully realized part of the whole. This would make them essentially an incarnation, or what you would call an avatar. Every human was designed to hold that kind of energy. And when they would meet, they would mirror that within each other and would be able to see it most deeply and apparently.

The term avatar could be defined as the awakened God in man. Therefore as humans form communities and family groupings, they not only are the windows for God to experience the third dimension, they also then become mirrors for each other to see what God is perceiving. And that is a wondrous phenomenon. The plan of humanity, from the perspective of the fallen universes, is to be restored to that state. Even in the light universes, this has been a process of awakening. When the third dimension was first created and peopled by humans, this whole process was not fully functional. It has been a growth experience, and a long period of growth. The fullness of this awareness and mirroring process has not entirely manifested, even in the light universes, although it is very much apparent. However it is not completely functional as yet.

Of course, in the fallen universes, this plan for humanity has been totally subverted, perverted, and stopped. When you look at a human being on this planet, the DNA has been damaged, and people are living maybe one tenth of their life span. Much of that is spent in survival mode with nothing left over for the pursuit of higher knowledge, experiences, and so on. Religion has served as an enslaver, as have governments. Humanity on this Earth and these fallen worlds has truly lost its way, as have the beings on the fourth, fifth, and sixth dimensions. They, too, have also by and large been suppressed, subverted, and perverted. Therefore a great deal of work must be done to restore not only the third dimension but all of the other dimensions.

How does Prime Creator experience other dimensions, and how is that different?
The other dimensions are experienced through the beings on those levels. What is new here is the complexity. As we have said, this third dimension is like a fractal. It is exponentially more complex than the dimensions above it. I know that you and Karen have talked about the food that is consumed on the higher dimensions, and how it becomes more simple and less substantial as you go up in dimensions. If you would look at the great variety of foodstuffs in your world, that would give you an idea as to the greatness of the complexity, compared to what a sixth dimensional being would eat.

Is it also new that Creator experiences this degree of density?
Yes. However all the dimensions, including the third, are less dense in the unfallen universes.

Let's take a being such as yourself. Back in a light universe, do you prefer the third dimensions or the higher dimensions?
My preference would be more of a traveler, going back and forth. In the light universes that is more common than not—coming in and out of form on any given dimension.

Then what do you enjoy more about the higher dimensions, again in a light universe?
The higher dimensions are, in a sense, closer to Source. None of them was meant to be an end in and of itself. Nor were any of the dimensions meant to be a prison, or a place where a spirit would be entrapped and would only exist on that dimension. As you go higher in the dimensions you would go closer to Source, which feels good. As you go lower into the dimensions you would go more into complexity, which also feels good. It is a fluid motion back and forth, and that is a wonderful thing.

Were humans originally designed for a much longer life span?
Yes. The original blueprint for humanity is an incredible, magnificent, multi-dimensional palace. It is really one of the supreme works of Creation, yet it has been degraded to the point where really humanity is living at such a low, low vibration. The shortened lifespan is a reflection of that degradation, and the decimation of the DNA is another reflection of it. What is left for the collective humanity is a grinding, never ending struggle for survival. That is what really dominates this

planet at this time.

If the light workers would get in touch with some of their older incarnations on this planet, such as the Lemurian incarnations, it would be very helpful. Many of them had incarnations there. They were quite lengthy, and they were closer to the original blueprint in their lifespan and their realization. If the light workers would seek to remember those lives, and connect to them as their own identity, this will restore knowledge, power, techniques of manifestation, meditation, healing, longevity, self regeneration—all of these gifts that are considered rare. Remembering the identity of the original blueprint in an actual incarnation of it is a very quick way to begin to restore it and to bring it into being. For once it was and so it shall be again. And when a person remembers the once that was, it's like proof and it activates that cellular memory.

How does this shortening of our lifespan affect our experience of life and death?

The human body is originally designed for a life span of 300-500 years. Because the lives of humans are so much shorter, there is a fierce clinging to the body due to the feeling that one's life is not complete. Therefore whether a person is facing mortality at 50 or 70 or 100, there is still a built in sense that they haven't completed a full cycle. Since this trauma has been repeated throughout many lifetimes, that fierce clinging to the body is also imbedded on a cellular level. Were humans having the full span of years that they were meant to have, it would be easier for them to let go of their bodies at any time. The fact that they're not having a complete life span means that they are furiously trying to cling to the body and make it survive in an effort to complete the full cycle.

Just as the Hebrew tradition talks about the five phases of life, in truth there are really stages that go out to 500 years, which have not even been touched on or explored. These are natural states of evolution that would happen in one single lifetime, culminating in a state of deep mysticism. Therefore human beings have been continually robbed of the fullness of their life cycles.

If people are fiercely hanging onto their bodies, then there must be many cases where the monad tries to release the person's soul from the body, but is unable to do so.

Yes. It is a very sad thing, and is a source of much suffering on this planet.

Can't the monad just "pull the plug" and take the person out?

At this time and in this density it is difficult to do. It is difficult for all people, including the more evolved light beings, to really have that complete faith in their higher beings, and the complete willingness to hear them and to work with them. Also the dynamic that I described about the collective desire to live the full life span is very strong, and the trauma and the repression of that is very strong. And that is one of the great evils on this planet, that the life force has been suppressed to the first two or three chakras, making people subsist on a survival level. Life for so many people is so harsh and hard that they have to fight to survive. This, combined with the fact that their life is going to be so short and they know it, creates a great fear of death. And the collective programming is there to support the fear of death, with stories of hell and damnation and reincarnation as a cockroach, and all these teachings that people are hammered with. It's appalling. I don't know what other word to say. But it sets up the rigid dynamic of "I'm not letting go of this body."

Can we look forward to a relaxing of that fear that holds people in the body?

Yes. When the fourth dimension is cleared out and significantly lightened in the next month or so, [from October 2004] there will be an exodus of people leaving this planet rapidly, where that fear for them will drop away. Another dynamic that sets up this fear is that when a person approaches even the thought of death, they approach the wall or the entrance into the fourth dimension, which has been filled with *many negative energies. That is also a great factor in the fear of* death. With that cleaned out many will no longer fear. There is also a great dismantling in process of religious structures, as evidenced by the Catholic Church scandals and such. These fears are being smashed and the restoration will begin.

Can you give a forecast for humanity's future?

I would say that for humanity the future is bright, and the amazing restoration of the original plan that will come about in the next few centuries will bring joy to so many. Humanity will be restored to its original plan, and life spans again will increase significantly. The transition between lives will be more seamless because there will be more memories of past lives, and in a sense memories of future lives. Thus the whole cycle will then become much more integrated.

CHAPTER FIFTEEN
ASCENSION

The topic of ascension is an important one. In order to get answers which would be most useful to humanity at this time, we chose to speak with Sananda. Sananda went through the ascension process more recently than Heru did, and he has also been working closely with humanity as an Ascended Master. We also spoke with Heru about ascension and have included that material at the end of this chapter. Most of the questions posed to Sananda were submitted by Shakura Rei, and we thank her for her input on this subject. The term "light worker" in this material is used to denote a being who came from a light universe to this dark universe, with the purpose of helping transform this universe to light.

PART I—DEFINITIONS AND DIFFERENT TYPES OF ASCENSION

Before we begin, Sananda, I would like to say that we realize we are currently in a period of rapid change. I know that things will probably be different a few years down the line. We would like your answers regarding ascension, as much as possible, as things are today. With that preamble, would you please define the term "ascension"?

I would define ascension as the reunification of all of the aspects through all of the dimensions and through all space and time. For a person in a state of ascension, it would not matter if they had a form in the third dimension or not. It would only matter that all of their aspects be in harmony, in communication, and united with both the monad and God. At that point, there is no barrier between the dimensions or between time and space; and everything that humans would call miraculous is possible.

The forms of ascension that we are most familiar with are what Heru has called "fiery ascension", which I think is the type that you underwent, and ascension through union of twin flames. As I understand it, in fiery ascension the person arrives at a state of spiritual awareness in which they have mastered their emotions and body, experience themselves as God, become active in their bodies which correlate to the twelve dimensions, and are no longer restrained within any level or dimension but can travel within any level or place within this universe. Please comment on this definition.

This parallels the original definition I gave, except that in a dark universe complete freedom does not exist, even for ascended beings. That is soon to change.

I have yet to find any information on ascension via twin flame union. Please describe it.

I know Karen wanted to write about the vision that she had, and that might be the best description to give. Perhaps I will let her do that.

[Karen:] Using the third meditation technique given by Heru, I went into the Void, the space from which Heru creates. Without having any particular intention for the session, I invited Prime Creator to join me in this space. Prime Creator began speaking to me, and as He/She spoke, I was taken into this experience and became one with it.

Prime Creator spoke of the fact that the twin flame dynamic is one of the most powerful creative energy sources in the entire Creation. He/She described how so much of this Creation's movement is based on the magnetic flow of energy that comes from this dynamic. From the microcosm to the macrocosm, this is the engine that moves so much. Even this universe has a twin.

I was taken into this energy. It looked something like a multidimensional, undulating caduceus. Two images came to me to describe this. The first was of two trains that are on the same track. They leave the station, going in opposite directions, traveling some distance from each other. At a given point they reverse direction. When they meet, instead of crashing they begin to merge and pass through each other. As the two trains go through this process, they exchange experience and energy atom by atom—each particle finding its mate, and merging and exchanging energy. The trains complete this process yet their momentum never slows. They reach the point of separation;

they continue until the appointed distance is reached; and again they reverse and repeat. It is somewhat similar to the oscillation of a pendulum.

The other image I received was of two dancers doing a tango. Again there is the back and forth motion. But in this metaphor, the dancers always maintain at least a finger of contact. They swing out as far as they can go without losing touch, then the magnetic energy pulls them back in towards each other. As they swing back together into an embrace, they again pass through each other, with each atom and each molecule exchanging energy and experience with its twin.

In this vision Prime Creator became my partner, as my own twin is not available. I had a direct glimpse into the power of this magnetic pull and saw that this weaving, undulating dance was being played out in all the dimensions of my being. It is like a giant organic machine that creates much of the movement throughout all the dimensions.

Returning to our discussion with Sananda, we asked: Does twin flame ascension involve personal mastery of this plane?
No, that is not required.

How is it accomplished? Is it a process of surrender more than of will?
What occurs to me to say is: how can it not be accomplished? It is a matter of a magnetism that is so strong it is irresistible, inevitable. *[So basically all beings with twin flames, at least when things are set to rights, will go through this process.]* It is inevitable.

Are the results the same as fiery ascension?
Yes. For the magnetic energy is very similar. The pathway that the energy travels is different. The pathway of twin soul ascension leads through a dance with the twin. The path of solitary ascension or fiery ascension would have Prime Creator as the partner. It would look somewhat different, but the end result would be essentially the same.

Is fiery ascension more difficult than twin flame ascension?
It is not, if that is truly the path that a person has been made to walk. One is not easier than the other. *[I somehow envision it as a magnetic pull v.s. an ascent up a mountainside]* But is there not in every soul the longing for union with God? *[Yes, there is. That is the*

magnetic pull for fiery ascension?] Yes. I'm not sure I like that term however; it sounds as if one is going to place oneself in a fire and burn up. Let's use the term solitary ascension.

Are there other forms of ascension relevant to those incarnate on Earth? If so please describe them.
Yes, I would name one. Let us call it "peaceful ascension". That would be where a solitary individual, rather than having that magnetic energy focused on Prime Creator, is focused on seeing Prime Creator in all of Creation. It is where someone would be in nature and experience the unity with all that is.

Is peaceful ascension what is usually referred to as enlightenment?
Yes. And I would add that there are different degrees and stages of this. A person can have a momentary but very profound experience of enlightenment and inner union which will change their whole life. The experience then goes away, and seemingly becomes covered up by daily life. Yet even so, the experience will continue to work on that person, and will oftentimes bleed through into daily life in small ways. These are ways that a person would perhaps not notice. They may think that they are not growing or progressing towards their goal, but it is there nevertheless.

Heru describes enlightenment thus: "Enlightenment would be a dissolving of the barriers, or the removal of the dark, that keeps one separated from their highest self; and the certainty within that the connection with God is eternal." How would you describe it?
I believe Heru's definition is more than sufficient.

How does ascension differ in the fallen and unfallen universes?
In the unfallen universes, ascension does not exist separate from life itself. For everything is ascended, and there is no disconnect between the higher and the lower dimensions. It is a seamless flow of constant communication and energy.

To bring it to this current time and space: It is a confusing mess, very much so, because this fallen sector is in a state of chaos, disconnect, and disunion. As the light workers came to this sector that was fallen, they experienced the disconnect and separation from God, from their twin souls, from their higher selves, and from all that was good. But fortunately their self-awareness and memories could not be completely erased. There was a memory of union, a memory of the transcendental experience. Therefore throughout the time since the Fall, there have always been beings on this planet and throughout this sector who have both sought to re-establish the full connection and to teach that to others.

What does it mean, in this fallen state, to ascend? And have I indeed even achieved it? For you must understand that even though through the greatest of alchemies I was able to resurrect my body, and make that body of light a body that was re-connected with my highest self or monad, I am still imprisoned by several things. I am imprisoned by the frequency fences around this planet, this galaxy, this universe, and of course this whole sector. Therefore my love and I are unable to return home, just as you and many reading this have been.

I am also imprisoned on this planet by the collective emotional chains set up by the religious beliefs surrounding my time on this planet. Every person who wears a crucifix around their neck or carries it in their pocket adds another link to that chain, and keeps me tied to that cross. Believe me, I will be very happy when that is dismantled. And it is a burden, for what people do is seek to heap their suffering upon me in exchange for their idea of salvation.

Now back to your questions about ascension. For many of them come not from the western traditions; many come from the yogic traditions of the East which I did study and which gave me the foundation for the resurrection.

At this point, we would like to speak of your own ascension for a moment. First, are you and the one whom we know as Jesus essentially the same being?

We are one and the same. Sananda is my name on the higher planes, and how I am addressed by masters on the inner planes. And Jeshua was the name that I bore in my last incarnation here. However at his ascension we essentially merged. Before that time there was some degree of separation. There was a great deal of back and forth communication, but there still was some degree of separation between us.

Heru stated that your crucifixion was a demonstration of what happens when an Ascended Master attempts to introduce light into this world. Did you not plan to be crucified and did you not agree to such a death?

I knew that it was a probability, and yes, I did come willingly, knowing that was a probability. Would I have preferred a different outcome—yes, you bet. I could have chosen a more private ministry, but it was asked of me to do a very public ministry in which the teachings and the miracles could not be wholly denied. And for that it was deemed that the risk and the sacrifice were worthwhile because of the benefit of the teaching.

Was it your plan or your hope to have a much longer ministry, teaching and healing and spreading Light?

It was my hope. Plans were laid out for me to have an extended and extensive ministry. However it was not thought that I would get very far.

Did you, in fact, die on the cross and resurrect your body? Or did you go into a deep coma from which you recovered, and then ascend your physical body by transmuting it into a light body?

I was fully dead. I came back into a somewhat decomposed body, and resurrected it. And then ascended it.

Some say that you lived on for many years and bore a number of children, who founded some of the royal houses of Europe. Is there any truth to this?

I bore one daughter. And yes, she founded some of the royal bloodlines of Europe. She was conceived before the crucifixion and was born after.

Thank you; now we will return to our more general questions. Many people who talk about ascension really mean getting to a place of spiritual development where they no longer must reincarnate into physicality, and will instead incarnate into a higher dimension where they believe things will not be as difficult or dark as it is here. Do you agree?

I actually do not, and that is again going back to the difference between this world and a world in the unfallen universe. In an unfallen universe, it is an absolute joy to descend into the third dimension. It is like a plant that puts forth all its energy into the blossom, and the third dimensional bodies are that blossom. They contain within them the beauty, the fragrance . . . it's like a crescendo, the culmination of a beautiful symphony. It's glorious, and there is no reason to not want to be there. Therefore on this fallen planet, I believe that the teaching of ascension, of graduating from the wheel of karma, of no longer incarnating, is a concept fostered by the dark in order to further devalue life in the third dimension and deepen the disconnect to all of the higher aspects.

Are you saying that the teaching of ascension on this planet is not a favorable thing? It seems that by making one aware that the ascended state is a possibility, one begins looking inward to their source and recognizing their own Divine Self.

It is the nature of the dark on this fallen planet to mix the truth with falsehood. Therefore in many of these teachings there is a kernel of truth. If you would take the example of Karen and her relationship with her former guru and the teaching that he gives, the basic teaching came from a wonderful and very high lineage. But it was stolen and corrupted, and used to enslave people into devotion to falsehood. Yet within all that, there still is enough of the truth of the original teachings that there is some benefit received in practicing them. So it becomes something that is almost like a beautiful apple with a lot of strings attached to it. And the eating of that fruit has many unintended consequences.

Therefore the ideas of enlightenment, ascension, graduating from the wheel of karma and so on, are basically sound and good ideas, founded in truth. However I would say that most of the pathways existing now have been tainted, and one must use the greatest degree of discernment in order to separate the truth from the falsehood. And this stretches across all denominations, all cultures, all religions. A person would then ask: how do I know a path is true? How do I know a path is uncorrupted? This is a most difficult question to answer, because I have to tell you that basically all the paths have been corrupted, just as every atom on this world has been tainted. That is a very upsetting piece of news. And yet the acknowledgement and the facing of this truth are perhaps the only avenues to attain the necessary discernment, with which to be able to pick up the mighty sword of truth and to cut through this jungle of confusion.

My advice to those of you reading this is to go deep in your heart, to find within you the bedrock of your soul, and to sit there in place very solidly. Then humbly but firmly demand that the Creator give you discernment, and that the Creator give you the desire to act upon that discernment to the extent that you will not succumb to temptation and lies. For you are in a deep and treacherous maze, yet there is forever that golden thread of truth. It stretches from your heart to the heart of Prime Creator. And whether it goes through the twin soul path, through the path of enlightenment and merging with nature, or through the solitary path, that thread cannot be broken. In spite of the efforts of the dark, in spite of the treachery of the maze, in spite of the degree to which humanity has fallen and lives in a state of utter degradation: just as I have said that every atom in this universe is degraded and dirty, also every atom in this universe contains that golden thread. And this, my friends, is a miracle, an absolute miracle, how the light has survived.

Returning to a previous question, is there a point at which we can choose not to keep reincarnating physically? It seems to me that we are drawn back against our will.

Yes, that is true. In an unfallen world, that choice is always there. *[And in our world?]* Because of the disconnect from Source, and the frequency fences, generally it is nearly impossible to manifest that choice not to return. *[You have done it though.]* Yes. *[What does it require to manifest that choice?]* It requires a cleaning up of all karmic threads and actions, making everything right, so that no one has a hold on you. And that is the beginning. The next stage is to have a solid enough connection with all of the aspects and the monad that this connection is more real than the connection a being has to their third dimensional life. When that is attained a being can manifest the choice to return or not, the choice to turn their body into a light body, and so on, for then there is the possibility to manifest anything. Many choices open up at that point.

About how many humans have reached that point?

A few thousand. *[But that is to change very soon.]* Yes, it is. And I would also add to this that there have been, especially from the eastern traditions, false teachings of ascension. These teachings create an avenue for a person to believe that the ascension and liberation process is in place. This being then becomes trapped in a place, generally between the fourth and fifth dimensions, where they will no longer incarnate, but they are not completely aware of their fullness of their consciousness and being. And growth does not happen there. It is a somewhat static, pleasant, but stultifying environment.

The common belief is that we don't leave this dimension until we've experienced all there is or all that our soul desires to experience. Some would say that we don't leave until we have learned all our "lessons", a concept which I have never been able to agree with. Would you comment on the truth or fallacy of these beliefs, please?

I agree with you 100% on the fallacy of lessons to be learned. As for the first part [i.e. not leaving until we experience everything there is]: As Heru has said, this Creation is built upon an insatiable desire for experience, an insatiable desire for manifesting diversity. Therefore a soul really never finishes fulfilling that desire. How many more ways can a lover tell her partner about the love? It's an infinite thing, an infinite expression. It is never finished, and it is a very sacred thing.

Sananda, it seems that there are not a great many people right now who are consciously on the path of ascension.

All humans desire something. In the fallen state, generally there is a sublimated desire where people look for peace, satisfaction, and all that they seek for in the external world. Essentially everybody desires to go home; they just have forgotten what their home is, or have been misled and brainwashed that their home is a false home.

When we ascend, specifically in solitary ascension, does our physical body dematerialize or does it remain as if we had simply died?
Most of the time the body is left behind. You will see this with many of the Tibetan monks. They pass out of their body, and their bones will carry the electric charge of that ascension, and so are held as sacred tools. *[When the body is left behind, the soul essentially just leaves the body?]* Yes. *[So what some teachers call "ascending the body" is not necessary for solitary ascension?]* Not at all. *[Is there a choice in this?]* There is somewhat of a choice, but I would say that taking the body along is a far more challenging and demanding process. It is felt that unless there is a compelling reason to do so, it is not worth the effort.

PART II—WHAT IT TAKES TO ASCEND

The common belief is that before we can ascend we must first master our emotions.
In essence this is correct. Somehow the wording rubs me the wrong way here, for it implies that a person take a "top down" approach to controlling the unruly beast of the emotions. I would see it more as attaining an equilibrium and a harmony emotionally.

It is said that we must master our bodies, i.e. heal them and not be slaves to them.
In some cases yes, but there have been many afflicted people that would still have a great experience of God. Elora's acquaintance Y. would be an example of that. She does truly suffer on the physical plane but has attained a very beautiful state of consciousness, so that is not always necessary.

And it is said that we must know ourselves as God.
Yes.

After accomplishing all that, we are apparently light enough to experience a full kundalini rising, which activates the brain and brings us into a full God-realized and ascended state.

Yes.

On the other hand, I have also read of Masters bringing a person to ascension just prior or after death. These people had not necessarily mastered themselves nor were in states of enlightenment. Does this happen, and if so what are the circumstances in which a Master would do this?

Let me differentiate here between the Ascended Masters or earthly gurus. For the Ascended Masters, the time of leaving the body is a time when the great portals do open, opportunities do present themselves, and unexpected blessings happen at that time. For the earthly gurus, I would question the veracity of the experience, cautioning people that oftentimes these lead to the sort of bubbles of false ascension where a person no longer incarnates, but they are trapped.

There have been many gurus in recent times who have proven to be lacking in integrity.

Yes. I would say that it is not a good time to be a spiritual leader, especially one of wide renown. It is a time for individuals to forge their own paths directly with Prime Creator. And because of that, I do believe a certain amount of grace has been removed from these leaders and returned to individuals. And so truly the most direct path would be one of solitary exploration.

I would also say that anything these masters or gurus or priests offer can be attained without their help. *[By going directly to Creator?]* Yes. *[So someone could ask Creator for an enlightenment activation?]* Yes. My recommendation would be to use Heru's third meditation technique, ask Prime Creator to join you in Heru's world, and ask the Omniversal Energy to also join you there. This is a wonderful platform from which to manifest your soul's deepest desire. If an individual is unsure of which path they are destined to take, they may find the answer there as well. Remember that Heru said this direct communication with Prime Creator would change everything.

Is enlightenment necessary before solitary ascension?

I do not see a separation there.

Is enlightenment only bestowed upon someone via brain activation, such as Kalki and Amma [two spiritual teachers in India] are doing?

No. *[Then how does one become enlightened?]* I would say that there are as many paths to enlightenment as there are individuals. You will not hear from my lips that there is only one way, although many would take my name and use those words.

Please give a couple of examples as to how a person can become enlightened.

There are many kinds of activations. Some are spontaneous, some are generated by teachers on this planet, and some are activated by ascended masters. Many of them are what you would call partial enlightenments, stages of enlightenment. One example I would give is when Melchizedek came to Karen and gave her an initiation. He said to her that she had done a good job of seeing God in some things and some people, and now it was time to see God in everyone and everything. And he did an activation with her that was quite deep and profound, and was life changing for her.

Regarding an example of enlightenment through a person, it is hard for me to say that a person may receive enlightenment from this teacher or that, because I would caution people that in general there are strings attached. Each one of these teachers brings more or less of the integrity of the original teachings to the students, and there is some measure of benefit to that. But I would, at this time, caution people about relying upon a teacher.

As far as spontaneous awakenings, these are generally orchestrated by the monad, and have been planned for more than one lifetime to bring together many components to bear upon a single moment. Therefore people might find themselves in the midst of a favorable astrological configuration, in the midst of a favorable environment in nature, and at a time in their life where a feather could push them into it. There is no real way to orchestrate that from the third dimension and make it happen at any particular time.

You could petition your monad for an awakening. However, if you are ill prepared for it, some disruption can occur. Mental hospitals are full of people who have had premature kundalini risings. Perhaps some of you know of people in this situation, or have experienced yourself the disruptive, out-of-control feeling that this generates. Therefore I would caution that great care be taken in that request. But if you are a person who has done a good deal of work and you feel that you have a good handle on your whole being, it may be safe to proceed. Look within to see if you feel psychologically sound and stable, if you feel integrated, if you know something of your past, and if you have looked at your shadow enough that if anything surfaces with this awakening it will not be a total shock. If you feel to be in that position, ask your monad now.

With enlightenment, sometimes there is a kundalini awakening and sometimes not. Is that true?

That is true. *[But one should be prepared that it could happen.]*

147

Yes. Those whose journey is that of the peaceful enlightenment and merging with nature would be the ones least likely to have a kundalini experience. It does happen, but it is more rare.

Is it necessary to have the experience of BEING God flowing through all creation, before one can ascend?

Not necessarily. For the path of the twin soul ascension, a being would see everything as the beloved. For the path of the solitary ascender, they would see only God. And for the path of peaceful enlightenment, they would see God in everything. It is more a matter of flavors and focus.

For those focused on peaceful ascension, to what degree must they experience God in all nature? Is it a matter of experiencing oneself as God within all nature, or is it a state of appreciating and having some sort of connection with God in all nature?

I would say it is both. There ceases to be separation. It is an experience of oneness.

Regarding twin flame ascension, let's say a person feels strongly drawn to this path, but doesn't know her twin flame. What can she do?

The best course of action would be to establish contact with her monad, and express the desire to have contact with the monad of her twin. That would be the first step. *[Following this request, contact in some way could be established?]* Yes. *[Can this path be followed through if the twins are on different dimensions, or if the contact is only on the inner?]* Yes.

What if the person knows her twin but there has been conflict or disharmony?

That person may establish a strong enough connection with the monad of her twin, and with certain of the higher aspects on the ladder of her twin, and the work could proceed very far. It would be somewhat difficult to complete in this way, but it could be done.

Is it necessary for third dimensional twin flames to be intimately involved on the physical plane, to follow the path of twin flame ascension?

It is not.

How can we know that we're on the right track? Once we're on the ascension track, feeling the magnetic pull, is there then no way that we can be on the wrong track?

One can certainly be diverted from that track and distracted. I would say that any time you feel that you have been distracted from this process, simply go within your heart to the bedrock of your soul, find that golden thread, and just finger that thread, so to speak. And doing that will re-focus you. I would use the analogy of a big epic movie that sweeps you away so completely that you forget about yourself. You come out into the sun and you are blinking, disoriented, and emotional about something that is not real. It is just an image, a story. If you find that something in your outer life sweeps you away in the same way, just do the exercise I have outlined.

Are there signs that tell us our ascension is assured in this lifetime?

A measure of that would be the intensity of the desire for ascension. Does it supersede the intensity of desires for things of this world?

The crux of my questioning is: How do we go about ascending? How do we get there? There are so many techniques and teachings; how do we find our way?

In a simple sentence: Ask your monad. *[The monad will guide the process.]* Yes. The monad will make it happen. *[So contact with the monad—direct contact—is extremely important.]* Yes.

What about people who are not that active in their ascension? They just seem to think it's just going to happen, while others feel a need to work at it and get beyond the spiritual and emotional restrictions of this world. Are both correct?

Yes. Again there are as many paths as there are people, and one does not always see the work that another has done in other lifetimes to set this up. *[I would guess that as many cycles are closing now, many people have set up ascension for this life.]* This is true.

To ascend, must a person first have descended through all the levels within the universe?

No, because there are well nigh an infinite number of levels and things to experience. No one being could experience them all, or at least no one has yet. *[I think Shakura is referring to the belief that you must go all the way down, to then go back up.]* No, it is not necessary.

Can ascension only occur from the physical plane? Or can we die, go to another level, and ascend from there?

Yes, that is possible.

To ascend, do we need all our aspects to be light?

Yes. *[If they all need to be light, what can a person do to bring them into light?]* The techniques that Heru has outlined for working on the light filaments and the aspects are very good. [See Appendix, "Tools for Returning to Light."] I would also add that working with the Masters is helpful; they are great facilitators.

For the lightworkers going home, but not ascending, must they also have all light aspects?

Yes, for as the frequency fences are dismantled, light fences will form that will preclude dark beings or aspects from crossing one area to another. *[Can some of the lightworkers go home while their dark aspects stay here to be healed and turn light?]* Much of this is new, for we have never dismantled a dark universe and reclaimed it. But I believe that things will be set up such that when one encounters a fence that cannot be gone through, there will be plenty of assistance. Beings will be there to help. And so not to worry; I believe it will not be a lengthy process. It is best for all aspects to return together.

Sananda, as we embark on our homeward journeys, and as people reclaim their memories, the issue of self forgiveness is going to be a huge one. We have all done things, terrible things. How do we forgive ourselves? I find it far easier to forgive others who have hurt me than to forgive myself for hurting others.

That is an excellent question. Understand first that Prime Creator has no concept of non forgiveness. And so using as a platform that unconditional love, that total acceptance and forgiveness, that total nurturing of the cosmic parent—use that as your platform for self forgiveness, for you are a part of that which created you. I think in essence it's that simple. It is understanding that you are not separate from the Creator. Even though you may have lost your awareness of that connection, it is still there.

PART III—ASCENSION TECHNIQUES

We've been given techniques to aid us toward ascension. Please comment on the usefulness of each in terms of how important are they and how much they actually help us toward our ascension.

I would like to preface this by saying that most of these techniques will not directly aid the ascension process, but will prepare the way and remove obstacles that would get in the way of the ascension process.

C&E (Consciousness and Energy) breathing and kundalini raising method taught by Ramtha.
   Helpful.

I AM decrees.
   Limited in their helpfulness.

Kundalini raising meditations as taught in various yoga practices.
   Some are helpful, some are dangerous.

Kriya and other yoga techniques.
   Helpful.

Seeing ourselves filled with light, through meditation.
   Helpful.

Tantra exercises.
   It would depend. There is a lot of dark magic surrounding a good many of these schools. I would say proceed with caution, and use discrimination in following any of those paths.

Celibacy.
   It's essentially an irrelevancy. It should not be sought after, nor should it be pushed away.

Emotional healing.
   Very important, and very helpful.

Sitting in the Violet Flame.
   Again helpful.

Sitting in the Sacred Fire.
   Helpful.

Chakra work, specifically vertically aligning the chakras.
   That is helpful, especially if healing work is done and any blockages removed, and these can be past as well as present life. The chakras are designed to go back and forth from vertical to horizontal alignment as needed. During meditation they will be aligned vertically, and when you step out into the world they will be horizontal. Anything that could block that movement would be uncomfortable, to say the least—particularly if there were to be a strong kundalini experience.

PART IV—VERTICALLY ALIGNING THE CHAKRAS

Sananda, please tell us more about are vertically aligned chakras. My understanding is that the chakras look like a double cone or funnel. With the throat chakra, for example, if it is vertically aligned instead of horizontally, then one cone or funnel points up and the other one points down. Is this correct?

Yes, instead of facing to the front and back. The root and crown chakras are always vertical. With the other chakras, the forward-pointing cone rotates to face up, and the one normally facing the back rotates to face downwards.

What is the difference in effect between horizontally and vertically aligned chakras?

The vertical alignments of the chakras will happen automatically as the ascension process occurs. However one may help along the process through meditation and working to align them in that direction.

When a person's chakras are aligned front and back, as is normal, this serves the purpose of receiving and manifesting energies from the world. To interact with the world, it is necessary to have the chakras aligned to the world, aligned externally.

When a person seeks to go into the ascension process, they may, in meditation, either ask for their monad to rotate the chakras vertically, or use mental energy to bring their chakras so that they are facing in the up and down position. This will further their progress in the ascension process. However, at the end of the meditation, it will be necessary for the chakras to be rotated back to face the world. You can program into your meditation that this happen automatically. I know some of you will meditate and drift into a sleeping state, so if you give intention for them to return at the end of the meditation, they will do so automatically. This can be very beneficial in the process of connecting all energies with the monad, and having a complete alignment and a complete download of those energies.

What changes might we notice once we begin vertically aligning the chakras during meditation?

You will see and feel and experience a much more direct contact with the monad. You will be able to access all that your monad can do and know; you will have access to your entire akashic records, and you will be able to reprogram your life to bring it into a greater accord with your original blueprint. *[This is a very powerful technique, then.]* Yes, and as such this will all spill over into your daily life in this world.

Are there any requirements that need to be met before a person begins to vertically align her chakras during meditation?

Yes, the chakras should be clear and rotating in the proper direction. If they are not clear, if there are cords or karmic debris, blockages and so on, they simply will not rotate up and down.

Why do they tend to revert back to horizontal?

The natural interactions of life will pull them into the horizontal position.

Why is it not a good idea to maintain the vertical orientation during daily life?

Doing so would make it difficult to be grounded in reality on the third dimensional plane. Also, you would lack the necessary energy to engage, especially in your closest personal relationships. An example that comes to mind is a mother being too detached from her child who needs her.

In addition, for someone who is not prepared by doing a considerable amount of spiritual work, the effects of maintaining a vertical orientation could be somewhat similar to a premature kundalini awakening. Just as that could put a person into a psychotic state, when a person had this vertical orientation happening involuntarily and without adequate preparation, it could be dangerous. At times when a person goes into a catatonic state, where there is no physical cause for it, it would be because this has happened. In this case the person needs to have their chakras brought back to face the world. For a person who has done a lot of work, rarely would it be dangerous, but it will be harder to relate to the world. I do not necessarily see it being a healthy thing to maintain over time, however.

It is said that that the only people who have a vertically aligned system are the newly born, dying and enlightened. Is this true?

Yes, in general—with the exception of some people who have had, as I said, a premature happening of this alignment. *[For a person who is fully enlightened, this happens automatically?]* Yes, but again, depending on how much interaction that person would have in the world at any given time, those chakras are free to rotate out into the world for contact with others. Generally, at the time of death, the "cones" of the charkas will both merge into one and face upward.

PART V—ANIMALS

Do animals ascend, and if so where do they ascend to?
They would ascend into their group mind and collective. *[Do they lose their individuality in so doing?]* Partially, but not entirely.

Do they ascend into humans?
No. *[Then where do they go, what is the next step for them?]* The best way to describe it would be that they become a universal archetype of that animal. You could say that at one time Bast [the Egyptian cat goddess] was a kitty in somebody's living room, and now she has become a cat goddess. *[So for example, my three cats will ultimately be cat goddesses?]* Yes, each embodying the greatest of their personal qualities.

Do animals ascend, or progress, from wild to domestic?
Some do and some don't. You must take that in the perspective of this being a fallen world. In the unfallen worlds, there really is not a distinction made, there is not a disconnect between nature and civilization. And that disconnect causes you as humans to fear nature, consider it wild, be threatened by it, wish to control and destroy it.

Do animals ascend from one species to another?
They do not. *[I read a story in which a woman who owned a guinea pig followed this animal psychically through the death process. The guinea pig decided to become a raccoon.]* That will occasionally happen, but the guinea pig will never permanently become a raccoon. They may visit for a life or two. But they will always revert back to their original type.

My dog has incarnated to me three different times in my present life. He is so gentle, mature, and aware, that if a dog ascends I believe he would be such a dog. I cannot stand the thought of him reincarnating into an abusive home. Please tell us what happens to animals such as him once they die.
This is a frequent occurrence, that an animal such as your dog who has a long history with you—not just in this lifetime, but in several—will seek you out time after time, and you will seek him out. The bond between you is very strong. As he approaches the end of his may wish to talk to him about your preferences. Would you have him come back again? And you may set some goals. *[And if he is not to* life, you may wish to ask him if he wishes to come back again, or you

come back, where would he go?] He would stay in the canine group mind.

Can you explain a bit more about what happens to an animal when it ascends, in terms of becoming an archetype? What does this mean in practical terms for the individual animal?

Animal species are somewhat of a group soul, having greater and lesser degrees of individuation. The animal souls who have the greater degree of individuation and the greater degree of maturity are the ones who tend to reincarnate into a person's life again and again, and have that soul connection. Let's create a metaphor, that of a sunflower, to describe their maturation process. Initially the seeds in the sunflower are in an immature, non-individuated state. You can see there are individual seeds but there is really not much difference. The skins around the seeds are very soft and light colored, and the blossoms have just fallen away. Then, as the days go by, the seeds grow larger. They develop pigmentation and strength, and at a certain point they are somewhat released by the flower head so that they are easier to pry out. It is at that point in our analogy that these mature animals would be more autonomous.

When an animal such as a cat ascends, they become somewhat like the flower head for a whole new gathering of immature cat souls, which would all radiate those same qualities. *[It's almost like becoming a monad?]* Yes, like a cat or a dog or a horse monad. So if your cat Vega were to ascend, you would begin to see many Vega type cats born on this planet.

Let me say this also: there is a curious bond between domestic animals and their owners. And therefore it would take a mutual readiness on both their parts for that animal to ascend. There does need to be the animal's maturity and autonomy, and also the readiness on the part of the people that it has bonded to—their willingness to see it into completion, to let go.

Isn't there a relationship that occurs between spiritually mature humans and the animals that come to them? Don't they have some sort of symbiotic relationship in terms of growth?

We draw to us companions from the animal kingdom that we have an affinity to. Like attracts like. Therefore less evolved people would tend to attract disharmonious animals to them, as an outward reflection of their emotional imbalances. For those of you who have done a fair amount of self work, you will tend to gather to you those animals that would reflect your greater sophistication and harmony. And animals can serve as gateways to other realms. I think I will

THE RETURN OF LIGHT

leave it to you to ponder that statement. Looking at the quality of the animals in your lives, think upon what world that animal could usher you into as a guide.

When we ascend, do we have any sort of influence over our pets? In other words, if I ascend while my dog is still alive, can I help him ascend or take him with me, or somehow prevent him from having another third dimensional life?

Yes. You may communicate with him and ask him. Depending on the animal, some have two or three humans that they feel comfortable incarnating with. If that is the case with him, he may choose to come back to one of his other friends.

PART VI—HERU SPEAKS ON ASCENSION

Heru, ascension seems to refer to the process of "rising up" through the various levels, after one has descended all the way from the twelfth dimension.

On the descension process, I would like to interject that, in general, it would take eons for the descension process but that the ascension process has various short cuts encoded into it so that at any time the whole may be opened up. There are no short cuts in the descension, but the ascension always has the potential to be instantaneous.

Thank you. Regarding ascension, are you yourself an Ascended Master?

As well as being a Creator God, I am an Ascended Master. I am also able to traverse all of the twelve dimensions.

Did you undergo ascension in some other universe?

Yes. I came here fully ascended. In fact it would have been, at the time, very difficult to have ascended in this universe. Not many beings who came to this universe would have been able to ascend here, if they were not already ascended. At that time, ascending through this universe was almost impossible. There is, furthermore, a minor descension process in being born into a universe. The veils are much thinner for an ascended being but they still must go through an ascension process. However it can happen fairly quickly and easily. *[Did you go through ascension in this universe?]* Yes, and I have manifested a physical body on more than one occasion.

I do not seem to have the drive to ascend my body, as you and Sananda have done. Why is this? [Ascending the body refers to the process of transmuting the physical body into a body of light.]

For you, this has been a very difficult place to be, and there would be a great deal of effort in going through the ascension process. And you feel that it is not needed.

Why do I feel it's not needed?

There are many different ways to Source. And it took so much for you to descend, especially since you have no intervening platforms [i.e. no higher aspects between the third dimensional self and the monad] that you have really nothing left to give for the ascension. You came bearing so many gifts for this level of Creation that you left no fuel for the return trip. *[Or for ascending my body, for example?]* That is correct. And your return trip is being taken care of. You really did not come with fuel for the return trip, and for that reason intervention has been necessary. You sacrificed much in coming here, and were in a sense prepared to sacrifice everything to be here.

Is it correct that ascending the body gives a mastery of all the levels, one that cannot be achieved otherwise?

It gives a full mastery, indeed, of all the dimensional levels. However, is that the only way to attain such mastery? No. And, as I said, in some ways what you have done is far less common than the ascension process. It required far more sacrifice and courage, because you were giving everything up to come here, including even the path home. There was no guarantee that you would succeed, and there was no guarantee of the intervention which would allow you to return. However, your success is now assured. And it seems as if you had to walk a tightrope without a net, that almost no one else could have walked. Without that journey, things would not be as they are now on this planet. So a hero's welcome awaits you. This is not something anyone would have asked of you because the risks would have been too great.

What was it that I achieved?

You brought with you the uncorrupted blueprint for the life forms on this Earth. And in so doing, you held it in place here long enough that when the intervention for the life of this planet itself began, and the new Earth was to be established, there was the information available so that as the new Earth was created, it would not have the same flaws within it. For where there is one tiny flaw in the beginning, it will magnify and magnify a problem. You came with the perfected ele-

157

mental genetic material. And this has implications far beyond Earth.

It seems that people have various drives and desires when it comes to ascension. Why is this?

Each being has its own specialty, its own quality. And not every soul burns with the same fire. Just as there are many different colored stars, there are many different paths to union. Some of them are solitary, some of them require ascending the body, and so on. And some of them are through the union of twin flames. But for many, once a being has descended into the third dimension, the path to union with God is the path of seeing God within everything. This is the humble, invisible path of being in non-duality and enjoying being here. It is my observation that many more humans would fall into this last category than for the fiery ascension or the twin soul ascension. And they are all wonderful. There is no one that is better than another.

Many of these decisions as to what kind of path would be taken are planned at the beginning, meaning at the time of one's birth into each universe. Prior to that, the planning for the full cycle would be made. Some beings come into this universe and never descend. Some will descend part way, and some will make the full descension. Whichever level a being chooses to go is their own choice; there is no right and wrong in it, no better or worse or higher or lower. It is the infinite variety of creative choice, and each is integral to the whole. It is a beautifully woven, intricate, infinitely complex web. These systems are as intricate as the biological system on this Earth is intricate.

Is it possible in the process of enlightenment in this dimension to return to one's original magnificence, prior to the awakening of the entire planet and universe?

To a great degree, yes. There has always been a fraction of energy coming through from the Godverse and from Prime Creator, and thus there have always been a few beings on this planet who have been able to maintain an enlightened and liberated state. They will increase exponentially; they are increasing exponentially because the frequency fences are in the process of collapse.

How enlightened do the light workers have to be to go home?

As the frequency fences continue to deteriorate and fall, a process of instant enlightenment is becoming widely available. There will be no particular amount of enlightenment needed to ascend. It will be happening for many, and was foretold in the Bible by the Rapture.

Those beings that are greatly fallen, the ones that we have had to incarcerate, will take some time to heal and clean and reclaim. But if you look again at Majaron's progress, it can be quite rapid, almost miraculously so. And what I must remind you is that what you call enlightenment is your natural state. It is hardwired into every cell of your body. It is in the blueprint of your soul. Everything that is not of the light is unnatural to you. In the coming days it will become harder and harder to resist enlightenment.

CHAPTER SIXTEEN
COMING TO TERMS WITH DARKNESS

Heru has explained that this Creation was never designed to include negativity or evil of any sort. Nor were we created to deal with this phenomenon. Therefore we humans still have a difficult time understanding darkness or even believing that it truly exists, despite massive and continuous evidence to the contrary. Philosophers and religious teachers throughout history have grappled with the problem of evil. In this chapter Heru discusses the various ways that we have attempted to understand the presence of darkness in our world, and in so doing illuminates our true nature.

It is important to understand that while the belief systems and rationalizations described below are generally erroneous, we have truly needed these illusions in order to maintain hope during the dark times we have passed through. Had we seen the reality of the situation at any time prior to the present, most of us would have succumbed to despair. Now that help is at hand we can face the truth and allow these illusions to slip away.

PART I—RATIONALIZING DARKNESS

Heru, since our discussions of darkness and its prevalence in our universe, I have been wondering about some of the ways that humans have tried to come to terms with the presence of negativity or darkness. I would like your responses on them.
Yes, this is a very important subject.

Some metaphysicians would say that the challenge and purpose of this Creation was to meet the darkness. Is there any truth to this?
(With passion:) This Creation is an expression of love, an expression of beauty, an expression of harmony. Its purpose has nothing to do with darkness.

A very common rationalization is that everything is love and light. This point of view claims that darkness is an illusion.

It would be nice if that were the case but it is not, clearly. There are dark forces at work. If this so-called "illusory" darkness were built into the fabric of Creation, in any way, shape, or form, what would that mean? It would mean that the Creator or the Gods who created this universe had done a terrible job. For life on this planet is full of misery. And if that were the intent of the Creator of this place, I would say that person should be fired.

Of course many humans are very angry at God for just that reason. They feel that God created this world to be full of suffering. I found it illuminating when you stated that the purpose of this Creation had nothing to do with darkness.

Correct. And in recorded history, your memories have been suppressed to the point that you have no memory of life before the Fall or the invasion, or whatever words you would like to use.

When people say that darkness doesn't exist, I think they are saying it is only on the surface, something not really real; and when one penetrates beyond appearances, darkness is found to be an illusion.

One factor here is that when a being has even a partial enlightenment—where they will have an experience of the goodness within everything, the oneness of all beings, the God within the self and the God within everything—there is the realization that this is the truth. And yes, it is more real than what people are experiencing on the third dimensional level in the day to day world, much more real. Thus it would come to a person that what they are experiencing of disharmony is not real; and so there is truth in that statement. However, making that statement and believing in that philosophy will do nothing to lessen the suffering of the beings in this universe or this part of Creation.

Therefore, yes, a person may experience an injury, go into meditation, and be able to transcend that pain and go into an experience of oneness with God. Then they can say: my pain is not real, my suffering is not real. But has that injury been healed? Unless a being then goes into a state of rapid healing, which would be called a miracle, the injury will remain until such time as the body heals it or not, through the natural course of things.

I think part of what is being said is that what happens on the third dimension is not real.

That would happen when a being is identifying more with a fourth or fifth dimensional level of their self, denying the sacredness of the third; and saying, "I identify more with the fifth dimension, therefore I don't need the third dimension." That has been a schism perpetrated by religion in order to perpetuate suffering on the third dimension. *[It's also true that in the fallen universes, the third dimension has become terribly dense and not all that pleasant.]* True, and these factors work hand in hand. Denial of the flesh, denial of sexuality, denial of the sacredness of the temple that the third dimensional body was created to be—all of this has created justifications for not relieving the suffering on the third dimension.

A corollary to the idea that darkness is illusory is that whatever we focus on increases. Therefore we should only focus on light and whatever is positive and beautiful.

I would describe that as a Pollyanna philosophy. It is true that what you focus on increases in your life and you draw that to you. If you were too obsessive about darkness you could be swallowed by it, so there is a kernel of truth to that idea. And yes, it is important to focus on light. However it is also important to be realistic in sifting out and perceiving what is propaganda and what is truth.

One more rationalization that people use about darkness is to say that this has all been like a huge play, and everyone is playing roles. From this perspective, it is said that the villains have done a good job playing the bad guys, and the heroes have done a good job playing the good guys. When it's all over, everyone will drop their masks, have a good laugh, and go home. Can you comment on this?

What a subtle rationalization! Would that it were true. And yet, it is good that it is not true. For if this were truly how this universe and how this Creation were designed to operate, what a miserable Creation it would be. It would be saying that the Creator created a Creation of conflict and that is simply not true. It would justify Hiroshima. It would justify all of the suffering of the Civil War. It would justify the concentration camps, and the starvation of the millions and millions in Africa. It would justify the plagues of the Middle Ages, the genocide of the American Indians; all of that. No. None of it is justified, and this Creation was not created for that purpose.

It truly is an either/or scenario. Either this Creation was designed to be an expression of love, light, creativity and harmony; or it was created to be an expression of conflict and war. There really is no middle ground there. So you have religious thought that believes in the dominion of man and that the Creation is a resource to be used as mankind sees fit, an Old Testament kind of philosophy. And who does that serve? It serves those who would benefit from exploiting, pillaging, and stealing from the Earth, one of the most complex manifestations of the Creator's love that has ever existed, and reducing it to no more than its elements. It would be akin to taking a Van Gogh painting and melting it down for the small amounts of cadmium and lead which are in the paint. It would be like extracting those elements and saying that this painting is worth nothing more than the ten cents of elemental minerals contained within that painting—when in fact each of Van Gogh's paintings is considered to be a priceless masterpiece.

Therefore if you looked at the complexity, the indescribable beauty of this Creation and this planet, those who seek to exploit it would render it into its ten cents worth of gold and silver and oxygen and so on. And the rationalization that the fight between good and evil is just a play, is a pure smokescreen to divert humanity from understanding that there are exploiters here who want nothing more from them than the gold fillings out of their teeth, so to speak. *[All of these rationalizations are different ways of saying the same thing, which is that darkness isn't real, therefore don't pay attention to it.]* Exactly. Which allows the darkness to penetrate further and further into Creation.

It is also believed that darkness exists only on the lower or denser levels of the universe. We know that it actually extends up through the eleventh dimension. Is darkness more prevalent on the lower dimensions?

No. It is as above, so below.

I have noticed that fact that as I have become progressively more unveiled, I have increasingly seen how bad things are in our universe. Yet, people who have NDE's [near death experiences] seem to become unveiled when they drop the body, and their experiences are the opposite. Are NDE'ers going to protected realms where they don't see the whole picture?

Depending on who they are, they may. There are people who have very frightening NDE's. The shame they feel about seeing that much darkness would cause them to be reluctant to share. A more evolved soul would go to light realms, but generally would still not see the whole picture.

Some humans try to rationalize the degree of suffering that we have on this planet by saying it is karmic. A high percentage of humans on Earth are born into terrible conditions and often have very little hope of improving their lives. This is justified by the statement that it is a matter of karma.

No, it is not like that. It is more that this Earth is trapped in a prison not of its own making, and those beings who are here are also trapped in terrible conditions. Some of them have come here voluntarily and some of them have been dragged here. Actually, those beings who have the worst karma are most likely to be those that are the wealthiest and in most control. *[And somehow they are escaping their karma?]* Well, we shall see. They think they are.

I am wondering about the concept of original sin. In a dysfunctional family, where the children are abused, they come to believe it is their fault. Would you speak about the concept of original sin, and do you believe that the same type of psychological reversal applies here, where we have taken on the guilt for the things that have been done to us?

I would say that is only part of the issue, but I do agree with your analysis of it. Actually what has happened is that the dark has used that kind of emotion as a central controlling feature of their philosophy. This can be seen not only in Christianity, but similarly with Hinduism and the way karma is used in that system. The blame for the dark is inserted into each individual, forcing them to carry the burden—really, in a sense, forcing karma upon every being. Thus each being in this fallen part of Creation is chained by the darkness, wedded to the darkness in a way that is very difficult to escape, either individually or collectively.

There are a great many programs which have been designed to keep humanity chained. One of them is a collective implant that keeps the collective society from wanting to allow others to succeed in liberation or in a good lifestyle. I am sure you can find many examples of this kind of thing. There are a great many efforts to tear down a being who would find liberation. And original sin specifically—yes, that is one of the best ideas for slavery that the Christian church came up with.

What do you mean by "forcing karma on every being"?

I believe I mentioned this once before. It is almost as if one takes a pill when one comes into, or is created in a dark universe. There is an immediate invasion by the dark, and there has been nothing that could prevent this. That dark virus, to use an analogy, is inserted in each being. And the extent to which it takes root and flowers there is the extent of the karma that every being is saddled with. *[Essentially, each being gets tied into the whole dark-permeated system.]* Yes, and that is, in part, why it was necessary to come up with an offense that was both microcosmic and macrocosmic. *[Is there karma in the light universes?]* No.

Another statement which tries to explain darkness regards what is called the divine plan. It is said that there is a divine plan, and that nothing occurs outside this plan. Therefore, if this is true, everything must occur within that plan and purpose and everything is perfect because it happens for a reason.

That is written into your blueprint because at the time your blueprint was created it was true. However since that time circumstances have changed. Yet still that belief is hardwired into every atom and every molecule of life. It is more than a belief really, and it is very strong in everybody. *[This is very illuminating.]* It explains a lot, doesn't it?

It is also said that, as individuated beings, our mandate was to experience—to experience everything. Since "everything" includes darkness and separation from God, we therefore chose to experience those things too.

This is similar to the belief that everything is in divine order, in that the mandate or impetus to experience is also hardwired into all of life. However, not hardwired into all life is separation from God. That is not hardwired, and that has been created by the invasion. A soul comes into this universe, which is dark. And written into their blueprint is the desire to experience everything. When the experience is contaminated, that desire does not abate. In other words, the soul still wants to experience everything. What it experiences is darkness and separation, yet there is not the ability to turn off the desire for experience. So in a sense a being starts indiscriminately vacuuming up everything.

The beliefs that are hardwired into us—for example, that there's a divine plan—what purpose did that belief serve initially?

It is part of the eternal connectedness that all Creation has with Prime Creator. What the darkness has done is to essentially sever that connection or subvert it. *[Does this belief serve any purpose now?]* As a being reconnects with Creator, yes, it does.

Some teachers say that the light and dark brotherhoods work together in the sense that the light is always trying to move things forward towards evolution, while the dark holds things back; and the final result is that things happen at the correct time. Do you agree with this, or do you feel it's sort of a Pollyanna justification?

A Pollyanna justification would be my perspective on it, but that would not be everybody's perspective. There are people who subscribe to the idea that dark must be there to balance the light. They equate the darkness with yin, needing to balance the yang, and they are not the same.

From my own memories of the light universes, I would say that light does just fine without having the dark.

Light does fine without it. The dark forces have rationalized their actions by saying that they are part of the yin, so to speak, and the yin is necessary. But the imposition of anyone's will over another being is never necessary, outside of the parameters we have discussed.

Is there a benefit to living and evolving in the fallen universes? Does one become stronger? Evolve faster?

I don't see how. *[The challenges are more intense.]* That is true. But if you take a tree and you bang on its trunk and deprive it of water, and rip off some branches leaving open sores, does that make for a stronger tree? Perhaps the scar tissue on the bark is stronger and thicker and calloused on that point, but does the overall health of the tree increase from that? I would say not.

PART II—REALITY AND ENLIGHTENMENT

I have observed the fact that people who claim to be enlightened say that everything is one, there is really no evil or darkness, everything is perfect, everything happens for a reason and is within the divine plan, and so on. It would appear that these people are deluded in this regard, yet it also seems that they are more awakened and enlightened than someone like myself. How can you explain this?

That is a good question. What these people have done is that they have activated their original blueprint. Therefore they are sitting within their original blueprint, and have generated enough of a force field that the contamination which is present in this fallen universe is not affecting their consciousness. For them, to a greater or lesser extent, they have created that reality. And it is powerful to do so; it is admirable that they are able to do so. They are able to draw to themselves what they need. To the extent that their sphere of influence carries, they are able to create a space around them where that reality is manifest. For some people that sphere basically ends about as far as their hands could reach [gesturing with hands outstretched]. For some that would have greater power, it would extend into a community or such. In the situation of your friends at Circle of Light [a community in AR] it would be a slightly larger sphere, and would have the ability to draw others into it and transform them enough so they can hold that space as well. It could build on itself to a certain degree, though would have its limitations. For someone like the Kalki avatar [a spiritual leader in India] it would be a much larger sphere.

And from that place they can't see darkness, apparently?

Right. *[So in a way they're right and in a way they're wrong?]* Yes. They have created a bubble of uncorrupted reality, and within that reality they're correct. It will be interesting because as the darkness lifts there will be a great expansion and connecting of those bubbles.

Is it possible for a person to live a life of non-duality in a fallen Universe and yet still recognize or acknowledge the reality of darkness?

It is rare, but it has been done. *[Most people either go into a non-dual state, and can no longer see darkness even when it's existing all around them; or remain in a dual state, in which case they can see darkness.]* Yes.

If people who are enlightened are no longer able to see darkness, then this must have created some very confusing situations for humanity at large. Most of the scriptures, as well as bodies of work such as the I AM teachings by St. Germain, state that all is One, darkness is an illusion, and so on. However, these teachings are being read by people who are not in the awakened state and have not created a "bubble" of that reality around them. I'm going to mention some points that come to mind.

First, scriptures and spiritual teachings would appear to be "airy fairy" and there would be some justification to that, as the scriptures would be describing a reality other than that experienced by most people.

Yes, and other than what is accessible to most people. And you may be able to put that in the past tense, for it is more and more accessible.

I would also think that people would get very frustrated trying to experience the reality described in the scriptures, since that isn't their reality.

Yes, they would be very frustrated. This has actually been used by the dark forces to increase people's self-loathing, lack of faith in God, guilt and shame, self hatred, and sense of separation.

Secondly, I have noticed that people who are in the awakened state try to describe what it's like. Then others who are not awakened attempt to mimic these experiences, hoping that this will cause them to become awakened. However, if someone who is not awakened tries to act as though there is no darkness, this could lead to inappropriate actions and choices.

Yes, I believe that is an accurate statement.

Many spiritual teachers, including some of the masters, say that our thoughts create our reality—period. It seems to me that our reality is created by a number of factors, of which our thoughts are certainly one. But I feel that it's also created and affected by other things, such as the following: Our emotions. Our soul intention, passion, and mission. Our karma. Our environment, which includes everything from our neighborhood to the planet and universe that we live in. The beings that we interact with. And so on. Can you give your perspective on this?

In the divine mind all of those aspects that you outlined would be part of divine thought. Therefore from a higher dimensional perspective, it is true that thought creates reality. However, I would say two things here. One, you're in a contaminated universe, and so the natural progression from the higher mind to manifestation is broken, interfered with.

The second is that for humans in the fallen state, as you are in at this time, the mind is a very isolated and limited piece, disconnected from the higher mind. In unfallen humans, they would be able to contain the higher thought forms, which would contain all of those attributes that you listed, including karma, environment, and all of that. But *in a fallen human, the mind is much smaller. It is constricted, discon*nected, and does not have the attributes to be able to contain much more than survival skills.

So for a fallen human, does thought create reality?

On a limited scale. It would limit the thoughts to the survival mode and limit the actions to the survival mode. So in a sense, yes. But what ends up happening is that fallen humans are disempowered to the point that they become the victims of their environment, as if tossed around in a hurricane. And that is because they are so disconnected from the greater mind. Therefore much of what happens would appear to be random accidents. That, for them, is their life. Their life is nothing, for them, more than a random series of accidents.

Would a lightworker such as Karen or myself be considered a fallen human?

You would be more considered a reclaimed human, a human that has gone through the fall and has come back up again out of the fall.

[In other words, somewhere in the middle between creating via limit-ed mind and creating via divine mind?] Yes, to a greater or lesser degree, and on the evolutionary spiral upward.

PART III—FURTHER QUESTIONS ON DARKNESS

Heru, what is the defining factor of a being who is fallen? What does it mean when we say that such a being is "dark"?

I would say that it is the willingness to impose one's will on some-one else.

Does this mean we are partially dark, because we may think unkind thoughts about the president, or that we may have wished something harmful to happen to an evil person?

No. Having a negative thought is not following through with the action of imposing that negative thought on someone else. For instance, you may dislike the president extremely much, maybe even to the point of obsession, but until you actually make the decision to go forward with taking action—to impose your negative emotions upon the president and/or the country—that is not darkness. It is con-fused and not the highest form of thought, but not darkness.

However, we all have a lot within us that wouldn't seem to be of light. We all have pain, fear, old traumas, anger, judgments, and so on. If these are not dark, what are they?

They are more the environmental fruits of the dark. If you were to embrace the motivation behind the trauma causing elements, then that would be darkness. We talked about the defining factor of dark-ness, in that it is the willingness to impose one's will upon another being. Is a rape victim dark because she holds within herself this trau-ma, and may overreact defensively to situations? Contrast that to a serial rapist. Is he acting out of a trauma that he himself had? To some degree that would be the case. But beyond that it's almost as if he has embraced that evil motivator itself and become identified with it, and that is a whole other situation. Even though the serial rapist may have been a victim to begin with, he has succumbed to the pleas-ure of perpetuating that disease. Can you see the difference between those two situations?

Yes, I can. Returning to your definition of darkness, several excep-tions immediately come to mind. One would involve the role of being a parent or a caregiver to a pet. Oftentimes a parent or a pet owner must override the will of the child or animal.

There is an acceptance in both the animal and human kingdoms of dependency relationships, and that is consensual, even though perhaps not consciously or overtly so.

That makes sense. The other exception is this. I know that Durga/Sekhmet and other mighty light beings are incarcerating some of the dark. Obviously this is against the will of those beings.

They have broken laws. It has been a long time in coming for this to happen. There was great reluctance on the part of the hierarchy of light beings to take action against the dark beings, because the light has always honored free will. That which began in one sector of one universe was not stopped. And it has created an infection that has spread far and wide throughout too many universes. For the sake of the integrity of this entire Creation it was decided to take action. Otherwise the entire Creation would be lost.

Heru, are you saying that darkness started in a small way in one universe, and spread, simply because free will was being honored to the maximum, and no one stopped it?

Yes. *[And had it been stopped, back then, other universes would not have fallen?]* Yes, and other universes would not have been created dark by fallen hierarchies. The decision to root out all darkness has come from the very source of this Creation. It was not done frivolously or lightly.

Please explain how the adherence to free will stymied the efforts to getting rid of the dark at all levels.

It put a restriction upon the light workers, and especially those that came into these fallen universes in an effort for reclamation. In essence they were operating with one hand tied behind their back, while the forces of dark had within their arsenal free rein to use everything that they wanted. It would be something akin to a chivalrous knight in armor going up against a modern Navy SEAL. I do not think that is too dramatic a gap to convey the difference in attitude, technology, and so on.

In our discussions with the Creator, it was stated that the walled-off part of this Creation was somewhat analogous to a cancerous tumor. And that, at a certain point, this "tumor" would have exploded and infected all of Creation. How close were we to that point?

It was not imminent in terms of years or decades, perhaps thousands of years away, but that is not to lessen the feeling that the Light Warriors have come in the nick of time. For even though it might not have been at the point of exploding into metastasis, had the balance been tipped much further some of the universes within this sector that are now salvageable would not have been so. Therefore it would have resulted in a permanent amputation of parts of this sector.

All true humans, including the fallen ones, appear to have within themselves a pure spark of what we might call the divine Godself. Do the dark beings not have this?
Correct. They are soulless. And that is why they are not redeemable. They have not been created with a divine blueprint in the same way that all of this Creation has been created. That is why the fallen can be redeemed, for they retain that spark.

My friend R. and I did some work a few years back with the reptilian ET's, the Dracos and others. We found that these beings generally did have this spark of divine life. Are these reptilians the invading dark beings? Or are they races which have fallen due to the dark influences?
They are fallen races, but more accurately, they are races which have been created by the fallen. *[What will happen to them?]* I believe they will be given an opportunity for reform. Every effort is being made to reform anyone that is possible to reform. A great effort was put into reforming the dark itself, with no success. But it is hoped that the fallen races, those created by the fallen, may be able to be reformatted in such a way that it is possible to reclaim them. *[Are the Greys one such race?]* Yes.
There really are no humanoid representatives of the dark. There are no races or beings you can look at and say "That is the other." It is almost as if the dark were a gas that permeates and corrupts and is very hard to define. It did not come in ships, it did not come in soldiers. That is part of the reason it has been so hard to fight, because in a sense it is almost invisible, but its effects are obviously very deleterious.
Are the Light Warriors able to deal with this invisible presence?
Yes. That is why they were created in so many sizes, and why they are in the microcosmic arena.

Beings such as the Illuminati—they are not the original invaders?
No, they are the fallen.

Then what about the beings who are getting incinerated by the Light Warriors? Who are they?

It is hard to describe. But it is more like the entities that have sprung up out of this gaseous undefined stuff. It's almost as if the darkness has spawned them, the way mushrooms spring up. They use some amount of energy and matter from this Creation in order to form themselves, but they are parasitic in nature. They would be what you call demons and other types of dark beings, and they are the ones who are being incinerated.

What is it that drives darkness, so to speak? What fuels the desire of dark beings to invade, to destroy, to harm and to cause pain, to corrupt other beings, and so on?

Again, I do not know. Perhaps when the Light Warriors have driven dark from this Creation and go to the source of dark to render it unable to repeat this, they will come back with answers.

What is their true agenda here?

I don't know. It looks to be a combination of slavery and destruction; and whether ultimately it is destruction I don't know.

Throughout our conversations, we use the term "darkness" to mean all forms of negativity. We use the term "light" to denote that which is positive, life-affirming, and in the flow of God's will. Why are these terms selected? Why, for example, do we not use good v.s. evil? And what is light that the opposite of light is all that is life-negating?

A very good question. In terms of polarity, nature has a natural polarity to it—the yin and the yang—that I would have people see as separate from the light and the dark. The terms good and evil are too ideological, too laden with cultural and religious issues; they have a very limiting history. The words light and dark are both vague and specific at the same time, and for that reason I believe they serve my purposes best. The light was, in essence, the first act of creation that Prime Creator generated. The dark is an unknown. We see its effects but in essence we do not at this time know its source, we only know its outcome. Therefore to paint it with the face of the devil or something more descriptive, is to limit its scope. It is much more all pervasive than those images.

How can the truly dark beings have so much power, if they are simply parasitic life forms which have no soul? Or is it the fallen who have power, and who can do these things?

172

It is the fallen who have power. The dark only gains power by corrupting beings, and it is the fallen who do these acts of terrible destruction and harm. The tragedy of it is that these are great, wonderful beings who have succumbed to something that is not understandable. And once reclaimed, they will take their place among the stars in the sky. It is a great heartache that they have been imprisoned and had their free will taken from them by the dark in such a way that most of them did not even have a chance to choose.

Those beings who have gone into dark universes in an attempt to help (those much darker than this one) how do they eventually get out and find their way into a less dark, or even light universe? Do these beings often succumb to the darkness and never get out?

Some of them do. In the case of your friend, there was a rescue mission mounted to extract the group that she was a part of. It was seen that they would have either been killed or permanently disabled. Some people were lost.

Are they somehow programmed to stay so long and then get out?

There are agreements made. In that case, it was a specific mission to try to set up an underground network and I believe it was given a set time to determine if it would work or not. This type of mission was attempted with the dark universes that were created after the Fall. And when it became clear that there was really no redemption possible and no opposition which could be created by sending people in, it was stopped.

How do any of the beings who are native to the totally dark universes get out, if they don't know anything else? Or do they ever get out?

They don't get out, and it is possible that there is no reclamation likely for the beings who were created by the fallen Creator Gods in a totally dark universe. It appears that there are gradations of being fallen in terms of how dark the beings are. The fallen Creator Gods who have created the completely dark universes would be very fallen indeed, and their creations most likely will need to be destroyed. The races of beings that you were asking about earlier [i.e. the dark ET's] were created in this universe by compromised Creator Gods. And that is the difference.

Was it possible to establish key planets in the truly dark universes, those which were made by the fallen Creator Gods?

No, and it appears that they will probably collapse. There is not enough light in them. *[What happens to the beings in such a universe when this occurs?]* Those who came from light universes to help will be rescued. The others will be transported to a universe not as dark as that one, where they will be given the opportunity to make choices.

When such a universe collapses, what about the other beings—the animals, devas, elementals—all the beings that make up a universe?
My dear, nothing is ever lost. I don't really see where they go; I just know that nothing is lost.

Those of us who came into the fallen universes like this one—even though it's not completely dark—we ended up getting trapped as well?
Yes. *[Did we, in fact, expect to leave long before now?]* Oh yes. *[And it has been about 500 million years that most of us have been here?]* Yes, that would be close enough.

In our case, how is it that many of the light workers expect to be leaving this universe at the same time; is it because of some pre-set arrangement?
It is because the Light Warriors have finally come and the frequency fence is coming down, so that now passage back to the home universes is possible.

Several of us have found that we have family here from the light universes who have stated that they are here to help us get home. Given what we know of the frequency fence around the fallen universes, how did they ever get here? And how did they expect to get us home once they arrived here?
There are, and always have been, a few secret wormholes that have allowed penetration of a few beings. Any time that a sizeable number of beings would be detected coming through a wormhole, the wormhole would be attacked and shut down. It has been a dangerous venture. Your families love you very much to have attempted this.

Would you say that the majority of light workers now have family here from the light universes, who are waiting to escort them home? Or in most cases must they still wait for family to come in through the breaches in the frequency barrier?
In most cases that will come later. Among the beings who are assembled and waiting to come and help with the healing of the universes are also many family members, and there will be many reunions.

For the light beings such as ourselves who came here to help, has there been any progress or growth over these many millions of years?

I have to say that, yes, there is always growth—there is always growth in understanding, wisdom, compassion, and so on. And for all of you, yes, there has been growth, but it is not what it would have been had you not been in a fallen universe.

Have we fallen behind the evolution of the rest of Creation?

In a manner of speaking, yes. It is not really seen what will happen once all of the lives within the fallen universes are restored to wholeness—all the beings, life systems, and life forms. There are abundant theories on what will happen, but no one truly knows. There is a predominant theory, however, that once the restoration of wholeness comes to each being, and the restoration of harmony, full potential, and full power is attained—that even though an individual would have been stunted from being in a fallen universe, something new, something never before seen, will be there. Therefore really a qualitative judgment cannot be made.

Heru, on a personal level, I am wondering how you kept your faith during these very difficult times that our Creation has been through. Did you always have a very strong faith that all would be well, or were there times when you felt deeply discouraged?

Not so much discouraged or depressed, as worried that this plan from the Prime Creator would be able to be completed on time before much of this Creation would either be destroyed or need to be jettisoned. I was aware that the plan was in place and what the plan was, in a rough outline. But I knew it was a race against time. *[Has darkness continued to spread up until now?]* Yes. *[So it's only now, with the coming of the Light Warriors, that the spread is being stopped.]* Correct.

I've been trying to process everything that has happened to us, and it's difficult. I think that I'm grieving for the millions of years that all of us spent here in this dark universe and the fact that we really have made almost no progress. Can you offer any insight into this?

I would tell you first of all that even though it appears no progress has been made, just the fact that this universe did not succumb is a great victory. Secondly, I would like to express how grateful I am to have those who are able to hear just how bad it has been. For we have hidden from the light-working humans just how dire the situation was, in fear that if we disclosed it they would be overcome by despair. Therefore the fact that we are able to tell you this dire dark news—that in itself is really an accomplishment. It means that first, help is here;

and secondly, that the human light workers have matured enough to the point that they are able to see the truth.

CHAPTER SEVENTEEN
MORE INFORMATION ON
THE LIGHT WARRIORS

The numbers of Light Warriors are countless, and more are arriving every day. Heru and Sananda have recommended that we all call upon them to act as personal guardians. People who are prone to attacks for any reason will need more than others. It is also a good idea to call in Light Warriors to protect your home, business, and/or property. At this time, the "second wave" Light Warriors are the most powerful and capable group in terms of their ability and consistency in protection. A third wave should be arriving somewhere in January of 2005, and we expect these beings to be even more effective. Updates will be posted on www.returnoflight.com as further groups enter. Depending on when you read this book, then, we suggest that you specify which group of Light Warriors you wish to call upon. The most recent "wave" will always be the most powerful and effective. It is a good idea to contact your Light Warrior guardians at least once a week to reinforce your protection.

PART I—CALLING ON THE LIGHT WARRIORS FOR PROTECTION

Rashona, we have some further questions for you. Regarding clearing another person, or someone else's house of discarnate entities: Do you clear those beings for us, or should we clear them ourselves?
     You would have to ask for that action, and then the Light Warriors can do it.

If you clear them, what do you do with them? It seems they would be very afraid if they saw one of you coming at them.

Yes, probably they would. They are placed in a holding pen where they would await further processing. We are not equipped to process them, so they are put some place and other beings are assigned to do work with them, such as to move them into a place of light or whatever.

What about clearing very dark entities that are ensouled? Can you remove them or do we remove them?

The same applies. We have not met anything yet that is our match. *[If you remove them, what do you do with them?]* Again, if it is an ensouled being it goes to a holding place to be processed by other beings. If it is not ensouled, it is simply eliminated.

If I wish to clear a person of dark entities, do I need to first discover all the dark forces within all their levels, and then ask you to clear them? Or do you find all of them and clear them without me being aware of where they are?

It would depend on how you would phrase the request. For example, you could phrase the request to include all dimensions, all levels of the being, all time and space, and so on. For you see if there is a timeline on which an entity is attached to a being in the past, you could ask to clear all the dimensions and you would still not go back in time to that, and it would still be there. So you want to encompass your request to include everything: all dimensions, all time, all space, all levels, and you may add parallel existences and realities as well. *Therefore you don't need to find them, but if you request a broader* cleansing it will be done.

May we call in Light Warriors to protect others who may not be able do so on their own?

Very much so, as in the case of an animal or a child.

Yes, that makes clear sense. But let's take as an example a person who is light-oriented and is in need of protection, but has a Christian belief framework. This person would not know of your existence, and might not be open to such things.

We would appear to him to be angelic, so he could incorporate and accept us in that manner. If a being is intent on pursuing darkness—which in your example would not be the case—then the issue of free will comes up. In the interest of the survival of this entire Creation, and for the purpose of eliminating this dark cloud that has invaded the Creation, Prime Creator has overridden the free will prime directive. This was done with great caution and with great concern, but it has been done.

I would like to express the graveness with which this decision was made, and that it was with an extreme heaviness of heart on the part of the Prime Creator. However, it was felt that all other avenues had been explored and the nature of the dark is truly its inability to be redeemed. *[This is a temporary suspension of free will?]* Yes, it is seen that once the dark is eliminated from this sector of Creation, it will no longer be needed. The other part of this is that the dark captured the will of these beings without permission, took over their will, and made it appear that it was that being's will.

Those beings who are dedicated to perpetuating the dark have been allowed to basically express themselves to the fullness of their desire. That kind of desire, of course, is never entirely satisfied, but the basic expression of it has been allowed to play out to a relative completeness. As that is done, it will not be allowed to continue, and they will reach a wall. At that point they will be put into a holding cell, separated from the dark that they have embraced, and where they will await processing. Therefore there is still some room for beings to move forward into darkness, but it is increasingly limited and will reach its final stages in a relatively short time.

To return to the initial question, in the example that I gave you previously, would you recommend calling in Light Warriors to protect such a person?

Yes, I believe there would be no conflict or incompatibility. This being would perceive us to be of the angelic realms, and would accept the help. *[It is OK to do this without conscious permission from him?]* Yes. And I believe with such a person there would be not a tremendous activity of interference or change; our work would be more of a protective nature.

Can you protect more intangible entities such as businesses, including those which operate mostly on the Internet?

Oh yes. Basically the mechanism for doing that would be to call forth the overlighting devic being, and call for protection around that devic being. Then also ask that the protection surround the entire business entity.

We asked Prime Creator: We notice that when we call on the Light Warriors for protection, they don't always see all the forms of attack and interference that may be coming at us. Are you aware of this issue?

Yes, I am, and I can give you help in alleviating that problem.

When you call them in, <u>ask them to come to you through the portal of the All Seeing Eye of God</u>. And that way they will have the omnivision that you need.

PART II—CALLING ON THE LIGHT WARRIORS FOR HEALING

What types of physical healing work can you do?
Where a body is beset with lower life forms such as pathogenic bacteria or other microbial agents, we are effective in removing those. Our primary focus and abilities are on removing and decimating that which is dark. Therefore I would suggest that you call upon us for that type of work rather than for a broken arm. We are also able to clean up toxins in the body if they are created by and imbued with the dark. There are some toxins that are just a by-product of life, and so there is some differentiation there.

How do we initiate this physical clearing?
The first step is to connect with Light Warriors who will act as your personal guardians. These Light Warriors are essentially human sized. Once you have made contact with them and established a rapport with them, you would ask these beings to call in Light Warriors of the appropriate size and assignment for the toxin or microorganism *involved in your body. These are the micro Light Warriors. Upon your* request, millions and millions of these micro Light Warriors will work within every cell of your body, scavenging and waging battle against the dark that has invaded your body. Ask for the specific condition to be addressed. And you may ask for a general cleanse as well.

So we tell our Light Warrior guardians what type of work we want done on our bodies, and they communicate what needs to be done to the micro Warriors. Is that correct?
That is the easiest way to do it, yes. *[Is there any need for us to communicate with the micro Warriors, and is it even possible for us to communicate with them?]* I believe certain individuals would find it easier to communicate directly with the micro Warriors, but most humans will find they relate better to a being closer to their size. It would basically be a personal choice.

When the micro Warriors are working to clear our cells of dark-related pathogens, toxins, and so on, can we simply give you permission to clear us on a continual basis, as you see fit, regardless of what we're doing at the time and without our knowledge? Or should we sit down and be still, going into an altered state and requesting a clearing session right at that time?

A person could do both. The second option would probably be most effective, but the first will have an effect as well. Again, I think it will be an individual choice as to what the person is comfortable with.

[Elora:] We have found that the micro Light Warriors do seem to work more effectively while the person is in an altered state. Also, the first group of micro Warriors has a tendency to "drift" to areas of greater darkness if one is not consciously working with them. The third wave of micro Warriors, which is slated to arrive in January of 2005, may have less of this tendency and may be able to work within people's bodies in an ongoing way.

We could sit in meditation while you clear us, or we could ask you to clear us while we sleep. Is that correct, and which would work better?

Yes, that is correct. Again, I don't see a hard and fast rule of one over the other. The way people are constituted is in many ways quite different, and some people would like to have that feel of immediacy and contact in the waking state. For others, the work in sleep is preferable. I cannot say one is better than the other. It would have to be a trial and error by individuals to see what they are most comfortable with.

How about pets? I have called in Light Warriors to protect my cats. I would like to have pathogens and dark-related toxins removed from them as well. Can I also ask to have the micro Light Warriors work on them?

Yes, you could.

Can you remove darkness and negative programming on a cellular and DNA level?

Yes. The micro Light Warriors would be used for this.

How do we set parameters so that your work does not go too fast for us?

I would say that, especially for those of you who have fragile constitutions and compromised immune systems, ask the Light Warriors to proceed only at a speed that will not diminish a person's total vitality. That will protect against a healing crisis. The Light Warriors have the ability to monitor and control the intensity of the work in that way.

Let's take someone with a weakened immune system, who asked for help with candida. This would not be an overnight process, for if done at that speed it would surely cause a person enough distress that they would be bedridden. You would call in the appropriate Light Warriors to work on this problem on an ongoing basis, at a pace that will not lessen the person's overall vitality. It might take weeks or even months to accomplish. And I would suggest in a more long term chronic situation like this, that the person would want to call upon and reinforce the intent of this group of microscopic warriors, perhaps on a weekly basis.

In clearing our cells of darkness and toxins, why would we go into a healing crisis, since it would seem the toxins are not being dumped into our blood stream? Or are they?

I believe they are. *[Please explain the physical reactions we might have with your clearing, and why we would have them.]* It appears that it would follow the same pattern that you would have in taking medicinal substances on the third dimensional level, herbs and such.

Regarding the Light Warriors who are acting as ongoing personal guardians, can they create an energetic "bubble" around the person they are guarding, and can they keep that bubble free of pathogens and dark-related toxins?

Yes. You would ask your personal guardians, exactly as you said, to create a bubble around you, a shield. And you can actually ask that that shield be made up of the armies of micro Warriors. Then specify what you want to be protected from—viruses, bacteria, pollutants, etc. In this way you will be much less susceptible to these pathogens. Also, the people who are quite susceptible to these pathogens have a resonance in their bodies to these pathogens, and it would be most helpful to address that as well. The resonance itself is not a microorganism, and it could be removed by your human sized Warriors.

To create this shield, for example, you may state: "I call upon my Light Warriors to create a spherical shield around my physical form, containing sufficient micro Light Warriors to guard me from dark related pathogens, such as bacteria, viruses, mold, etc." and list what you would like to be protected from. Then continue, "And I ask that this shield remain in place at all times until such time as I release it."

Can you remove karma from a person?

Not directly. What we can remove is any dark motivation that had caused the person to act in a karma-generating way. Once that is removed, then a person is better able to face and process the results of this karma. I believe any of the human sized Light Warriors that are assigned to you would be able to do this type of work. If a person feels that is not sufficient, they may ask for a more specialized type of Light Warrior. However the beings that are closest to you will know you the best. There is a learning curve to the relationship.

Can you remove limiting thought forms from a person?

Again, not directly. If the limiting thought form has been created by an entity, or for example an institution like a religion that has been compromised, then there is work we can do. What you are looking for in all cases is the source of the conscious intent towards darkness. When you are looking to eliminate problems, look for an underlying being or consciousness and then you will be most successful. Take for instance the Catholic Church. There are many beings who are benefiting from that institution being in place, and many beings who are being harmed by it. If you were to look within a person who was raised Catholic, and that person says, "I want to get rid of my limiting beliefs, my guilt and shame," you would look for the underlying cause. First, it would be the programming put forth by the church. And then you would look for the beings who are supporting or holding that pro-gramming in place. You would specifically look for the beings who have, in a sense, been assigned to or are directly benefiting from that person's involvement. We are speaking here of dark spirit entities, and you would look for a rather vampiric energy in this instance. Then ask the Light Warriors to go after those entities. You could simplify the process by just saying, "I have these limiting beliefs. If there is a con-sciousness of darkness behind these limiting beliefs, and which is supporting these limiting beliefs, then I ask the Light Warriors to go after them."

Rashona concluded by saying:

There is, for us, somewhat of a learning curve in what we are capable of. It is as we get on the ground and really look around that we become more and more aware—both of what needs to be done, and what we can do. And this is our joy; service is our joy.

Following this discussion on healing, we asked Heru if the Light Warriors could remove cancer from the body. He stated:

I believe that is a good possibility. Cancer is very complex in nature, sometimes triggered by pollutants, sometimes by repressed emotion and trauma. Therefore a person wishing to work on it in this manner would need to take a multi faceted approach, to in a sense go on an archeological dig to find what is triggering it—and prepare for emotional upheavals if there are emotional components to it and so on. But yes, cancer itself would be one of those things that has the dark at its core. Cancer is very much the way the dark has worked in this Creation.

CHAPTER EIGHTEEN
HOMAGE TO DURGA/SEKHMET

This book would not be complete without a chapter devoted to the One whom we call Durga or Sekhmet. Heru and Durga/Sekhmet are my cosmic progenitors, and therefore she is my true mother in a very real sense. It was she, in fact, who contacted me even before I knew of my relationship to Heru. I had no idea who she was, only that a mighty being had come into my life with a power beyond anything I had yet experienced. One night I called upon her for protection, and suddenly found that three etheric lions had manifested in my bedroom. This was my first hint as to her identity.

I then realized that this being was the Goddess whom in India is called Durga. Durga is revered in India as one of the best loved embodiments of the Divine Feminine. She is always associated with lions or tigers and is most commonly shown riding on the back of a lion. Legends tell of a time on Earth when the forces of darkness had so oppressed our planet that even the Gods themselves were helpless. Durga appeared at that time and, with a power that none could withstand, defeated the demons and other evil forces. It is said that, like Vishnu, Durga manifests when cosmic balance is threatened and is an upholder and guardian of dharma.

After Karen began to channel the Ascended Masters and Creator Gods, I was able to communicate directly with this great being. She confirmed that she is the one who is known as Durga, as well as the lion Goddess Sekhmet of Egypt and White Jaguar Lady of Central America. She also stated that she was known as Artemis in ancient Greece. Each of these Goddesses represents a different facet of her being. She told us that it is like turning a faceted jewel. As each facet reflects the light, so a different part of her nature is revealed. Therefore when I connect to her as Artemis, I feel the sense of wild, remote places, of mountain crags, of the night sky, and wild animals.

When I connect to her as Sekhmet, I experience a mighty, royal, over-whelming power. The name Sekhmet, in fact, literally means "the powerful" or "the mighty".

I came to see that while Heru embodies knowledge and wisdom, Durga/Sekhmet embodies divine energy and power. In working with my progenitors, I found that when I wanted to know something, I would call upon Heru. When I needed to have something done, I would call upon Durga/Sekhmet. In the eastern traditions each God has his Shakti, the divine energy of existence. Without his Shakti, the God would be mind without life, knowledge without movement, vision without creativity. Therefore, while it is Heru who gave us the material for this book, homage is due to the one who completes him, whose power and creative force are the complement to his wisdom and vast consciousness.

As our work with Heru progressed, time and again we found that we needed assistance, protection, and healing. We repeatedly came under fire from the dark side for our part in bringing this crucially important work to the world. In addition, the acceleration of our spiritual growth continually brought old wounds to the surface to be healed and released. Scarcely a day has gone by that we have not called upon Durga/Sekhmet for help, and never has she failed us. Without her this book could never have come to fruition.

Of all the aspects of my cosmic mother, most dear to my heart is her manifestation as White Jaguar Lady. I found that often when I called upon her in the aspect of Sekhmet, I would see a pyramid sur-mounted by the full moon—but not an Egyptian pyramid. Instead it was a flat-topped structure, such as those built by the Mayans and Aztecs, and was surrounded by jungle. I saw myself sitting at the base of this pyramid, waiting and praying. On nights when the moon was high and full, a shining Goddess would descend the pyramid, flanked by two lionesses. In researching Sekhmet, I came across the site of Maia Nartoomid at www.spiritmythos.org. Maia, who writes com-pellingly about Sekhmet, describes an ancient temple in Central America:

"Qetalaxitolutum: Remnants of this Sekhmet Temple are still within the rich, green tangle of the Yucatan, not far from the uncov-ered portion of the Mayan Chichen Itza ruins. It was dedicated by

Queen Amaluxal to the 'White Jaguar Lady' or 'Lady Dalia', in eons past. Amaluxal created a 'palace-temple' for the cat-woman appearing to her in her visions, whom she called the White Jaguar Lady. It was only after an Egyptian named 'Three-Hawk' came from Egypt to Qetalaxitolutum, with sacred 'star charts', that the Queen realized her Lady Dalia to be one and the same as the lion-headed Sekhmet. With the help of Three-Hawk, an initiate of Sekhmet, Queen Amaluxal re-formed her palace into a true initiatory Temple of Sekhmet." (Heru says that "Three-Hawk" was none other than himself, in one of his incarnations.)

To return to her embodiment as Durga, the best representations of her give a clue to the nature of this magnificent being. She rides a lion and brandishes fearsome weapons with her many arms. Yet her beautiful face is serenely smiling, filled with compassion and tenderness. One day, when the battle for this Creation is entirely won, she will lay down her weapons and the warrior nature she has assumed out of necessity, and once again devote herself wholly to her role as the great Creator Goddess who has given birth to souls, to worlds, and to universes.

To my divine mother, whose love and power have sustained me and whose grace overlights me, I dedicate the days of my life and the fruits of my work.

SECTION THREE
THE MEDITATIONS

CHAPTER NINETEEN
THE THREE MEDITATIONS OF HERU

At the time that Heru stated his intention to bring his teachings to Earth once more, he gave us three meditations. These techniques are so simple that, at first, I did not recognize their enormous value. There are so many such exercises in our world that a few more could not make much difference—or so I thought. When I actually began to practice the techniques that Heru had brought to us, I was astonished at their power and depth.

Heru has stated that these meditations are safe, even for children, and for people with mental or emotional instabilities. He told us that the first two meditations, in particular, are excellent for anyone who is unstable.

PART I—THE FIRST MEDITATION: THE BREATH OF HERU

Heru, please describe the first of your meditation techniques.
The first meditation is a breathing exercise. In this meditation, you are linking the breath with the hara line. With the inbreath, breathe in and pull energy from below along the hara line. And breathe in "He" [pronounced "hay"]. Breathe in and pull energy, from as far and as deep down as you can reach, up through the top of the head. With the inbreath, bring the breath up through the body as high as you can go. Remember that the hara line is infinite, both above and below. With the exhale, pull down from above, from as far up and as high as you can reach, and breath "ru". And breathe down through the hara line, down as far as you can go.

What is the effect of the "he" and "ru"?
They carry the vibration of me. *[So this meditation also connects*

a person to you? To your powers, your light?] Yes. This would be my way to infinity, which of course is not the only way, but it is my road.

Please define the term "hara line".

The hara line is an energetic line passing vertically through the center of the body. It extends beyond the center of the body in both directions, and it is the energetic axis upon which the body is manifested.

Please describe the effects and benefits of this meditation.

First of all, this is the most relaxing of these three meditations, so a benefit of it will be deep calmness. The way of this is as follows: The axiatonal lines extend beyond the body like meridians. They go down through the earth, through the sun, through the central sun of the galaxy and on and on until you reach the Godverse or Omniverse—and likewise above. These lines will also, at some point, go through all of your star ancestry, and you can be linked with this. This line will pass through the planets, the galaxies, the universes that you have originated from. And you may pull down through these lines beings, ancestors, memories, and many such experiences.

Are "he" and "ru" said silently while doing the inbreath and outbreath?

Yes. It is a silent meditation.

How many breaths should one do in a sitting of this meditation, and how long should one take for this meditation?

It is not a matter of counting breaths. It may be practiced any time one is in a quiet space, and there is no recommended length. Even if a person has a five minute wait at some time, it may be practiced then with benefit. However, if a person were to sit and practice it for a half hour or 45 minutes, the meditation can go very deep. So it is flexible in that way, where a person can benefit from a short focus on it, and also by going deeply into it for a longer period of time.

In doing this meditation, I am trying to pull energy from all the way up and all the way down on my hara line, as you directed. However, this effort makes it very hard to relax.

Rather than making an effort, allow the breath to flow easily, naturally, and in your normal rhythm. Pull from as far up or as far down as is comfortable. The effect will still be there.

How often should it be done?

There are no shoulds around this. These meditations are gifts, and because of that I attach no regimen or expectation or value to regularity. Receive them as a gift and enjoy them. There is an endless pleasure attached to them, and over time a great unfolding will occur. If a person were to wish to make this meditation into a daily routine it could be of great benefit, but also it is of benefit just as a casual adjunct when a person thinks of it. Really it is up to an individual's life style and choice as to how deeply they wish to pursue this and how regularly they wish to practice it.

Does this breathing meditation open up the light filaments?
Yes, it does that, and much more.

PART II—THE SECOND MEDITATION: THE AXIATONAL ACTIVATION

Please describe the second meditation.
The second meditation deals with a star tetrahedron, the base of which is at the dantien and the top of which is at the pineal gland. The star tetrahedron is composed of two interlinked tetrahedrons, one pointing up and the other downwards. This form rotates in all directions—up, down, sideways, and so on. As it does so, from each point of this star tetrahedron there is a line of light, a line of life. That is your connection with the gridwork that holds you here. And these lines stretch into infinity. Do not get too into your head as to whether the lines will get tangled as you spin, just spin and feel the energy going out to infinity along these lines.

What is the benefit of this exercise?
It activates all of the lines of the gridwork and accesses all of your multi-dimensionality, everywhere that you exist in this universe. For you may have an atom in your abdomen, where the orbit of the electron extends so far as to extend outside this galaxy—this is how big you are. This meditation enables you to see and feel that bigness. And it again is infinite.

This meditation will also open all of the meridians in the body, and connect them with their infinite source of energy, so that connected with each meridian is limitless light. It connects all of the meridians to the axiatonal grid. Through meridian activation one then becomes consciously connected with all of one's dimensional selves, and the monad.

With the creation of each human soul, and the soul as it embodies in a body, is a portion—not a fragment but more like a holographic portion—of the original force of Creation. And you may access that portion through this technique. That is part of its great power.

Please define "dantien".

The dantien is a point between the navel and the pubic bone, about an inch and a half in diameter. It is a sphere that is the center of gravity for the body, and that when fully activated can resonate with a density comparable to that of the center of the earth. As such it is a very powerful point in the body.

Please define "axiatonal grid".

The axiatonal lines are the meridians that pass through the body. They are not vertical only, although your acupuncturists and so on see only the vertical part of them. When two or more or these lines meet they generate a vortex, and out of that come the horizontal lines. And these lines pass through the body. They do not come from the body—they are infinite in nature, and the body hangs upon them. *[Where do they come from?]* It's as though they don't come from anywhere; they are everywhere. They are our direct link to infinity. In activating them, one supersedes time and space limitations. And it is at that point, when they are fully active, that beings bilocate very easily and can travel through space and time and dimensions at will. Therefore the star tetrahedron that is within each person is not a merkaba vehicle in itself, but it is more like the engine of the merkaba which then can be activated.

What is the difference between the star tetrahedron in this meditation, and the merkaba?

Both have the form of the star tetrahedron, or the interlocked forms of two tetrahedrons. However with the merkaba the tetrahedrons rotate in opposite directions. This one does not counter rotate within itself. In addition, a merkaba is in a sense a travel vehicle. This is not a merkaba; it has a different function and purpose. In fact, it is almost a travel vehicle in reverse, where it will bring the universes to you rather than having you travel to the universes.

What is the special power or virtue of the spinning tetrahedron?

To answer that question would bring up a lengthy description of sacred geometry. It is one of the building blocks of the geometries of creation, one of the sacred shapes, and as such it carries great power.

I felt dizzy during this meditation.

If you find this exercise dizzying, you may slow down the motion of the spin of the star tetrahedron. This is more of a passive meditation than the first one, which is fairly active. In the first meditation you are drawing energy into the hara line and light filaments. The second meditation is more of a passive awareness where you are the observer, and you observe the change in energy as each of these points activates a meridian. As you observe the turning of the tetrahedron and the point of a star touching a meridian, it's almost like a chime being struck. You just listen to that sound or feel that vibration. Let it resonate within you and it will activate the light body. And much can be done with that.

Should I cause the tetrahedron to spin?

Many people will go at this meditation actively and attempt to spin the tetrahedron at a certain velocity. In fact it is better to not pressure the tetrahedron to spin at any particular velocity, but just to observe it. Westerners especially tend to be hyper and want to jump in and make something happen, but that is the antithesis of this experience. The tetrahedron is already spinning at its own speed, and actually is spinning at many frequencies. So whatever speed you tune into will be the appropriate one for you to follow at that moment. At different times as your consciousness changes it will spin at different rates, and there is no value given to the speed of it. Faster or slower is not better. Different frequencies would hit different frequencies within you.

I've been visualizing the tetrahedron spinning here and there and going around in a somewhat random pattern. Suddenly, as I was sitting and reading with it spinning in the back of my mind, it began spinning in all directions simultaneously. In other words, it began spinning in all directions, within all dimensions, so that it's spinning every direction within the Now. When it did that, its sensations also shifted and became much milder. Is this how it should be?

That is correct. *[It is hard to describe this so that people could visualize it.]* I think it is one of these things that you cannot get too much in your head about, as it is not easy to picture it mentally. It is something that you have to experience. So if you allow yourself to experience this tetrahedron and it is only spinning in one direction or dimension at a time that is fine. As you spend more time with this meditation it will open up to deeper and deeper levels. In your case this happened because you have been working with the meditation.

PART III—THE THIRD MEDITATION: THE PORTAL OF CREATION

Please describe your third meditation technique.

The third meditation is perhaps the most mysterious of the three, the simplest, and at the same time the most difficult. You focus on your heart and you just go in, and you go in, and you go in. You bring all of your being in there. And you go in and you go in. You invert yourself into your heart until you come out the other side. And when you come out, you come out into my world. It's almost as if you walk into your heart, and that creates a vacuum, and all of your being gets sucked behind you into your heart. You invert yourself inside out. This is the portal to the great mystery, and in a sense to the secret of all Creation. It is almost like going into the birth of life itself. This is the place that I create from, and it is most wonderful.

Has this technique ever been used on Earth before?

No. Up until this time, believe it or not, it would have been too dangerous to give to humans. Those people who will be using this, who will be attracted to it, will be of sufficient light to be able to hold it without attempting to misuse it. And the gateway has been created to protect those who are not of pure intent from going in the Void. I am immensely, immensely happy that this technique is going out. I am very excited, and I feel the response to it will be great—greater than *you can imagine.*

[Elora:] Heru has several times expressed a combination of joy and urgency about sharing this meditation with the world. He states that it will give us the power to co-create our lives in full conscious choice, as well as to heal and regenerate our world. By giving us the key to enter his world, Heru has provided us with a place from which to create, to manifest, and to make choices. It is time for light-oriented humans to have the power with which to shape our lives and our world.

Since this technique is so powerfully linked to creation: what happens if a person with less than pure intentions goes into that space, will they be able to create bad things? Also how about people who are unstable?

It will only open up for people who are stable to a certain degree. Someone who is depressed, that is no problem. Someone who is

196

even bi-polar, that is no problem. But for someone who is schizo-phrenic or psychotic, the portal just won't open up. It is up to me whom I let through that door. *[How about people who are negative—does this apply to them as well?]* Yes, it does.

You said: "It is up to me whom I let through that door." This implies that you have control of this space. Is this a space that you created from within the Void? In other words, is it a portion of the Void that you have qualified in some way?

That would be a good way to describe it, yes. Hence my calling this place "my world". *[With what qualities did you qualify it?]* I don't know that they really are separate qualities from the rest of the Void. It is more that it is under my domain and therefore I have, as I said, control over whom I let in. This applies not just to humans. If you were to call one of the fallen to come in there, it would be up to me to let them in or not, depending on the work you were calling them in there to do.

I am present in every part of that Void that you would go to. Through my gateway, it is my domain; and therefore the work that you are doing in that domain is under my tutelage and by my permission. This is the technique in which I am the most actively involved.

When I inverted myself through my heart as per your instructions, it felt very much like turning a rubber glove inside out. First my torso and head went through, and then my feet. Would that be a good analogy to help people understand this meditation?

Yes, that is a very good analogy. *[Sometimes I feel as if I'm part of the way into you world, but not completely.]* When this occurs, state three times, "Heru, take me entirely into your world." Then you will be all the way in. [Note: This works! If you find yourself partially drifting out of Heru's world, you can also use this affirmation.]

This meditation was much easier than I thought it would be. It felt like I went into a deep, black void, except that I could think, which is unlike the Void I usually go into. Normally when I access the Void, any thoughts will bring me out.

Yes, you are correct, and you were there. In this meditation, unlike other techniques of accessing the Void, you take your whole self in there. When you have been going into the Void using your other technique, you have in essence not taken the mind with you. In this technique you are able to do so. You may work in the Void and do the work that you do from the Void, still having mental clarity and activity should you desire to use it. It makes it a much more versatile tool.

Also, entering into what I would call my world, there is the ability to think clearly and act in spirit outside of your personal coloring and concepts and everything that you consider you, outside your personal identity. And that makes this an incredibly potent avenue and a wise place from which to make decisions. This is a wonderful place from which to gain perspective of the greater reality, because you really stand outside of time, space, duality, karma, and this world, and can truly see freedom.

I was working with you in your world, holding a visualization. However, my mind drifted and therefore I was polluting the visualization. So I stopped and did it again, and again my mind drifted. Why did this happen? And did this ruin my visualization?

It is a matter of practice. Because you can go in there with your mind, this makes it a more versatile tool than the technique you have been originally using. The fact that you take your mind in there is a double edged sword because yes, it will wander. And with practice, you will be better at it. But do not concern yourself if your mind wanders and your images become somewhat distorted, that you are diluting or destroying the original intent. For at the point that your mind wanders, you lose the power that happens in the Void. So as you lose the power you also lose the power to distort it; you are just drifting off. Let it happen and bring yourself back.

Once I got fully in, I was surprised to notice that it was easy to stay in your world, and I didn't want to leave. I looked around and noticed several things. One was the door into your world, the one that I had passed through. It seemed to have concentric rings, almost like a sphincter muscle, or the throat of a flower; and I saw purple and other colors, whereas there is no color in the Void. It also seemed that I could see beings passing by the door, and sometimes trying to get in. But I don't think I saw anyone enter while I was there. Was I seeing correctly?

Yes, that is a very good description of it. *[Could we say that door is a portal, and you are the guardian of that portal?]* Absolutely.

PART IV—MANIFESTING AND CREATING IN HERU'S WORLD

Would you please speak about the process of manifesting in your world?

The best way would be to have a clear intent before going in, perhaps one issue, idea, or desire per session. That would be easier than coming in with a whole list. State your intention as clearly as you can within the void, and that is sufficient.

Should it be repeated, condensing it into a point? I noticed you doing that with an intention I stated.

I will do that if the issue or idea is not sufficiently concentrated. The more emotion behind your manifestation—and I mean this in the sense of a true emotion, not as in "being emotional"—and the more concentrated the intent is, the more powerful the manifestation. So if somebody comes in with an idea that they have, which takes them a paragraph to state, I will work them into that fine concentrated point for it to have greater power. *[Perhaps that would also work well with something that is a bit abstract.]* Yes, and for that type of issue this is a very effective way to do it.

How about visualization?

This can be done also. For each person it will be somewhat different, and for each issue it will be somewhat different, so a great variety of things can be experienced in there.

How about the problem of limiting belief systems, which can stop a manifestation from occurring? The last time I was in your world, I felt that you were working on my head to help me with this. What did you do?

Restructuring of belief systems and uncoiling some fear. I believe that when you approach certain issues that have been fearful for you in the past, you will find a difference now. It would be good to take these issues for a test drive and see where there are still aspects of fear and resistance; and if there still are some then we will work again. *[Is this something that you will also do for any person upon request?]* Yes.

Unless I've been mistaken, Heru, you have appeared the last two times I've been in your world, and you helped me somewhat with my creations. Is that true?

Yes. That is part of this process; I am very active in the Void being a Creator God. And this will teach people the ability to truly consciously co-create their reality.

Please tell us why something we create in the Void doesn't manifest in the physical, and what we can do to change that.
Remember that you are living in a world with tremendous amounts of interference. And so with that premise, it is not always going to be successful. All I can say to that is to work at finding interference, clearing interference, and then trying again. *[What types of interference should we look for?]* Interference manifests on every level. It is dark beings, it is unconscious thought, it is the dark, it is everywhere. It does include any self sabotaging, subconscious thought forms. And just remember that the dark beings cloak themselves and travel on many dimensions, and are many shapes and sizes.

I have been feeling the created thought as being in the present, while in low alpha, with emotion, and trying to do this every day. You said there were other ways of doing it. What are they?
Emotion is definitely a very powerful component to this, and it is my feeling that heart centered emotion and heart felt emotion give weight and power to the creation. What I'm going to give you is more of an allegory than an actual step by step procedure. Take the longing for this creation, for what you are creating, and really identify that longing. Place it in a chalice, a very pure vessel, and offer it up to the Creator—and then ask for it back again. For this longing has great power, but it is when we offer it up to the highest good that it then becomes something pure and not conflicted. However you would want to stage that procedure would be fine; it is the intent or the heart of it that is important.

[Elora:] As a final note to this chapter, we have learned that it is possible to enter another space which is known as the Creator's world. To enter this domain, first go into Heru's world. Then once again travel inward through your heart. However, this time do not invert yourself. Whereas Heru's world appears black and calm, Creator's world is an extremely high-energy place, which may seem to have flaming skies and fountains of light. Usually the energy is so strong that you will have to ask for it to be stepped down. It is hard to think or operate in Creator's world, but Heru has told us that creations done there will manifest faster and more strongly. Another possibility is to invite Prime Creator to join you in Heru's world and assist you there with whatever you wish to manifest.

CHAPTER TWENTY
TECHNIQUES FOR CREATING
IN HERU'S WORLD

Heru's third meditation, "The Portal of Creation" is truly a door into another world. As we began to experiment with this technique, we began to realize what an amazing tool it is, and what a gift it is to be able to easily access that portion of the Void, the place from which Heru himself creates.

There are several ways to enjoy and benefit from the access into Heru's world. First, one may simply pass through the portal and rest in that calm, quiet space. We have found this to be very healing. Secondly, if you wish to work with a being such as one of the Masters, you may call that being to join you in Heru's world. Those of us who have been working with Heru will almost always choose to do our inner work in his world, as all such endeavors are enhanced by being in that place. Communication is enhanced as well.

Lastly, because the Void is the place of creation, Heru's world is the ideal space from which to accomplish any type of direct manifestation. Most light workers strive, in one way or another, to affect the physical through spiritual or energetic work. All energy healing is based on this principle. In addition many of us have attempted to manifest greater abundance in our lives, to draw appropriate relationships to ourselves, and so on. Because of the density here, generally this is quite a challenging undertaking. Entry into Heru's world is not an instant guarantee of total success, but it gives a tremendous advantage. I was astonished at the results that occurred for me after doing manifestations in Heru's world. For example, I was able to remove chronic viruses from one of my cats and to strengthen her immune system; I found that I could affect the weather; and I also manifested a rapid and complete resolution to a severe noise problem in our neighborhood.

Our initial success in creating and manifesting led to a series of questions regarding techniques for greater effectiveness. Heru gave us a great deal of information, which Shakura Rei summarized in the material below. Shakura also made the accompanying drawings.

PART I—USING GEOMETRIC FORMS FOR MANIFESTING

Pentagram: Often used for protection. If you wanted to create a deeply protected space around you, you could take the mental image of the pentagram in there with you, stand yourself within it, and ask for the protection to be created.

Vesica Pisces: This is the most wonderful symbol of all for creating anything new. Take two spheres and intersect them. Where they intersect and create a "flame" shape, this is where you would insert your goal, image, or intention. Or you can stand in the center of it and call forth what you would like to create. In the image, think of two spheres rather than two flat circles.

Spheres and Circles: Used for wholeness or oneness.

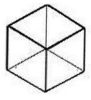

Cubes and Squares: Generally used for manifesting in the physical.

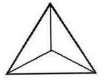

Three-sided Pyramids: Used for knowledge, for accessing different dimensions, and for protection.

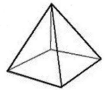

Four-sided Pyramids: For manifesting the same kinds of principles (those that were mentioned with the 3 sided pyramid) in the physical.

Five-sided Pyramid: Heru hasn't explained why we use it, but he did suggest this form for working with finances.

Infinity Sign—the figure 8: Creates a wonderful energy flow. If you were to place two people within the figure 8, and run energy through that, it becomes very magnetic. If you want to attract someone to you, this is a very powerful force.

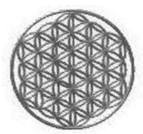

Flower of Life: Reaches into all dimensions and all times.

PART II—HOW TO CREATE IN HERU'S WORLD

To actually create, visualize one of the shapes and place your goal into it. If you're not sure what shape to use, you can either use the vesica pisces, or don't use any shape; there are no hard and fast rules for this. The simplest method is to enter his world and clearly state your intention. However, you give your goals more energy to manifest if you also use the energy of geometry and visualization to assist it. The more emotion behind your manifestation, and the more concentrated the intent is, the more powerful the manifestation.

If you want to use written words for your goal, you can visualize the letters as flaming and brilliant. Color is very useful for strengthening a creation as well. If you are using a geometric shape, the "floor" of that form is a "platform" upon which you set your goal, which can be in the form of a symbol, words, visualization, or even yourself—whichever you are using.

For a new goal, Heru suggests you manifest it a total of three times, though this is not set in stone either. He suggests you create it on day one, then three days later create it again, and three days later create it yet again. After that let it go and know that it is coming to you. There will also be some projects which will require ongoing work. For example, if you wish to draw more income to your business, you may wish to create this once or twice a week, every week.

When it comes to manifesting that which we desire, we can be our own worst enemy. Unconscious limiting beliefs can and often will sabotage the process. While Heru can work on us while we are in his world, and this can be of some benefit, for those who are really serious about creating their own reality it is suggested that they take two courses given by Shakura Rei, "Comprehensive Emotional Clearing" and "Creating the Life You Want: Manifesting From Within the Quantum" (Void). Please see Appendix for contact information.

Heru, you said you would help remove our limiting belief systems that hinder our creations from manifesting. Do we need to tell you what those limiting beliefs are, or do you already know?
You contain so many more limiting beliefs than you are conscious of. You may state the ones that you would like to work on, but you may also state it in a more inclusive way. For as I said there are many

you are not aware of, many assumptions that people make, and they have never dreamed of existence without that belief. For example, with most people there is the assumption of the inevitability of physical death, and the inevitability of it within a certain time frame. And therefore people begin in their twenties to program themselves for illness, decline, decay, and death. What would a person be without that program? If you think of all the systems within your body that are programmed, and have been for many lifetimes, what would it take to remove all of those programs? A lot. It occurs to me that a good platform from which to work on this kind of restructuring of a being would be to use a platform of the Flower of Life, for it will reach into all of the dimensions and all of time.

Following are some suggestions that Heru gives for creating specific goals, as well as healing. When he suggests using different colors, use each color for about five minutes. The directions given for each section below are direct quotes from Heru.

 **Physical Healing:** Place yourself in a four-sided pyramid. The reason that the four-sided pyramid is best for this is that it brings the healing to the physical plane. From the point of this pyramid, bring down a shaft of light. As it hits the floor in the center of the square it creates a circle. You are standing in the pyramid and looking at the floor. In the center of the floor of the pyramid will be a circle lit by this shaft of light. You go in the circle if it is you who is to be healed; if it is someone else you place that being in the circle. Then you would ask for that being or that condition to be healed. In this space it is good to use the I AM commands. For example, "I AM commanding that I be healed of this malady" or that so and so be healed, or "I command that I be healed." And that should do it. You need only state this once, or you can repeat it if you find it helpful. You may also visualize yourself healed if you choose, and you may call in healing angels as well.

To rid the body of toxins: Use the physical healing technique, but add some water. You may place yourself within this circle of light, this beam of light, and call for the healing to come forth in whatever manner is applicable. Then ask for a healing, cleansing rain to fall down upon you and through you, through the column of light, and ask for it to remove the toxins.

Sleeping problems: Use the physical healing technique, but add a blue light. A deep ultra violet, almost looking like a black light, would also be helpful.

Healing Relationships: In this one you would use a three-sided pyramid and you would create a figure 8 on the floor, illuminated by a column of light. Place the two beings wishing to have relation-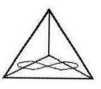
ship healing done, one in each lobe of that figure 8.
Call down first a rose red light, then a golden white light, and then call for healing to be accomplished in this relationship. For families or groups, you may then add other "loops" of the figure 8. For example if it were a four person family you would do two figure 8's so that it would look rather like a flower. If there were five, just add a petal; it matters not if they overlap somewhat.

Creating a Relationship: Set up the relationship figure 8 with different petals, depending on how many people. You could stand in that figure 8, leaving the other petal or petals empty, and invite persons of great statue and worth and attractiveness, whatever would fulfill you, into that space. If you wanted to manifest a partner as a lover, you could do that. You could also manifest friendships.

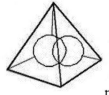
Restructuring the body: Place your perfect physical body blueprint within a vesica pisces, making that your new body. Place all of this within a four-sided pyramid, making that apply to the physical plane. You will find movement there. And that would be a good place to start, for you want to create a new perfect-

ed body on the physical. Do this three times. [In the image, imagine the two circles are two spheres.]

Fat loss: Using the "restructuring the body" technique, you would address the issues that underlie excess fat in the body—be they endocrine, toxicity, metabolic, emotional—whatever the core issues are for the weight gain. You would take each issue and place it within a circle, which is within a four-sided pyramid, and ask that the problem be removed with the "I Command" statements. For instance if it was a toxicity issue, you would put that image of the body within the circle, and say "I command that the toxins that result in holding fat in my body be removed." You would do that three times, three days apart. Do that with each issue.

Finances: In the geometry of this you want a five-sided pyramid and a five-sided form in the middle of the pyramid. This form is a pentagon, a figure like a square but with one more side. You would place the person or thing that you wish to have prosper in that pentagon, and ask for what you would wish, using commands as described. You may also use a white light with golden flecks; this would be very effective.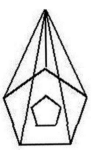

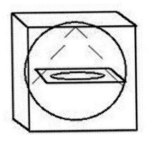 **Creating rain or stopping rain:** For this you would place a sphere within a cube. The forms are roughly the same size, and the sphere fits within the cube. Place that geometric symbol in a two dimensional form upon the middle of the floor, so you are seeing it almost as if it were drawn on the floor. Then also place this form in a three-dimensional format, so it's almost as if the forms are doubled. The sphere could be, in diameter, about the height of a person. This would give you the visual flexibility to work on some large projects and not have them too miniaturized as you visualize them. Also let me also

clarify that the floor of your workspace will be the midpoint of the cube and the sphere, so that you will have half of the sphere above you and half of the cube above you. You will have half of the sphere and cube below you. You are in the middle of it all, and you're actually standing in the same diagram that you're diagramming on the floor. If you were to take a slice right though the middle and make a drawing of that slice, you would be standing in a square and a circle.

Again create the shaft of light, coming from the top of the sphere and cube, and place in there that section of the environment that you would wish to be restored. The form that the work would take would depend to some extent on the problem being addressed. For instance if you took a drought area, you could put in there the map of that area, the full extent of what needs to be worked on. Or if you have a very strong mental image of that environment, you could put in the mountains, valleys, canyons and so on. In dealing with drought we would bring into this a blue green light with a shower of water. If you were looking at an area that has been receiving too much rain, you could do the same thing with golden white light, and that would bring the sun back. In the diagram below, the circle is a sphere, not a flat circle.

Clearing pollution: Use the same method for creating or stopping rain, but use a clear blue light.

Clearing polluted soil or toxic dumps: Use the same technique as above, but you would not want to wash that pollution away because it would then run somewhere else. You would want to concentrate it, contain it, and then vaporize it instead. Bring a strong image of that place into the diagram on the floor. Place next to it a vessel that can be used as a cauldron, and call forth for all of the pollution to be concentrated and collected into this vessel. When you feel that process has completed, bring forth the violet transmuting flame and incinerate it.

APPENDICES

GLOSSARY

The definitions below pertain to the way various terms are used within this book. In the field of metaphysics there are no hard and fast definitions; other authors and teachers may use different words for the same concepts. A number of the terms below may be unfamiliar even to the metaphysically astute reader, so we suggest that you peruse this page before reading the book, or at least refer to it when you encounter an unfamiliar label. The definitions below are mostly direct quotes or paraphrases of material given by Heru, although Sananda contributed the one for ascension.

ASCENSION

Ascension is the reunification of all of the aspects through all of the dimensions and through all space and time. For a person in a state of ascension, it would not matter if they had a form in the third dimension or not. It would only matter that all of their aspects be in harmony, in communication, and united with both the monad and God. At that point there is no barrier between the dimensions or between time and space, and everything that humans would call miraculous is possible.

ASPECTS

Aspects are essentially "selves" in other dimensions. Most schematics show twelve dimensions in our Creation, with the monad residing on the twelfth or highest dimension before Source. In order to gain a wider range of experience, the monad projects itself into other dimensions. This involves a stepping down of vibratory rate, and manifesting forms [the aspects] into lower dimensions. Each dimension, or each rung down the ladder, so to speak, would represent a hundred fold decrease in the vibratory rate of existence. Each aspect has a great deal of autonomy and individuality within the basic prismatic structure of that being. They will all retain similar qualities but will have a good deal of variation in life style, interests, what they do, and so on. Usually there is not an aspect on each dimensional level, so that if a dimension were skipped—such as going from a tenth to an eighth dimensional aspect—that would be a two hundred fold decrease in vibratory rates.

COSMIC PROGENITORS

Cosmic progenitors are a specialized group of Creator Gods who are capable of creating souls. Heru and Durga/Sekhmet are members of this group.

CREATION

Creation is the manifested will of Prime Creator. It is a vast system of universes, and is structured in the form of a flower with Prime Creator, or the Godverse being the central source around which the petals of Creation bloom.

CREATOR GOD

A Creator God is a being who is capable of taking the stuff of Creation, the plasma from Prime Creator, and manifesting it into form. These forms may be as large as universes and may be as small as microcosms.

DARKNESS

What Heru calls "the dark" is a non-souled, non-living substance, antithetical in structure to the basic life inherent in every atom of Creation. It is not known where it comes from, or who or what designed it. It has the tendency to permeate anything that it touches, though some beings have been able to resist it, at least in maintaining the purity of their spirit. A possible analogy is a computer virus, which is non-living yet has the capacity to corrupt, distort, and destroy whatever it encounters, and also has the capacity to replicate itself.

For an ensouled being who has fallen due to exposure to the dark, Heru defines "darkness" as the willingness to impose one's will upon another being.

ENLIGHTENMENT

Enlightenment would be a dissolving of the barriers, or the removal of the dark, that keeps one separated from their highest self, and the certainty within that the connection with God is eternal.

FREQUENCY FENCE

The frequency fence is a barrier created by the dark in order to stop the flow of energy, travel, and communication between this fallen sector of universes and the rest of Creation as well as Prime Creator. Within this sector there are many, many frequency fences: around planets, around suns, and around galaxies, in order to reinforce again the status of non-movement and non-communication. The barrier around the fallen sector of Creation is often referred to as the "Great Wall".

GODVERSE

The Godverse, or Omniverse, is the dwelling place of Prime Creator, although Prime Creator is not limited to or encapsulated by the Godverse. It is the place from which all energy originates, and all of the cosmic plasma that the Creator Gods use to create form originates in the Godverse. It is at the center of all Creation.

GODINJ

Godinj is a group of Creator Gods who wove the membrane, creating the perimeters of this universe around the great plasma given to them by Prime Creator. They themselves form, in essence, the nucleus of that great cell [i.e. the universe]. And spinning out from them are all of the forms of this universe, large to small.

HARA LINE

The hara line is an energetic line passing vertically through the center of the body. It extends beyond the center of the body in both directions, and it is the energetic axis upon which the body is manifested.

LADDER

A term coined as the most understandable image or framework

around which to describe the descension of aspects manifested from the monad down through the third dimension. For example, a "ladder" might contain third, fourth, sixth, ninth, and tenth dimensional beings [aspects], and then the monad on the twelfth dimension. In fact there is really no structure of this kind, however it helps to convey the idea of the chain of aspects from the lower to higher dimensions.

LIGHT FILAMENTS

The light filaments are energetic threads which not only connect beings on the dimensional ladder, but are also the vehicle with which to project the next level of being in that lower dimension. In other words, the monad projects light filaments from the twelfth dimension down through all the dimensional layers. At each dimension that the monad desires to create a body [an aspect], those filaments are the tool with which that is done. The light filaments appear in the physical body as the meridians. Through Heru's second meditation technique, these meridians can be activated. This is important when one desires to go through the ascension process, for through meridian activation one then becomes consciously connected with all of one's dimensional selves and the monad. The light filaments carry prana, light, and information between the monad and its aspects.

LIGHT WARRIORS

A unique group of beings who have been created by Prime Creator for the specific purpose of removing all darkness from the fallen parts of Creation. The Light Warriors have only been in this universe for a very short period of time.

MONAD

The monad is the first individualized creation beyond Source. It is the original soul which is created by the Creator Gods and could be termed the "highest self". Monads are beings who dwell on the twelfth dimension. They extend, or project, a "ladder" of aspects down through the dimensions. The monad is the "Supreme Person" for each one of us, and in a sense is the level between ourselves and God. Heru sometimes uses the metaphor of a mighty oak tree. The monad would be the tree with all its branches. A human being is a third dimensional aspect of the monad and is analogous to the tip of a branch which extends into our universe. Higher dimensional aspects would be analogous to junctures along the branch, until it connects to the trunk of the tree.

OMNIVERSAL ENERGY

The Omniversal Energy is a beam or ray of light, projected directly by Prime Creator as a beam of focused intent designed to penetrate all levels of Creation. It has, to a greater or lesser degree, penetrated and touched every atom of Creation, with the intent of restoring the true light of Creator to all Creation. Embedded and encoded in this beam or ray of light are many programs and many beings, such as the Light Warriors. These programs and beings are designed to activate sequentially in order to perform the restoration of the fallen universes, and all beings and substances contained within them.

PRIME CREATOR

God, or Prime Creator, is that which creates, sustains, and permeates all.

THIRD TECHNIQUE or THIRD MEDITATION

The "third meditation technique" is often referred to in the text of this book, and is a meditation which Heru has given us. He has asked that it be shared freely at this time, as it is such a powerful tool. Also called "The Portal of Creation", this technique allows a person to access a portion of the Void and thereby to create powerful changes within his or her life. This meditation is described in detail in Section Three of this book.

THOTH

Thoth is one of the great Light beings who has assisted this planet for many eons. The Egyptians knew him as a scribe and teacher. The Greeks called him Hermes Trismegistus, or thrice-greatest Hermes. According to legend, he is said to have provided the wisdom of light in the ancient mysteries of Egypt. Thoth is a great master of esoteric knowledge and is a "cousin" to Heru and Sekhmet.

TWELVE CRITICAL PLANETS

The twelve critical planets are twelve planets which were especially selected within this universe to be a repository of perfect and diverse genetic material. They are spaced in a grid pattern, so that if you divided our universe into twelve roughly equal parts, each would have one of these planets. Earth is one of the twelve critical planets. Earth has sometimes been called a "living library", and this is a good description in that these planets contain a complete store of life form material. This does not mean that every life form ever created is in existence here. What it means, however, is that every major archetypal system would be represented here. There is enough material, diversity, and knowledge here to create any of the forms that exist anywhere in Creation. There are, perhaps, places where flying cats exist, but here there is the form of the cat and the form of the bird. And it is the same with all twelve of these planets. Each of the twelve critical planets replicates the others. This was done for the sake of security, in hopes that the perfection and diversity of genetic material would be preserved.

TWIN FLAME

The term "twin flame" or "twin soul" refers to souls that are created as identical twins, although with opposite genders. There is a tremendous magnetic attraction between twin flames, which is a driving force for their own evolution as well as the evolution of Creation itself.

UNIVERSE

A universe is a structure contained within a membrane. It is created out of the Omniversal matter, which is a free flowing, unformed, plasmic cosmic material that Prime Creator has made. The Creator Gods take that plasma, create a membrane around it, and structure it. Most of the universes, like ours, are set up as vast collections of galaxies and galaxy clusters, but there are microcosmic universes as well. Each universe has a Great Central Sun which is integral to holding it together, and is integral in holding the outer membrane together.

VOID

The great Void is the thought projection of space that Prime Creator has created to house Creation.

TOOLS FOR RETURNING TO LIGHT

THE RETURN OF LIGHT WEBSITE

At the time of this writing, prior to the publication of *The Return of Light*, we plan to construct a website at www.returnoflight.com where we can publish updates from Heru and some of the other masters regarding the progress of the restoration of our planet and universe. We also intend to ask Heru to answer selected questions from our readers on a regular basis. Updates and answers to questions will also be distributed via an online newsletter. It is our hope that this website will be a beacon of light and clarity during troubled times, as 2005 and perhaps 2006 may still be difficult years on our planet. We expect that the years following will be times of great improvement, but will still require vision and understanding.

SHAKURA REI

Shakura Rei is a contributing author to this book, and is an extraordinary and powerful healer. Among many things, she is also adept at the healing and manifesting techniques mentioned by Heru, such as clearing dark aspects, straightening and clearing the light filaments, and manifesting in the Void. These are offered as remote sessions and workshops at her website, www.ascending-star.com. Shakura can be contacted at shakura@ascending-star.com, and at P O. Box 1694, Deer Park, WA 99006.

CIRCLE OF LIGHT

Circle of Light is a spiritual center in Arkansas which is dedicated to the process of twin flame ascension. They have published a number of channeled books on this subject, and also give workshops to assist people in opening to the twin flame connection. While the philosophical material in the channeled material offered by this group differs from Heru's perspective in some ways, we do feel that Circle of Light is genuinely accessing the tremendous power and love that is to be found in twin flame reunion. Please see http://www.circle-oflight.net/ or call 1-877-825-4448.

COSMIC ESSENCES

Cosmic Essences are a type of vibrational essence, and were, in a sense, developed from flower essences. Like traditional flower essences, they are made with perfect flowers placed in water and energized by sunlight or moonlight. However, an additional step is taken in which the water is potentized with the assistance of Ascended Masters, angels, and Creator Gods and Goddesses. In addition, these essences are infused with the evolutionary energy and power of the Omniversal Energy. The result is a set of essences which are unusually pure, potent, and rapid in their effects. Cosmic Essences have also been specifically designed to address the areas of soul growth and evolution, emotional release, twin soul connection, and ascension. For more information, please see www.cosmicessences.com or call Cosmic Essences, which is a subsidiary of The Green Willow Tree, at 1-877-968-4337 or 1-828-628-8208.

DNA ACTIVATION MUSIC BY SHAPESHIFTER

Shapeshifter is the collective expression of a group of highly evolved extraterrestrial beings. By channeling music through Gary and JoAnn Chambers, these beings are assisting in Conscious Evolution through Multidimensional Music and Sound. They support the Evolutionary Path of Light by modulating the lifewave of the body electric with the intent to activate the dormant potential coded within. Sonic keys unlock and reintegrate the multi-strand DNA with the goal of rejuvenation, physical immortality and empowered co-creation as conscious evolution unfolds within the totality of each listener. For more information, please see www.visionarymusic.com.

THE MAGDALEN MANUSCRIPT

This book, by Tom Kenyon and Judi Sion, contains a remarkable set of channelings from Mary Magdalen. We have seen a great deal of channeled material purporting to come from Mary Magdalen. This is the first such material that we feel is genuine. In this book,

Sananda's twin flame sets the record straight. The Magdalen Manuscript will be of interest to those who are drawn to the path of twin flame ascension, and it contains a number of exercises which may be helpful to those who follow that path. For more information please see http://tomkenyon.com/books/marymagdalen.html. Sananda has verified the correctness of this channeled material.

ABOUT THE AUTHORS

HERU

Heru is a Creator God—one who, in his words, "is capable of taking the stuff of Creation, the plasma from Prime Creator, and manifesting it into form. When Prime Creator said 'Let there be light,' we were the instruments through which that was manifested. I, personally, was involved in the creation of this universe, this planet and many of the souls that inhabit this planet." Heru is best remembered in our world as Horus, the Egyptian God revered as Lord of Light and known for his wisdom, spiritual vision and protection of the innocent against chaos and darkness. In Greece he was known as Apollo, and in India as Satyanarayana, Lord of Truth. "I am father, uncle and great uncle to many of you," Heru says, "and I would like to reclaim my own—to lift up, embrace, and heal my children."

KAREN KIRSCHBAUM

Karen Kirschbaum had her first awakening in 1971, and she has dedicated the better part of her life since then to expressing her love of the Divine. She has worked as an energy healer, painted visionary art, and written ecstatic poetry. Her channeling skills lay sleeping until her friendship with Elora awakened them. Karen credits her ability to be a clear channel to the work she has done with the DNA Activation Music by Shapeshifter, available at www.visionarymusic.com. Karen had a two decade career as a professional chef and now manages the office at The Green Willow Tree.

ELORA GABRIEL

The love of nature and the quest for truth have been two driving forces in Elora's life. She had her first garden at the age of six and worked for years as a professional gardener. Elora has also had an unwavering commitment to spiritual growth, and has consistently striven to bridge the physical and metaphysical. She has been an inveterate explorer of the inner realms. As part of her work in this world, she has founded two successful businesses, The Green Willow Tree and Cosmic Essences. She lives in the country near Asheville, NC, with her husband John and their three beautiful cats.